# F<sup>TO</sup>ISH HUNT MAINE

## BOOKS BY EDMUND WARE SMITH

*RIDER IN THE SUN*
*A TOMATO CAN CHRONICLE*
*TALL TALES AND SHORT*
*THE ONE-EYED POACHER OF PRIVILEGE*
*FROM FACT TO FICTION*
*THE FURTHER ADVENTURES OF THE ONE-EYED POACHER*
*THE ONE-EYED POACHER AND THE MAINE WOODS*
*A TREASURY OF THE MAINE WOODS*
*FOR MAINE ONLY*
*UPRIVER AND DOWN*

# TO FISH AND HUNT IN MAINE

*The Classic Stories of*
EDMUND WARE SMITH

*Introduction by*
**THOMAS A. KINNEY**

YANKEE BOOKS
Camden, Maine

© 1991 by Thomas A. Kinney

All rights reserved.

No part of this book may be reproduced or transmitted in any form or by any means, electronic or mechanical, including photocopying, recording, or by any information storage and retrieval system, without the written permission of the publisher, except by a reviewer quoting brief passages in a magazine, newspaper or broadcast. Address inquiries to Yankee Books, P.O. Box 1248, Camden, Maine 04843

Cover and text design by Amy Fischer, Camden, Maine
Cover and interior illustrations by Jack Barrett, Portland, Maine
Typeset by Typeworks, Belfast, Maine
Printed and bound by BookCrafters, Chelsea, Michigan

Library of Congress Cataloging-in-Publication Data

Smith, Edmund Ware.
    To fish and hunt in Maine / Edmund Ware Smith : [editor and] introduction by Thomas A. Kinney.
    p.  cm.
    Includes bibliographical references.
    ISBN 0-89909-336-1
    1. Outdoor life – Maine – Fiction.    I. Kinney, Thomas A.
II. Title.
PS3569.M53425T6  1991
813'.52 – dc20                                           91-2445
                                                                                CIP

10  9  8  7  6  5  4  3  2  1

*This book is dedicated to my great-grandfather Harry L. Getchell, hunter, fisherman, carpenter, and woodsman of Smith's era. He provided much of the inspiration for this work.*

Thomas A. Kinney

# Contents

*Acknowledgments viii*
*In Search of Edmund Ware Smith*
   *by Thomas A. Kinney    ix*

*An Ode to Spring Fever    1*

**PART ONE**
*The Saga of Third Chain Cabin    7*
*A Rifle Named "Sleigh Bells"    19*
*Jake's Rangers Hunt the Whitetail    30*
*The Jinx and Uncle George    41*
*"Old Come-And-Get-It"    52*
*The Magic Woodsman    64*
*Death of a Haunted Tent    73*
*Jake's Rangers vs. Spring Fever    83*

**PART TWO**
*Appointment With Death    97*
*Weather Prophet    107*
*The Tenderfoot Who Wasn't    117*
*Last Trip Together    129*
*Some Have to Get Hurt    134*
*The Last Hermit of the Maine Woods    148*

**PART THREE**
*Old Lady in Waiting    159*
*The Warden, the Rum, and the Preacher    171*
*The Long Night    181*
*The Diary of Death    193*

**ENVOY**
*Ghosts of Old Campfires    207*

*Bibliography    213*

# *Acknowledgments*

I am grateful to the many people who gave freely of their time, advice, and encouragement in the preparation of this book. Many thanks go to James W. Smith for information about his father, and to Helen Dennison Blustin for recollections of her life with Edmund Ware Smith. McClure Day, Margaret Eipper, and Agatha Rowland were all very generous with their time, and their remarks proved very useful. I deeply appreciate help from Bud Leavitt, Bill Caldwell, and John Gould. Editorial assistance came from Linda Spencer, Bob Farnsworth, and Lance Tapley. Without their help, the road from initial concept to publication would have been much rougher. My hours spent reviewing Smith's papers at Colby College were made pleasant because of the efforts of librarians Fraser Cocks and P.A. Lenk, and Megan Sloane provided invaluable assistance in the final proofreading. I would also like to thank two people who provided encouragement and feedback on my efforts from the very beginning: Margery Wilson at the English Department of the University of Maine, and Sanford Phippen.

# *In Search of Edmund Ware Smith*

Most of Maine is forest. From Thoreau to the present, authors have delighted in describing the Maine woods: the hushed solitude of a cedar swamp, the pristine clarity of a northern lake, or the craggy majesty of Mount Katahdin. Such passages enhance for many readers their vision of Maine. But the picture remains incomplete without the people, for they tell us more about a place than all the rocks, trees, and rivers combined.

Edmund Ware Smith shared with Maine woodsmen, hunters, fishermen, camp caretakers, and hermits the experiences of a lifetime. He enjoyed their company, admired their skill, and valued their friendship; as a writer he found them an almost inexhaustible source of literary inspiration. Smith loved the natural beauty of his adopted state, but he always wrote with the people in mind. In doing so, he preserved in his stories those characters whose living counterparts exist today, to a sad degree, only in memory. The fictionalized and factual lives of people such as Pappy Thornton, Roy Bailey, and Uncle George Whitehouse have left an indelible impression upon a host of readers.

I grew up in a family of readers and outdoorsmen, and I was influenced by Smith's kind of characters both in print and in reality. I idolized my great-grandfather and his cousins, inveterate outdoorsmen all, and their influence on me was reinforced by reading Edmund Ware Smith's books. My research on Smith and his writing was a way to learn about the stories behind the people and places that were an intrinsic part of my youth. Looking back over all his writing, I see him emerge as a skilled portrayer of Maine people and a preserver of the true flavor of Maine hunting and fishing. His literary excellence and characteristic professional aplomb brought these people and their activities to vivid life.

Edmund Ware Smith was born in Plantsville, Connecticut, on December 10, 1900, into a family of academics that included several ministers and the founder of Atlanta University. He felt tension between his family's ambitions for him and his own interests, and this may have been one of the factors that caused him to go out West, where he spent part of his early youth. Smith attended several prep schools and colleges both in the West and back East, but he never received a degree from any. By 1925, he had married Helen Dennison, daughter of the head of a noted New England manufacturing clan, and was writing seriously. His experiences with his new in-laws provided grist for some of his earliest works, for Smith's father-in-law, Henry "Pop" Dennison owned a camp on Sysladobsis Lake in Washington County, Maine. Smith enjoyed spending time there and at an outlying camp on remote Third Chain Lake. Pop Dennison was an interesting personality, and Smith found in him a source of inspiration and encouragement.

The early 1930s found Smith working for Boston outdoor magazines such as *National Sportsman* and *Hunting and Fishing*, where he wrote both articles and short stories, and worked as an editor. By 1935, he was living in Northampton, Massachusetts, and had decided to make his living as a freelance writer, which he remained until his death. During the following years he contributed articles to a huge variety of magazines ranging from *Redbook* to *Esquire*. As time went on, he created a niche for himself as a Maine writer.

In 1946, Smith and his second wife Mary fulfilled a lifelong dream by building a cabin on the shores of secluded Mattagamon Lake, and for the next decade he divided his time between this spot and Dearborn, Michigan, where he was an editor for the Ford Motor Company's *Ford Times*. By the time his advancing age forced him to sell his remote cabin and move to coastal Damariscotta, Maine, Edmund Ware Smith had become a nationally known writer with hundreds of stories and several books to his credit. He spent his twilight years in Damariscotta, continuing his writing and editing, and his last book, *Upriver and Down*, appeared in 1965. He died two years later.

Smith had a flair for describing interesting Maine people he met throughout his life; in his early years he found plenty of people who provided inspiration for his work. He always spoke fondly of Washington County guide Roy Bailey, whose skill with rod, rifle, and canoe pole spurred Smith on to become a better woodsman himself. Smith dedicated an early book, *Tall Tales and Short* (1938), to Bailey, hinting of the importance of local people for his inspiration when he wrote that Roy "showed me a great deal more than fish and game. He showed me a way of life, and, best of all, a people who require no other way." Even greater sources of friendship, instruction, and story material were Charles "Pappy" Thornton and his wife Kate, the caretakers of Dennison's camps. Skilled woodsman and woodworker, Pappy Thornton spent many hours hunting, fishing, cutting wood, and telling outrageous stories with Smith, who referred to him as "my gaunt, long-jawed collaborator." The early years at Dobsis provided for Smith material for nearly a lifetime of stories. The people from this part of his life are featured in "A Rifle Named Sleigh Bells," "The Saga of Third Chain Cabin," and "The Magic Woodsman."

Not only did Smith excel in accurately portraying the nature of actual individuals, he also distilled many of the mannerisms and habits of Maine people into his most famous fictional character, Thomas Jefferson Coongate, the one-eyed poacher. Smith incorporated many stories about local hunters, guides, and poachers into Jeff Coongate, resulting in a character that represents much of the nature of some hard-bitten Washington County woodsmen of an earlier day. And this is significant, for whether Edmund Ware Smith wrote about an actual person, or created a stylized persona, all of his stories contain the element of truth. Margaret Eipper, Smith's sister-in-law, declares that he was an utterly honest person, and though Smith himself claimed that some of his works were "wantonly fictitious," they still contain a core of "real life" truth, especially in the sketches of people.

Of course the characters that people Smith's stories wouldn't be nearly as intriguing if it weren't for the activities in which they engage. Maine's vast woodlands and countless lakes have not only provided income for her people, but also a source of recreation. When I was 14 years old, my father took me to a family deer-hunting camp in a remote part of Washington County. I can recall with utmost clarity both my excitement during those few days and the exotic activities that stimulated it: waking up at 3:30 A.M. to the clatter of someone firing up the ancient Queen Atlantic, hefting a relative's weighty .35 Remington, and recounting the day's adventures beneath a hissing Coleman lantern. Edmund Ware Smith wrote tellingly about many such experiences, and his descriptions of camps he helped build, of trips he took to far places, and of the fellowship of a close group of outdoorsmen all ring true because he experienced things that many of us enjoy. His description of the Maine sporting scene not only puts the stamp of authenticity on his stories, but it preserves a common heritage of annual trips, of deep woods camaraderie, and of a sporting tradition with a long, long, history.

Edmund Ware Smith's Maine was one of fewer roads, fewer people, and more game — a wilder Maine. The newest inductees to the rites of spring at a favored trout stream may never know what it means to have to pole a canoe for miles to reach a good spot, but by reading some of Smith's works they will be able to have a taste of it. Today, only the wealthy use guides, but through Edmund Ware Smith's stories we can relive an era when the Maine guide was less rare and more accessible. Thus, an accurate portrayal of traditional Maine sporting activities will only grow in value as with each successive generation they become just memories.

Smith has uncanny verbal deftness; his descriptions of nature surpass those of many of his contemporaries: "The stream spoke among the stones in a small, careless way." This stylistic ability allows Smith to lend vivacity to his character portrayals: He remarks that the lean and genial Uncle George Whitehouse was "virtually one-dimensional — like a canoe pole," and Pappy Thornton "was a gaunt poet, re-reading a sonnet he had written with a broad axe and crooked knife." Smith's writing is full of such memorable phrases, indicative of skill far exceeding that exhibited in most "outdoor writing." This skill wasn't lost on his fellow contemporary authors, as John Gould comments in the introduction to Smith's *Treasury of the Maine Woods:* "Those of us who have tried variously in our own ways to put the Maine woods in print will again look at a Smith book with a 'wish-I'd-said that'."

In a long writing career, Smith wrote 10 books and hundreds of articles and short stories for a wide variety of periodicals. In addition to his reminiscences of the Dobsis years, in this volume I have also included some of the one-eyed poacher tales and a few of the well-known Jake's Rangers stories. Shorter works, such as "Ghosts of Old Campfires" and "An Ode to Spring Fever," further illustrate some of his writing skills. Among the lesser-known works are some nearly forgotten stories from his earlier books. "Weather Prophet," "The Tenderfoot Who Wasn't," and "Last Trip Together" are all excellent examples of the art of the short story and are some of his very best writing.

Much time has gone by since Smith passed from the field, and a new generation of Maine writers is now presenting a more balanced image, painting a picture of natural beauty, but with pigment from the dark, but equally real palettes of poverty, crime, and domestic strife. While Smith does present Maine in a very favorable light, I do not feel he romanticizes it. In any case, Smith never attempted to sum up Maine in his works. Indeed, the bulk of his stories deal with a narrow band of the total spectrum of experience—people engaged in traditional activities, happy with their lot in life.

It should be kept in mind that Smith was born and brought up in southern New England, not Maine, and he wrote about Maine from the perspective of someone "from away." Armed with this bit of knowledge, some Maine people might discredit the man entirely because he wasn't "one of us." While this sentiment is extreme, being raised in the state of Maine does have something to do with how one perceives life here and, consequently, writes about it. Take the issue of firewood. In one of his stories, Smith notes that he enjoyed working up wood by hand, "thus deriving moderate exercise together with a pleasing sense of identification with men like Robert Frost and the late Bernard Shaw, who also cut and split." Now for someone who requires only small amounts of wood for seasonal visits, time at the woodpile may take on this recreational flavor. But for others who have to produce 10 cords of cut, split, and stacked firewood to ward off the effects of an overlong winter, it is quite another matter. I grew up "luggin' wood," and while I have suffered no ill effects from the experience, my view of the matter tends to be more prosaic.

This book is the result of my search for the nature of a man who died three months before I was born. Edmund Ware Smith deserves his spot in the renowned lineage of Maine writers, and I hope that I have contributed to his placement in those ranks for the benefit of readers who admire a tale well told.

Thomas A. Kinney<br>Orono, Maine

# An Ode to Spring Fever

According to *The Old Farmer's Almanac,* spring begins on March 21st at 4:36 A.M. But spring fever, respecting no clock or calendar, no living man, nor his wife, nor his children, may find its victims any time after the winter solstice, which is but a few days before Christmas.

The timing, contagion, and nature of spring fever passeth all understanding. It is a siren hope and loveliness, a sorceress, an ache in the heart, a flame of revival in the human soul. It is a monumental dream of green pastures and still waters; and it incites grown men to throw away their hats, to perpetrate sonnets in fervid secrecy, or to practice chip shots with rusted Nine-Irons on the snow which lies dying in the streets of the town.

No one is wholly immune, though many do not succumb till they smell hot pine or asphalt, or see the first dust frolicking in a lane. Still others resist even unto the day of the Kentucky Derby or the Indianapolis Five-Hundred-Mile Auto Race, or the Maine Lobster Festival. In contrast, the fisherman is often stricken prematurely, as witness my friend, Frank

Reck. Frank's 1956 Christmas card depicted a basket of trout on a brook bank. The card bore the following legend:

"Only 126 more days to the opening of trout season!"

One year in the city, with winter but a few days old, my wife announced that she had noticed the lengthening of twilight.

"Impossible," I told her, and offered her the almanac. "Look here. Only three or four minutes difference."

"Then it *is* longer!" she cried. "And besides, I heard a bird sing."

"It was a sparrow."

"A sparrow is a bird—and it sang to the growing light."

It may have been this incidence of voiced longing that led us to inquire into the nature of spring fever. We have found no conclusion, save mystery; and mystery is implicit in the beauty of spring.

Spring fever is composed of ingredients sifting through the mind and heart of a human being, at home or far away; and the human being and his mind and heart vary immeasurably. So do the ingredients comprising the litany of spring, for among them are the scent of wood smoke; the light in the eyes of a farmer as he touches a melting furrow with his boot toe; the imagined song of the leaping, ice-free river of your dream; the flow of maple sap; the wild geese charging the moonlit sky with drama; the subtle change in the bark of trees; the swelling under last year's matted leaves; the tendrils of music from peep frogs in a twilit swamp; the sway and color of the weeping willows; the scent of earth; the crack of a baseball bat; the changes in the voices of children on the playground at recess; a man in a window oiling a reel on a sleety Sunday morn; the florist shops and the hats of Easter time; the photograph of a swimming hole; or your own, small son begging desperately for matches.

"What for?"

"I have to build a fire—just a little one."

"But, why?"

"To see the smoke, and the light, and feel warm."

But perhaps spring fever is not so much an ailment as a moment in time. Perhaps it's when cats cry out in the dawn hours in the torment of life and its procreation; and bears creep from their dens in the wild canyons; and a partridge drums on a giant log in the forest, returning each day to drum again in the mystic language of its wooing.

Perhaps it's when the ice breaks up on the Penobscot River; and when men in the back rooms of Bangor talk about old days on the log drive; and when you suddenly see a foal and its mother lying in the young grass by a white fence; and when you find the blue, broken shell of a small egg and know that a young robin has hatched in a nest invisible in the elm branches waving above you.

Or maybe spring fever is when an old man, lame and gray, plans a canoe trip to Hudson's Bay and the Arctic Circle. He forgets that his comrade on the trip is long dead, as he gets out paper and pencil and writes out a supply list for the trip he knows he will never take. In late summer he finds the list stuck between the leaves of a book which should be titled *Of Time and the River*. The old man thoughtfully rereads the list, beginning: "Canoe, paddles, tent, axe, blankets, bacon, flour, salt, whetstone, compass, matches . . ."

He says to himself: "I guess I had it pretty bad last spring," and, smiling inwardly, drops the list into a wastebasket and relights his pipe.

Late in March, I think especially of the power of spring fever as it must affect the woodsmen in the isolated, snow-banked cabins in our Maine wilderness. Fred Walker? Clair Desmond at Telos Dam? Fred Harrison at Hudson Pond? They live alone, and the long icicle of winter must be stabbing their hearts with loneliness, and with longing for spring. One of them will see a crocus in his cabin dooryard; another a chipmunk giving forth an uproar of cheer; another a tiny patch of open water on his lake. Something will swell their hearts, and there will be gratitude, restlessness, a wild elation, and a dramatic trip to town.

But now, in the city, it is only January, and my wife speaks yearningly of seeds for the cabin vegetable garden, but as yet no seed catalogues have arrived. And when I remind her that we have many brown envelopes of seeds in the cabin left over from last year, and the year before that, she says:

"The mice might have eaten them."

But so far the accumulating seeds have not been eaten, and gleefully we buy more each year in homage to spring and growing things.

This year the fever seems more virulent than ever before, but that is an annual characteristic of the ailment. A few days ago, the fever caused me to walk moodily through a sleet storm to the nearest hardware store to buy a new jackknife. There is no excuse for my laughing at my wife, or at my fisherman friend, Frank Reck; for I am eleven hundred miles and one hundred and fourteen days from the log cabin where I will use the knife to whittle cedar shavings to kindle the first fire of spring in the wood stove. And I even bought a whetstone to put a razor edge on the knife. Right now, that jackknife will shave the fuzz off a peach!

What is the instant of your true realization that spring has come? What is the act, the scene, the scent, the incident? Do you know? Did you ever ask yourself? My wife says that, for her, spring comes when she opens the cabin door and steps inside. There's the tar smell, and the kerosene lamps with paper bags over them to keep their chimneys gleaming. Beyond that, she can't describe it, and neither can I.

Sometimes I think the moment comes as I walk down the path to the spring and dip the first pail full. Sometimes I think it's the first loon call. Or another time it's when we discover the first white violet, or light the fire in the stove, or when the first rain falls, and we carry in armfuls of the dry, split wood we cut the fall before.

We don't know; except that the moment is a mystery, and a time of immeasurable joy. What you *do* know is that spring will always come, and its reality is invariably finer than your anticipation. You can count on it! There will be a day, a moment, a combination of the ingredients of spring that you never dreamed of even in the very height of your fever. And that heart-lifting moment will be more wonderful than your total dream.

# Part ONE

*Such stuff as dreams are made on*

The Tempest

# The Saga of Third Chain Cabin

The rifle shot on the ridge back of Third Chain Cabin blew a tunnel through the November stillness. In the kitchen doorway of the cabin, where I stood listening, it seemed as though fragments of the sound split off and drilled smaller tunnels through the forest, and these fragments again divided, and were diminished and muffled, until somewhere in the solitudes the shot achieved a kind of reincarnation in the miracle of new silence.

There were only two human beings who could have heard the shot. I was one. The other was Henry Dennison, who had fired it. Even distorted by distance, the characteristic "blump" of his Winchester .44-40 carbine was unmistakable. And we were the only two deer hunters in Wilderness Township Five, Hancock County, Maine, at the time.

We had built the cabin on Third Chain Lake in 1926, hunted from it each fall for twenty years, dreamed of it in winter, cherished it, talked of it with a shine in our eyes and a lilt in our voices. But this trip was like no other, because it was our last.

"I think," Henry Dennison had said to me, "that this trip better be the swan song."

He was sixty-five, and a lot of us had been calling him "Pop" for a long, long time. The canoe trip from the comfortable headquarters camp on Dobsis Lake in to the isolated cabin on Third Chain Lake had been getting harder for him each fall. Once a challenge and delight, this twelve-mile trek had become an ordeal. He got tangled in blowdowns on the two portages — blowdowns the like of which he had once vaulted with a pack on his back. The sweat glistened on his eloquent skull, and it wrung my heart to see him try to keep his balance in a canoe when his pole slipped on bottom in Second Chain Stream. But his allegiance to the wilderness he loved was a moving thing to see and feel, and some of it rubbed off on all of us.

The sad part was that Pop's old hunting companions had dropped out, one by one, pleading game knees, sore backs, or family obligations. Pop accepted this with outward good humor, but you knew it hurt him just the same. The last of the original hunting party, Al MacMasters, had defaulted the year of our swan song hunt. Pop had showed me Al's letter, which is significant. It read pretty much as follows:

> Dear Harry: (Pop's generation called him "Harry") Susan insists on a European jaunt this fall, and I'm afraid this means that some younger fry will sleep in my old bunk at Third Chain Cabin. Say "hello" to the big ridges and the wind in the pines, and tag a ten-pointer. But *not* The White One!

We had seen a white buck every two or three years ever since we had begun hunting from the cabin. Of course it couldn't have been the same deer, but we always called it The White One. Tom Compus Mentis, the wonderful old Indian who had helped build the cabin, had first sighted the deer. And it was Tom Compus Mentis who had created the freewheeling superstition around the mysterious, exciting creature.

"You shoot The White One," Tom had said, "and you never shoot another deer for seven years. Hear what I say."

So The White One, or one of his offspring, had become not only a symbol of hard luck, but a topic of cabin humor. There wasn't one of us who wouldn't have given a new canoe for a shot at The White One, hard luck or not. But there had been several incidents which bore out Tom Compus Mentis's dark forebodings.

In 1928, Harley Fitch got a ghostly, twilight shot back in the Second Chain Burn. He missed, but two days later upset in his canoe in Second Chain Stream and lost his watch and tobacco.

A couple of years later, Pappy Thornton got a perfect standing shot in

Killman Pond Swamp. He was dead on, but his bullet stopped in a big cedar. He hadn't seen the tree at all, just The White One. It made no difference that the deer was untouched. Within a week, Pappy slipped on a wet root and wrenched his hip.

So Al MacMasters' farewell letter to Pop Dennison, with its reference to The White One, was in the Third Chain Cabin tradition. Pop had stuffed the letter in his pocket, and he had said to me:

"Well, that's the last of the old bunch. But I've got to go back to Third Chain just once more. Will you come with me? Just the two of us?"

"Okay, Pop. I'll be your guide."

"You guide *me?* Why, you could get lost on a billiard table."

"All right. Then I'll do the cooking."

Pop said he could survive my cooking one more time. This last interchange was a routine of long standing between us. We had said the same thing in almost the same words every fall for twenty years. We were in Third Chain Cabin a week later. It was our last trip together.

When Pop's rifle shot merged back into primeval stillness, I leaned in the doorway listening for a second shot. There wasn't a second one. All you could hear was silence, and it seemed to me then, as it does now, that the phrase "dead silence" is a mistaken figure of speech—because silence is alive. Things leap to your mind out of silence. It's as if all your senses were on tiptoe, and there is a faint ringing in your ears which could be your memory tuning up, humming like a tight wire.

The cabin stove was cold. I took some cedar kindling and a stick of dry beech from the wood box and started a fire. Then I looked up the trail we'd spotted. It led through immense white pines, and on up across the lonely beech ridge to Killman Pond Swamp. There wasn't a red squirrel, a bluejay, or a moose bird in sight. Not a branch stirred. Not a pinecone fell.

Should I go up the trail to find Pop? Or should I stay where I was? Had he wounded a deer? Had he decided to track it alone? Had he missed? Or was he dressing one out with the old, bone-handled knife that Pappy Thornton had made for him out of a flat file and a piece of moose horn?

I pictured the knife. It made me think of the irrepressible Pappy, and that made me glance at the alarm clock on the kitchen shelf. It had stopped, but my watch said ten o'clock on the button. The alarm clock was a hurt and crippled thing. You had to wind it every few hours, or it would conk out. The timepiece had sustained a direct hit from a seven-pound flat iron that Pappy Thornton had aimed at me. It was a justified attack, for I had hidden two of these flatirons in Pappy's knapsack, and he had unknowingly lugged the superfluous heavy metal all the way in from the Dobsis Lake camp. It had seemed very funny at the time.

The cabin stove was warming with the fire I'd built. It made expansion noises, and a tired old bolt let go with a snap. I closed the damper in the stovepipe. Then I took the alarm clock down and wound it. I couldn't get those flatirons out of mind; and I could feel my face grinning as I remembered old Pappy's Homeric rage when he had discovered them in his knapsack.

What do you do with two flatirons in a hunting cabin? You can scarcely imagine anything more futile except an electric razor. But in a kind of boomerang way, those flatirons came in handy, as I shall explain.

The front door of the cabin, facing Third Chain Lake, was built of heavy pine boards, double thickness. It was hung crooked. In fact, I hung it myself. It opened inward, and it would swing shut of itself — silently and with seeming belligerence. Harley Fenlayson's hand was once caught by the swinging door, and his blast of free speech was of such high octane that Pop Dennison recorded it in the cabin diary. Macey Armstrong's dog, Carrots, got his tail pinched in the door, and when freed went yipping off toward Unknown Lake, returning after two hours with his face like an old, old man's — bewhiskered with porcupine quills.

So it came about that one of the errant flatirons did service as a doorstop, until the night Pop Dennison got up sleepily and walked out to take a look at the stars. On the return trip he kicked the flatiron with his tender big toe, and his wail of anguish wafted into the night and set the loons to hollering on the lake.

No one could get back to sleep, so we all got up, had an early breakfast, and went hunting. Just after daylight, Roy Bailey got a running shot at The White One on the Pistol Lake tote road. He found white hair, but no blood. That very afternoon, while splitting firewood, Roy cut his knee with the axe. He traced the blame back to the flatiron, which he flung to oblivion in a quagmire in Unknown Swamp.

That leaves the second flatiron. One fall a guide named Amos Berry used it for a drag on the chain of a trap he had set for an elusive porcupine. A night or two later we were all aroused by a commotion outside near the cabin dump. You'd have thought it was raining old coal hods.

"You've got your porcupine, Amos," said Pop Dennison. "Go and tend to him."

Amos took his rifle off the wall pegs and went out barefoot into the frosty moonlight. The roar of his shot danced off across the lake and caromed around the ridges. The night was simultaneously defiled by as dense and penetrating an odor as ever outraged the nostrils of man. Poor Amos! His porcupine had turned out to be a large skunk with a twin brother. Roy Bailey thoughtfully asked if Amos had dynamited the privy.

"He fired the shot smelled 'round the world," said Pappy Thornton.

## The Saga of Third Chain Cabin

You never saw anyone lose friends as fast as Amos Berry. We quarantined him in a tarpaper shelter up the trail and passed him his meals on a long board. We made him hunt downwind of us for days. Pop Dennison found a piece of haywire, hooked it to the tainted flatiron, went out on the lake with it in his canoe, and buried it at sea. I doubt if any two flatirons ever caused finer furor.

I looked again at the alarm clock ticking away on the shelf. What with its ruptured viscera, it sounded as mournful as a slot machine digesting your last quarter. It was two minutes past ten. That meant Pop Dennison had fired his shot three or four minutes before. A lot of things can happen in your memory in four minutes — especially when the history of an old hunting cabin is coming at you from all four walls and the smoky rafters.

I went into the main room of the cabin, after folding the blankets on my bunk in the kitchen under the skylight. On this trip only one bunk in the main room had blankets. That was Pop Dennison's, and I smoothed it up, and hung up his old, gray sweater and the stocking cap he wore to keep his bald head warm on cold nights.

The other bunks looked lonesome and deserted — Bill Howell's, Roy Bailey's, Al MacMasters', Harry Wheeler's. Harry Wheeler had killed the first deer on the very first hunting trip, twenty years before. Harley Fenlayson was guiding Harry at the time, and they were in Harley's canoe on Second Chain Deadwater, when a superb eight-pointer stepped out on a grassy point in the stream. Harry had fired from the bow of the canoe. It was a clean neck shot and the buck dropped instantly, and there was wild rejoicing when the other canoes came around the bend and saw Harley and Harry dressing out the game and announcing liver and bacon for supper.

I went over and looked closely at Harry Wheeler's bunk. None of his belongings had been on the bunk for years — but there was his ashtray, an old coffee can cover, wedged between two wall logs. While I was thinking of Harry and his buck, a little white-foot mouse ran along a log and sat down in Harry's ashtray, his whiskers twitching as he watched me. I went back to the kitchen, my footsteps muffled on the deer hide rugs, and hunted around for a mousetrap. I decided against setting one. If this was our last trip to Third Chain Cabin, why not let the mouse live to inherit it for a winter home?

The business of living and letting live reminded me of a strange episode that occurred one frosty afternoon on the Key Road — an abandoned lumber road that ran along the west shore of Third Chain Lake. The old bunch had been intact, then, and everyone had got his deer except Pop Dennison. It seemed ironical that our host, the man who had built and provisioned the cabin and planned all the trips, should have been denied a fair shot at a deer. But in eight days of hunting, Pop had seen nothing but the white flash of a tail. He always liked to hunt alone, because—as he said:

"That way, you can breathe the wilderness deeper."

But on this afternoon, I had persuaded him to hunt the Key Road with me. He had finally consented—just to please me, I'm certain. But I was proud of the chance to show him a deer.

He was having trouble with the circulation in one of his legs. It was partly numb, and it made him awkward. He kept stepping on dry twigs. I didn't see how we could get near a deer.

I was ahead, cat-footing over the moss and through the spruce saplings, wishing Pop wouldn't make so much noise. I came up over the brow of a pine knoll, and there in the straight road ahead stood the most magnificent buck I ever saw—but one. I'm not positive, but I think he was a twelve-pointer. His ruddy-gray flanks shone in the low-slanting sun rays. He was standing broadside about eighty yards away—a perfect shot.

I signaled to Pop with my hand. He came up beside me, saw the buck, cocked his rifle silently, and aimed. I thought my heartbeat would knock the buttons off my shirt. I never knew such suspense. I thought Pop would never pull the trigger—and he never did. What he did was to lower the hammer to half-cock, take the red bandana out of his hip pocket, and wave it at the buck. The deer stiffened, wonderfully poised, four feet braced, head high and imperious. Then he cleared a blowdown from a standing start, and vanished, his hooves thudding off through the forest.

"What the hell happened, Pop? Why didn't you shoot?"

"Well—we've got all the meat we can use," Pop said, "and I don't need a trophy."

"But you *always* need a trophy."

"All right." He tapped his forehead. "I've got the trophy right here. I'll have the fun of remembering that animal just as he was—and not the way he would have been if I'd pulled the trigger."

I put another chunk of beech in the cabin stove. Then I took a damp cloth and wiped off the oilcloth-covered table where we'd eaten so many meals; where at night we'd told of the day's hunt, where we'd been and what we'd seen; and where, at breakfast, we'd planned where we'd hunt during the day.

The teakettle sang its familiar song on the stove, and I washed all the lamp chimneys in the hot water. Why? I would never see their light again, and Pop wouldn't. But I took special pains with the lamp Pop had read aloud by all those nights. How many nights? Six or eight nights a year for twenty years. Say a hundred and fifty nights, with the guys lying in their bunks after supper; and while Pop read on, the snoring would start, and I'd lie in my bunk under the kitchen skylight identifying each sleeper by his snore.

When most of the boys were in dreamland, Pop would close his book, using for a bookmark a thin piece of sweet-smelling cedar that Pappy Thornton had whittled. Then he'd turn the lamp down and blow it out, and you'd hear the springs of his bunk as he turned in. You'd hear his sigh of comfort, and you'd remember how the lamplight gleamed on his head. And you'd remember how wonderful the light in the cabin window looked, when you'd hunted too late, and the dark overtook you.

Finally, lying in the kitchen bunk, you'd see the stars shining through the skylight, and the crippled alarm clock would tick away, and maybe a pinecone would come down ker-whack on the tarpaper roof. So all this is why I washed the lamp chimneys so carefully.

Or maybe I washed them partly to please the mythical Little Man. He might want to winter here, along with the mouse. The Little Man was a figment of Pappy Thornton's fantastic imagination. Pappy Thornton was Pop Dennison's resident caretaker at the Dobsis Lake headquarters camp for many years, and those were the most hilarious years at the cabin, as well as at the main camp.

Pappy claimed to have seen The Little Man hunting out of season one Fall when he and I went in early to Third Chain Lake to open the cabin and cut firewood. According to Pappy, The Little Man was about eighteen inches tall. He had a little rifle in proportion, and wore a fur cap and mackinaw to size. He haunted the forests, and appeared out of nowhere, standing in the middle of the trail, and terrifying intruders in his domain. For years, every strange sound, every eerie tapping on the cabin roof, every scurrying of mice was attributed to Pappy's bizarre Little Man.

Pappy, who, with a crooked knife could create anything out of pine, cedar, or whole cloth, fashioned three separate Little Men, each with its little rifle, cartridge belt, and clothing sewed by his wife, Katie. When he and I went in ahead of the main party to provision Third Chain Cabin, we positioned one Little Man athwart a blowdown on First Chain Portage, and another on Second Chain Dam.

Amos Berry and Harley Fenlayson, two extremely superstitious guides, thought The Little Man was hounding them. They were certain of it when they found the third Little Man sitting on the cabin porch when they arrived. They didn't find out till later that Pappy had whittled *three* Little Men, and meanwhile were certain that the hunting trip was jinxed. They wouldn't step out of the cabin alone at night; and in the daytime, when they were eating lunch back on the ridge, they'd sometimes look up and see The Little Man peering down at them from a tree where Pappy had suspended him in advance. Pappy knew where to plant his creation, because lunching spots were usually announced at breakfast.

Since Pappy and I invariably hunted together, I was party to these high jinks. As hunters, our score was not high. We had too much fun. We'd still-hunt along the nut-smelling beech ridge for an hour, then sit on a stump or a sun-warmed boulder, talking in loud whispers, then in natural voices. Pop Dennison figured that our laughter frightened a lot of game away, and he finally called a halt.

"Henceforth, as of now," Pop Dennison announced, "Pappy Thornton and Ed Smith are separated."

This was a sad blow to Pappy and me, but we'd earned it. How Pappy got us back together again is part of the Third Chain Cabin saga, and a fine sample of Pappy's devious schemes. It kept the hunting personnel in a state of ferment for days.

Shortly after Pop Dennison had separated us, Pappy came into the cabin bearing his axe and a burden of abject misery and hurt. His saddened eyes showed pale blue behind his gold-rimmed spectacles as he called everyone close to examine his axe. It had a nick in the blade as big as a crescent moon.

"Look what Ed Smith did to my axe that I've loved an' cherished through the years," Pappy said.

It was true that I'd been using his axe, and I knew how he treasured it. I was horrified to think I'd ruined the historic implement.

"I'm sorry, Pappy," I said. "I'll grind it down for you when we get back to Dobsis."

Pappy turned away from me, his eyes downcast and forlorn.

"Mr. Dennison," he said to Pop, "please tell him (meaning me) that I don't wish to speak to him again—nor I don't want him to speak to me. This is the end, between us."

"Pop Dennison repeated this ultimatum to me—and from then on, all verbal contact between Pappy and me was through a third person.

"Ask him (meaning ask Pappy)," I'd say to Pop Dennison, or Roy, or Harley, "where he put my extra cigarettes."

And Pappy, replying through a middleman, would say:

"I don't know a thing about his dang cigarettes, nor I wouldn't touch anything that his hands has touched."

The middleman, or interpreter, as we came to call him, would repeat the message direct to me, and Pappy and I would go into a brooding silence, with everyone else laughing. This went on for two or three days, until finally Pop Dennison said:

"I see no reason why Pappy and Ed shouldn't resume hunting together. Since they're not speaking, we have a guarantee of reasonable silence on the ridges."

The bunch all gathered on the cabin porch to see Pappy and me start off together again.

"Ask him," I said to Bill Howell, "if two sandwiches are enough for his lunch. That's all I made for him."

Bill Howell relayed the question to Pappy, who relayed his answer back through Bill to me.

"Tell him," Pappy said, "that I ain't had any appetite since he ruined my axe. Nor I couldn't eat a sandwich he'd made if I was starvin'."

His face a gaunt mask of tragic aloofness, Pappy took his rifle and started up the trail. I followed. We walked an hour in this painfully maintained state of enmity till we came to a favorite beech blowdown, where in the past we had sat together telling stories, smoking, whittling, and breaking all the rules of deer hunting.

This time, not a word or a smile passed between us. Wondering how Pappy would resolve the situation, I sat down on one end of the log. Pappy walked the full length of the log away from me and settled himself, his back toward me. I got out the venison sandwiches I'd made, went to Pappy's end of the log and put one near him. He didn't touch it till I'd gone back to my end. I was having a serious time keeping up the show. I wasn't the actor Pappy was. We ate in silence, back-to-back, not once looking at each other.

Then, suddenly, I heard a noise overhead. I turned my eyes upward, and there, dropping from an overhanging beech limb, right in my face, was *The Little Man!* It startled me out of my wits. Pappy had suspended the thing with black thread, patiently planning for days for this single moment — and when he saw my eyes pop he could contain himself no longer. The forest awoke and resounded with laughter. We both stood up and came together, raining blows of affection and reunion. And in the very midst of our rejoicing, two deer broke cover from a patch of shoulder-high spruce, and danced out into the open ridge. We jumped for our rifles, and fired simultaneously. Both deer dropped. They weren't over fifty yards from us. One was a spikehorn, the other a small doe. Obviously, the two critters had worked up to us during our silence on the log before The Little Man arrived by air.

Pappy confessed that he'd nicked the axe himself, deliberately, as part of his conspiracy to get us together again. We dressed out our deer, and lugged them down to the cabin. Pop Dennison and the rest of the bunch were in when we arrived. Pop said he could hear us coming for a mile. But a big cheer went up, and Pop wrote in the diary for that year:

"Best trip to Third Chain ever. Silence can be golden."

It was twelve minutes past ten in the cabin, and through the window just to the right of the front door, I could see the frost melting on the bottom of the canoe turned up on the lake shore. Through that same window, I had made the acquaintance of the biggest buck I ever saw. It had gradually become my duty at Third Chain Cabin to police the camp after the hunters scattered in the morning. On that particular morning, we'd had pancakes for breakfast, and Macey Armstrong had spilled some maple syrup on the end of the table nearest that front window. It just goes to show how narrow are the rails of destiny — especially with regard to deer hunting.

I had a got a dishcloth, wet and soapy, and walked from the kitchen to the end of table and had started scrubbing. I glanced through the window, and dropped the cloth, every muscle tense. I'd looked from that window a hundred — maybe a thousand times, and seen nothing but the pine needles and rocks on the path down to the lake. The path was thirty-seven steps long from the cabin porch to the shore. This time, standing in the lower end toward the lake, I saw the buck.

He was heavy in the neck and shoulders, and almost as red as the pine needles — but with a gray throat and gray muzzle. His rack of horns was so fine a spread of points it took my breath. For me, this was it — the chance of a lifetime. And what would the boys say when they got home after hunting all day, and found me with this record breaker, tagged right from the cabin doorway?

I slipped my rifle off the wall pegs, and gently eased a couple of brass-gleaming shells into the magazine, and one in the chamber. The buck stood perfectly motionless, but when I opened the door he tensed, turned his head directly toward me, and snorted. I saw the bead front sight settle low in the rear sight notch, felt the stock tucked against my right cheek — and the next instant the front door, swinging shut behind me, hit hard against my right heel and leg. I haven't the wildest idea where my bullet went — high, low, or to either side.

The great buck knew when his luck was in, and disappeared into the dense cedar growth along the lakeshore before I could gather my senses and jack in another shell. I unloaded my rifle, put it back on the pegs, finished wiping the maple syrup from the oilcloth — and then I hauled back and kicked the front door as hard as I could. It didn't bother the door a bit. And it made me feel only a little bit better.

Now, on this final hunt with Pop, so many years later, I could remember the big buck and smile. And now I could remember to open the front door and hang onto it, letting it close gently as I stepped out on the porch. I stood there looking at the mist on the lake — and a second or two later, I heard a footstep in the cabin. It scared me for a second, till the door opened again and Pop Dennison stepped out beside me on the porch. He'd come down the trail off the ridge, into the kitchen, and on through the cabin. And his eyes were bright and triumphant. He held a fresh deer heart and liver skewered with a beech twig.

"Pop! You connected!"

"Yes. Let's go up and lug the critter down. And —" he hesitated, and went on — "what do you say we put the shutters on and go out for good this afternoon? I've got my deer."

"All right. We can make it to Dobsis before dark — if the lake stays calm. What'd you shoot?"

"A buck."

"That's a good way to end it, Pop."

He looked at me and grinned. He took his felt hat off, and mopped the sweat from his head. I didn't notice anything strange about his grin at the time. I was just thinking of lugging his deer down, shuttering the cabin, putting the cover on the skylight, the lard pail over the stovepipe, emptying the teakettle, packing all the freezeables to take out —

"What you been doing all morning?" Pop asked.

"Remembering. Your shot came practically on the button of ten o'clock. It's twenty-eight minutes past ten, now. I've remembered twenty years in twenty-eight minutes."

"So have I," Pop said. "Good — all good. Let's go."

He led the way, limping a little on his bum leg. Less than a quarter of a mile from the cabin, he stopped, reached back and grabbed my arm. He pulled me a couple of feet to one side, pointed, and said:

"Look there!"

The deer lay in a depression in the deep green moss. It was hidden, unless you looked just right through the cedar fronds.

"My God, Pop! *The White One!*"

I could feel my hands starting to shake and my throat getting thin and tight. I went closer to look at the deer. It wasn't a big buck. It was a spikehorn, beautifully formed, and wonderful to look at — as white as summer clouds, except for a few brown spots an inch or so in diameter.

"The White One," Pop said. "Don't you see the point?"

All I could see was that this old man had wound up his last hunt at his beloved Third Chain Cabin with the deer — or one of its offspring — that was part of the soul of the place. I didn't know the right words to tell him that. So I just looked away at the deer.

"Don't you see?" Pop persisted. "Don't you remember what old Tom Compus Mentis said? 'Seven years without a deer if you shoot The White

One?' I've fooled the jinx! This is my last deer anyway! Because it's our last trip!"

There isn't much more in the saga of Third Chain Cabin. Just the way it looked with the shutters on as we pulled offshore in the canoe on the way down to Dobsis; just the strange feeling of putting the cabin key in the milk bottle, and putting the milk bottle in the hole under the big pine root near the porch; just thinking of it now and then, in winter with the snow on the roof, and the pines moaning in the wind, and the mice snug inside ... and maybe The Little Man, too.

But there is a little bit more, at that. When Pop Dennison died in 1952, he willed the Dobsis Camp and Third Chain Cabin to his son, Jim. And Jim gave Pop's old deer rifle — the Winchester .44-40 that downed The White One — to Pappy Thornton, and tears came in Pappy's eyes. One of the big pines fell in a gale across the roof of the cabin and crushed it like a shell, and so Third Chain Cabin is sinking back, down, molding into the earth in the wilderness from which it grew.

# A Rifle Named "Sleigh Bells"

Any rifle has a history—a story—and many rifles have strangely begotten names. This is the story of a rifle named "Sleigh Bells." It begins on a warm, still morning in May when Al Foster boated me across Grand Lake in Penobscot County, Maine, to my cabin on the wilderness shore. I had no inkling that I was on my way to discovering a secret concerning a buck deer I had shot almost thirty years before. There was something weird and haunting about it, because the secret was Henry Dennison's. "Pop" Dennison was my father-in-law—and he had been dead for more than four years!

I have no convictions about communication after death, one way or the other; but I hope Pop knows I have found him out, and perhaps he does. To me, it's a heartwarming thought. He was such a vital and dynamic personality that I don't have to listen very hard to hear the echo of his *basso profundo* chuckle over my discovery. You could call it leftover laughter.

Pop Dennison, more than anyone, got me interested in deer hunting, the Maine woods, and log cabins—including the one that loomed closer over the bow of Al Foster's boat that day in May 1956. But when Al put me ashore, I wasn't thinking about Pop; and the buck I'd shot so long ago down on Second Chain Lake had been totally out of mind for years. Presently, I was to do some intense thinking about both, but for the moment I was preoccupied with the purpose of my trip to the cabin, which was to take an inventory of its contents with the idea of selling out—lock, stock, the works.

My wife and I had built this cabin, and many of the things in it, mostly with our own hands. We had lived in this remote and beautiful spot for ten incomparable years, and it was high in our hearts. The decision to sell had been tough to make and hard to take. But it made sense. We had reached the age where a gale on the lake was a hazard, rather than a bright challenge; the toting and hauling a burden; and the twenty-nine miles to a telephone too far for peace of mind. But, as I waved good-bye to Al Foster and walked alone up the path to the plank porch, I thought of the rich experience of our life here, and it pulled hard.

The wake of Al's boat followed along shore, and you could hear the little waves breaking. In the distance, the boat was a speck, and its motor sounded like a bee under a derby hat. I looked straight across at the long, dark peaks of The Traveller Range rising three thousand feet above the lake, saw the snow patch on Big Traveller, and the bald eagle doing a slow, superb lazy eight in a thermal above Birch Point. Then I turned, opened the cabin door and stepped inside. And the ghosts came stalking, one by one, with their sad whispering. They were nudging me toward Pop Dennison and his secret about that buck deer, but of course I didn't know it at the time.

Just inside the cabin door there was a loose floorboard. It had been loose for years. I went in and stepped on it to see if it would make its familiar squeak. It did. Then I walked into the kitchen and looked at the wood stove. This spring there would be no ritual of lighting the first fire in this wonderfully familiar stove. What manner of man would succeed to the ritual? Would he love it, as we had? Whoever he might be, I said to him:

"Mister, you've inherited one hell of a good cook stove."

I had said it aloud, and the sound of my voice startled me. This was no good. If I didn't get going on the inventory, it would be but a matter of minutes before I'd be talking to myself—and *believing it!*

Al Foster had agreed to pick me up at noon for the trip back across the lake to my car. I had about two hours to finish my melancholy job. So I got out a pad and pencil, started by itemizing everything in the kitchen, and worked systematically through the cabin. I wound up in my den, where my deer rifle hung on the wall pegs.

This rifle is an old model .32 Special Winchester, half magazine. It has a sling ring on the receiver, and when I took the rifle down, the ring tinkled in the lonely stillness of the cabin, and the sound gave my memory a terrific clout.

It's ridiculous what an insignificant stimulus, like the "plink" of metal on metal, can do to a man's thoughts. On second consideration, it isn't ridiculous at all — because memory is one of the great marvels of life. For example, by a simple exercise of remembering, you can be in two places at the same instant. Actually, I was standing in my log cabin on Grand Lake. But the sound of the sling ring had given me such a yank that to all intents and purposes I was also a hundred-odd miles away, down in Hancock County. The time had changed, too. It was early in November 1926 — thirty years ago. And I was standing in Pop Dennison's deer hunting cabin that we had built the summer before.

We had built the cabin at the head of Third Chain Lake in what was then virgin deer hunting country. It was twelve hard miles by canoe from Pop's permanent camp at the foot of Dobsis Lake. Pop's annual hunting trip at the Dobsis camp had already been an institution for years. The select personnel, known as "The Old Bunch," consisted of Harry Wheeler, Bill Howell, and Pop. The guides were Harley Fitch, Harley Fenlayson, and Roy Bailey.

The 1926 hunting trip was extra special, extra exclusive, because it was Third Chain Cabin's christening. The trip's planning, which began weeks in advance, had a pioneer zest that was contagious. I had dropped heavy hints for an invitation, but Pop didn't field any of them.

"I haven't seen the big woods in fall yet, Pop. What are they like?"

"Wonderful," said Pop, and described them at length.

"I hope I cut enough firewood last summer," I said.

"If you didn't, we'll cut some more."

Just because I was a mere kid of twenty-six, with no deer hunting history to speak of, I was excluded from this all-important trip. And I had spent most of a treasured summer vacation helping Roy Bailey build the peeled spruce cabin where these over-privileged old characters would be sheltered. I had patched and painted the canoes they would use, toted in their cook stove, tar papered their roof. And they had cast me aside, depriving me of my rightful adventure.

The crowning misery was when Pop showed me his nonresident Maine hunting license with the deer tags. But no! The crowning misery was when, as though conferring an honor, he asked me if I'd like to drive "The Old Bunch" from Framingham, Massachusetts, where they lived, to the night train at the North Station in Boston, where they would embark for Maine — and Third Chain Cabin.

If I wasn't green with envy and frustration, I felt that way. I helped them aboard the train with their duffel bags and rifles, and wished them luck, while inwardly hoping the cabin roof would leak and the stove would smoke. When the train pulled out, I stood glumly at the gate, reading the scheduled stops on the bulletin board: Portland, Bangor, Lincoln, Mattawamkeag, Forest Station, Vanceboro, St. John, Halifax, and all those wonderful places I couldn't go to. Then I drove home through the frosty night, bruised with self-pity.

Three or four days later, I received a cockeyed telegram from Lincoln, Maine. As near as I can remember, it read like this:

> GALLOP THE SHALLOP AT FIRST CHAIN WEDNESDAY
> (signed) POP

Some telegram! But what else could you expect from that artful, bald-headed, stumpy-built bundle of wisdom? It is a known fact — a matter of written record — that Pop Dennison wrote some of his annual reports to his stockholders in blank verse. If you don't believe this, and I don't blame you, check the reports prior to 1950 of the Dennison Manufacturing Co., Framingham, Massachusetts.

The whole shenanigan of the 1926 hunting trip is characteristic of Pop Dennison and the way he did things — always with careful staging, and elements of suspense, mystery, and surprise. He'd probably been planning his stunt for weeks. Rather than say outright: "Ed, you join us at Third Chain Cabin after The Old Bunch has had a few days together," he had sweated me dry, just because he knew my ultimate delight would be magnified by ten.

Incidentally, it was no cinch in those days to get from Third Chain Lake to the town of Lincoln to send a telegram. And, just as Pop had intended, the telegram itself took some decoding. After about an hour's mystification and torment, I figured it out for what it was: a command invitation to take the Tuesday night train from Boston to Lincoln, get a ride from Lincoln to the head of Dobsis Lake Wednesday, find someone to boat me down Dobsis to First Chain Lake Carry, where, if I hunted in the right place, I would find a "shallop," which meant canoe. "Gallop" meant hurry. By means of the canoe, and several hours paddling and poling through the three Chain Lakes and their connecting streams, I would eventually arrive at Third Chain Cabin.

Thirty years later, in the den of my Grand Lake cabin, I could feel myself smiling. I was smiling at the sound of Pop Dennison's voice. It was almost as if he were actually speaking, saying to The Old Bunch that fall at Third Chain:

"Wait till Ed gets that telegram. His lid will fly off."

It had, too. The telegram reached me Tuesday afternoon, a few hours before train time. And I didn't even own a rifle, let alone a Maine hunting license or a ticket on the night train. I asked and got permission from my boss for a few days off, including that Tuesday afternoon. I telephoned my wife and found she had been in on the scheme all along. Then I went down to Federal Street in Boston to the late Bob Smith's Sporting Goods Store and bought a hunting license and a secondhand rifle. The rifle was an old model .32 Special Winchester, half-magazine, with a sling ring on the receiver.

Because of my intense remembering of Pop, it seemed weird and spooky to be holding that same rifle, now, in my own cabin. Pop had spent a night in this cabin. His hands had held this rifle. Would I list the rifle on my inventory, leaving it to the unknown future owner of this beloved place? How would I describe it?

"One (1) .32 Special Winchester carbine, excellent condition."

No! The description was vastly oversimplified. It ought to tell how, after I found the "shallop," or canoe, on First Chain Lake, I laid the rifle along the gunwale, tossed my knapsack in the bow, and paddled up the lake; how the shod canoe pole sounded on the rocky bottom of Second Chain Stream; how the shell-iced puddles cracked under my moccasins on Third Chain Carry, and the middle thwart of the canoe bit into the back of my neck as I lugged across into Third Chain; and then the big moment when I hauled the canoe ashore under the leaning cedar at the cabin, and Pop Dennison opened the front door and waved both hands, and hollered:

"Hello, boy! Hello! Hello! I see you made it."

I couldn't remember when I'd been so happy.

"Where's the bunch, Pop?" I asked.

"Hunting. They'll be back."

"Do they like the cabin?"

"They're bats about it. What you got there? A new rifle?"

"Sure — new secondhand."

I handed it to him. He checked to see if it was loaded, and I awaited his distinguished approval of my pride and joy. No approval of any kind was forthcoming — nothing but a frown, and a stern look in Pop's steel-blue eyes.

"What's the matter with it, Pop?"

"The essential of still-hunting for deer is stillness."

"Okay, I'll be still."

"Not with this," he said, shaking the rifle so that the sling ring tinkled. "You might just as well go forth to the beech ridges with a bell dangling from your neck."

"What'll I do? Hunt with a slingshot?"

"No. I'll fix that confounded ring."

He got a piece of soft, white grocery string and wound the ring all around. When he had looped the end under the last two turns and cut it off, he shook the rifle again, and you couldn't hear a thing.

"There," said Pop, handing me the rifle, "from now on, it's up to you."

It was too late in the afternoon to hunt the long beech ridge back of the cabin, so we sat on the porch and watched the sun get low over Duck Lake Mountain; and, as the shadows lengthened, the hunters drifted in, and told their several tales. Bill Howell, with Roy Bailey guiding, had shot a buck where Killman Pond Stream came into the lake. Harry Wheeler and Harley Fenlayson had fallen asleep in the sun and dry beech leaves. When they woke up and stirred the leaves, three deer broke cover within a few yards of them.

"Just another 'caught napping' episode," said Harry.

Harley Fitch, hunting alone, brought in a fat, dry doe; and we had fresh liver for supper. Pop told about the noise my rifle made, and the Old Bunch promptly named the rifle "Sleigh Bells."

"Ever had buck fever, Ed?" Bill Howell asked.

"No. 'Course not."

"Old hand, hey?" Roy Bailey asked me.

"Sure."

"How many deer all told have you actually accounted for?" Harry Wheeler asked.

"Four — so for."

No one believed me — which was fair enough, because I had multiplied the truth by four.

"Wait till tomorrow," I said. "I'll bring one in. You'll see."

Pop Dennison said: "The steam that blows the whistle never turns the wheel."

"How many people at home did you promise venison to?" Bill Howell asked me.

"Just three or four guys in my office," I said.

"Poor, starvin' guys," said Harley Fitch.

As the kid member of the party, I was the target for all the jokes, and I had talked big. I had better produce. But, in two days hard hunting, my score was three porcupines, and Pop wrote in the cabin diary:

"Ed Smith and his rifle, Sleigh Bells, are doing well in Quill Pig circles."

The third afternoon I came in early, my moccasins soundless on the pine needles on the path to the kitchen door of the cabin. I heard voices in the cabin and stopped, not intending to eavesdrop, but getting trapped into it. Pop Dennison was talking to Roy Bailey, and this is what he said:

"I'd dearly love to have that boy get a deer. Will you take him with you tomorrow?"

Roy said he would. He said he knew where there was a big buck working in the old burn over toward Second Lake. Then Pop said:

"Make it casual, Roy — so Ed won't suspect us."

I ducked back up the path, and started whistling, and they came to the kitchen door to greet me, none the wiser.

That night I couldn't sleep. Pop Dennison wanted me to get a deer even more than I wanted it myself. I had to make good — for Pop. I was suddenly weighed with responsibility to this devious and exciting old man, who was my father-in-law. I was no longer hunting for myself. I was hunting for Pop — and for the vicarious triumph he would derive from my success — if any.

The next morning at daylight breakfast, Bill Howell said his feet hurt.

"I think I'll take a day off," Bill said.

That left Roy Bailey free to guide me, and I knew that was the way Pop had rigged it. None of them had any idea I knew what was cooking; and so, just out of devilment, I said to Bill Howell:

"I'll stay in camp with you, Bill. We can play cribbage."

When I saw Pop Dennison's face, I could have bitten out my tongue. He was hurt and shocked by my implication that I had quit cold, or — worse — didn't like deer hunting.

"It's your last day in camp!" he said. "Did you forget?"

I said: "For a second, I did. No cribbage for me — just the long, brown ridges."

"Good! Good for you. How'd you like to go with Roy?"

"Wonderful," I said. "I'll make some sandwiches, and we'll get going."

I made the sandwiches with thin slices of cold deer liver left over from breakfast. Pop followed us a little way up the trail back of the cabin. Then he slapped me on the shoulder, and said:

"Good luck to you," and turned back; and Roy and I were alone, cat-footing through the ghostly gray beeches.

I had already known Roy Bailey for several years. We had fished salmon together on spring trips, and been on canoe trips in summer, and worked together building Third Chain Cabin. But Roy was a hunter at heart, and still is, and I caught the fever from watching him work — three or four slow, careful steps, then a pause, and his head turning slowly, eyes searching, peering, listening. His rifle was an old favorite — a .45-70, the cartridges almost as big as your forefinger. Sometimes, when the angle was just right, I could read the number of his guide's license carved in the stock of his rifle. It was "8820."

We were traveling east toward Killman Pond swamp. We crossed the swamp and turned north toward the old burn, where a fire of years before had reached Second Chain Lake. We had entered the burn a distance of a hundred yards or so, when Roy stopped, tense. He moved his hand in a beckoning motion, and I knew my chance had come, and I started shaking like a twig in a current. Roy beckoned again, and as I moved up to him, I stepped on a dry stick — and a deer blew, blew again, and I heard the animal's hooves thud as he took off.

Roy looked around at me, a small, wry grin on his lips. I was sick. Anyone that would step on a dry stick at a time like that wasn't fit to be in the woods. What would Pop think, when he heard about it?

Roy pointed to a nearby spruce blowdown, and we went over quietly and sat down on it.

"I'm some still-hunter," I whispered.

"Never mind," he whispered back. "Take it easy. Let's eat our sandwiches."

Roy took a big bite from his sandwich, and it bulged his cheek. I nibbled at mine. The new growth after the burn was dense, and black stumps loomed here and there. A jay screeched and a red squirrel chattered — and behind us we heard a crash, and the thud of hooves. Something caught the corner of my eye, to my left — beyond where Roy was sitting. It was the motion of a spruce branch, and I focused on it. The growth was so thick that it was like sighting through a pipe. The branch moved again, and I saw the magnificent head and neck of a buck.

"I can see him!" I whispered.

"Go ahead and shoot," Roy whispered.

I reached down and picked up my rifle and cocked it. The ivory bead front sight settled into the notch of the rear sight — and the shot broke open the silence, and Roy and I were standing up, our liver sandwiches lying on the green moss where we'd dropped them.

"Did you see the deer?" I asked.

"No. But it must have been the same one — circling to get us sized up. Did you hit him?"

"No. When I fired, he just disappeared."

"Where was he?"

I sat down on the log again, and sighted the spot with my rifle. Roy got the line, and walked slowly to the spot through the tangle.

"Come on over here," he called back, and I did — and the big buck lay on the green moss, dead from a clean neck shot, and Roy was shaking my hand, and laughing. I thought of Pop Dennison and couldn't wait to tell him.

"Fire three shots," Roy said. "Pop'll hear them, an' come. I'll bet he ain't far."

Pop heard the shots, and came. He was all out of breath, and his head gleamed with sweat.

"Boy!" he said. "You're white as a sheet. Go and sit down. What a wonderful head — the buck's, not yours."

Now that it was all over, I felt weak as a starved kitten. I sat on a stump, while Roy and Pop bled the deer and dressed it, and skewered the heart and liver on a forked alder.

"Hey, Pop," I said. "You got here awful quick. Were you following us?"

"Oh-o-o-o-o — well, not exactly. Thought I'd like to be around."

What could you ever do to repay a guy like Pop? What he loved best, outside of home and family, was hunting. He had just given up a morning's hunting because of me. He had given up another day of it so he would be at Third Chain Cabin to greet me when I arrived from Boston. And he had made the long hard trip out to Lincoln, personally — to send me that crazy telegram. I would never catch up with him, and I would be a long time understanding his works and ways. But, sitting on that stump, looking down at my buck, I had what I then thought was a flash of pure inspiration. Much as I wanted that handsome trophy for myself, I would have it mounted by the best taxidermist I could find — and I would give it to Pop! It would surprise hell out of him. He'd think I was having the nine-point head mounted for myself, but all the while it would be just for him.

Now, after that inspired moment on Second Chain Burn, I know the secret of the deer head, and how Pop kept it locked for all the years in his eloquent skull. If it weren't for the tinkle of the sling ring on old "Sleigh Bells" that morning in my cabin, I'd never have found it out. The string that Pop had wound on the ring had been long since removed by a gunsmith who had reblued the rifle, otherwise no tinkle.

I put the rifle back on the pegs on the wall of my den, and listened. I could hear Al Foster's boat coming, but I couldn't see it yet. I was thinking of the literally open-mouthed astonishment in Pop Dennison's face when, in the winter of 1927, I had presented him with the deer head, beautifully mounted.

"No!" he said. "Oh, Ed — No! You can't give me that."

"I could give you anything."

"But — this is *yours*."

"No, Pop, it's yours — for keeps."

"Do you really mean it?"

"Sure. I want you to have it—and I really mean it."

My mother-in-law, Ma Dennison, was with us at the time of the presentation. She looked quizzically at the mounted head, and said to Pop:

"Where will we put it?"

"Over the fireplace in the dining room," said Pop, unhesitatingly—and, until Pop's death, the big buck of Second Chain Burn looked down for about twenty-five years on every meal that was served at the long, oak table in the house on Juniper Hill in Framingham; and sometimes Pop would interrupt his carving, turn and look up at the head, and say:

"That's Ed's buck—the one he shot on Second Chain Burn."

I looked from my den window out over Grand Lake and saw Al's boat rounding a distant point. My time was about up, and I thought of the last time I saw the deer head. Pop Dennison died in 1952, missing his seventy-fifth birthday by four days. He lived an unusual life, and died on an unusual day—a day which occurs just once every four years—February 29th, Leap Year.

Some months afterwards, Pop's widow gave the deer head to me. I was quite touched. But at the time I had no place to hang the head, and no place to store it, and I suspected that my wife didn't regard it too highly as a decoration for the cabin. So I gave the head to Pop's first cousin, Lew Bement. Lew gave it to a friend of his named Jack Wechter, who has a kind of club room, and at this writing it hangs in Jack's place near Greenfield, Massachusetts.

As Al's boat drew closer, I tried to visualize the deer head hanging in Jack's club room; but I could just see it where it hung originally, for all those years, over Pop's dining room fireplace.

"Harry," Ma Dennison must have said, innumerable times, "I don't like that deer head. We ought to have an oil painting of a ship."

"What? Don't like that head? Why, it *belongs* there. And we've got a ship painting in the living room."

There was something wrong with that dialogue, even though it was imaginary. Pop's secret was right on top of me. Why would anyone want a trophy that he hadn't shot himself, unless he was furnishing a museum or a club room? Pop Dennison never cared much for trophies anyway—except the white buck he shot on his last hunt, just a few years before his death.

"Pop," I said to him, "now I know! You thought I'd be hurt if you didn't accept that deer head. So you made a twenty-five year show of liking it and no one ever knew you didn't, least of all me."

Al's boat had landed, and I took old "Sleigh Bells" down to the shore with me, and Al saw me lugging it, and said:

"This isn't deer hunting season."

"The hell it isn't!" I said. "I was just on a hunt down on Second Chain Lake."

Al looked up at the cabin, then back at me.

"Say," he said, in a puzzled way, "did I hear someone laughing? Just a moment ago?"

I did a double take. Of course everyone will say that Al heard me laughing at my discovery, but it might have been Pop Dennison's leftover laughter that he heard, because I think I heard it myself.

# Jake's Rangers Hunt the Whitetail

W hether you call them "The Trail Blazers," or "Whitetails Limited," or simply "The Old Bunch," it means the same thing when the leaves begin to fall in the little towns in the deer-hunting states of our nation. Whatever the name, and there usually is one, you are talking about a group of men, young and old, who gather each fall to hunt the whitetail deer.

The personnel of these groups often is so varied in age and walk of life that individual members rarely meet during the rest of the year. But with the first frost and the foliage bright on the ridges, there comes a flurry of eager telephone calls. Meetings are held, the trip is planned; and, when you reach your hunting camp, you are reunited like brothers. Your rifle stands in the gun rack where it stood last year. Your sleeping bag is on your old bunk or bed. You are fraternal in the glow of lamplight, sharing the familiar warmth of the wood stove with the old bunch, and talking of just one subject — tomorrow. For tomorrow is opening day on deer.

Each fall, the phenomenon of the deer-hunting groups grows

deeper into the country's grass roots. In Pennsylvania, New York, the Virginias, the Carolinas, Michigan, Maine, and perhaps other states, there are groups that were first organized well over fifty years ago. Rich in tradition, and sometimes in ritual, this annual gathering of the deer-hunting clan has become an American institution.

I suspect that my own bunch is typical of at least a hundred others. We call ourselves "Jake's Rangers"; and, in this description of the Rangers' fourteenth annual hunt, I believe you will find striking similarities to your own hunt, and perhaps a kinship between your group and ours. In fact, in what follows, you may even read words that you have actually spoken or heard spoken at night around the stove in your own hunting camp. For example:

"I was standing in a little spruce knoll, when I heard this deer coming."

That opening line, with minor variations, has been uttered at least once for every whitetail deer sighted, heard, hit, or missed, since deer hunting began. It can't be copyrighted, for it is always an inspired original to the hunter who is telling his story. Certain of Jake's Rangers will be speaking the magic line presently, but first I must explain who we are and where we hunt.

Officially, there are seven Rangers. Guests bring the total to ten or more. All of us reside in, or near, the small seacoast town of Damariscotta, Maine. Typically heterogeneous, our membership includes Damariscotta's postmaster, its veterinary surgeon, its Railway Express agent, a leading physician, an insurance man, a cabinetmaker, a grocer, and an artist. We have named ourselves for our leader, Maurice "Jake" Day, known to his Rangers as "the Colonel." To the rest of the world, he is Maurice Day, artist, naturalist, and authority on the woods and waters of the Pine Tree State. His nationally known watercolors of wilderness Maine are considered important regional documents, and in many of them, his favorite wild animal appears. Appropriately, it's the whitetail deer.

Every group of hunters, by tradition, has to have an old-timer, a colorful character, or highly developed curmudgeon, who is an unfailing source of camp anecdote and humor. Our candidate in this field—the man who sets Jake's Rangers apart from all other groups—is Uncle George Whitehouse, age seventy-four.

Uncle George, who used to be a boat builder and almost everything else, weighs in at around a hundred and six pounds. In build, he is virtually one-dimensional—like a canoe pole. Despite the spareness of his frame, his feats of strength and conquests of all types, as reported by himself, are without equal. He has rigged more topmasts on more four-masted schooners, felled more trees, shot more and bigger deer at greater distances, and run wilder rapids in smaller canoes — or just on logs — than any man alive. He doubts nothing that he says. His chief characteristic is his halo of invincibility.

Jake's Rangers regard Uncle George as an endowment. He is in residence the year-round in the deer-hunting camp at Sprague's Falls on the Narraguagus River, near Cherryfield in Washington County. This is fortunate, because when the camp — an old farmhouse — showed signs of sagging at the sills, it was nothing for Uncle George, alone, to hold the building off the ground with one hand while he shored it up with the other.

Annually, before departing for camp and Uncle George, the Rangers go through a stage of high-octane anticipation. It has become a kind of ritual: listing and packing supplies, sighting in rifles at the local rifle range, airing sleeping bags, applying the whetstone to hunting knives, switching from white handkerchiefs to red ones.

Bentley Glidden, Damariscotta's postmaster, invariably squeezes rare juices of drama from these preliminaries. He telephones his fellow Rangers at odd hours. You pick up the receiver. A sepulchral voice comes over the wire:

"Is your waterproof match safe full?" Or, "Have you remembered your compass?" Or, "Only *you* can prevent forest fires."

Bentley is a rotund, merry, and uninhibited organizer. If you step into his Post Office in mid-October, with the opening of deer season still two weeks hence, your name is sure to be called loudly and jubilantly. Bent will snatch you into his back room, and read you the camp menu for the entire ten days:

"Friday, first night in camp: hamburg, onions, mashed potato. Saturday, opening-day night: deer liver (?) and bacon, or baked beans."

Sometimes, without a word, Bent will hand you a slip of paper, turn his back on you, and disappear into the darker confines of the Post Office. This year I got the paper treatment twice. The first listed the personnel of the trip as follows:

Jake (our leader), Mac (McClure Day, our veterinary surgeon, who is Jake's son), Eddie Pierce (who owns Damariscotta's Yellow Front Grocery), Dr. Sam Belknap (The Rangers' physician), Jack (Bentley's brother, our insurance man), Bud Haugland (Railway Express agent, a newcomer), Louis Doe (mayor of the nearby village of Sheepscott), Ed Smith (yours truly), and Bentley Glidden.

The explanatory parentheses are mine. The final words addressed to me are Bentley's. They follow:

Please remember that you were inducted into Jake's Rangers during "Be Kind to Animals Week."

The second paper that Bentley slipped me was a command that I obeyed with pleasure. It read:

Have your station wagon in the alley back of Eddie Pierce's store at three-thirty, Thursday, October 30.
[Signed] Sgt. B. Glidden, Jake's Rangers.

The loading of grub and supplies in Eddie Pierce's back alley is always a ceremony. It's the last act in Bentley's anticipation byplay and is attended by all Rangers able to sneak a few minutes off from work. Bentley had read the camp menu to all of us, and now — passing carton by carton over the tailgate of my wagon — was the reality: a colossal turkey, an Olympian ham, a classic corned-beef brisket, enough hamburg to equip a diner, bacon, flour, canned fruits, juices, vegetables.

As the last parcel was loaded, a bystander remarked with heavy sarcasm:

"You poor guys are going to starve up there in the woods."

"Oh, no," said Bent, airily, "we'll eke this out with venison and partridge."

I locked the tailgate carefully over all this bounty, drove home, and locked the wagon in my barn as a double-security measure. I was to pick up Bentley at daylight, and we were to drive to camp ahead of the others in order to make things ready and establish peace with Uncle George.

We had had five straight days of rain, but Friday morning was as clear as a bell, with mist veils hanging low in the valleys, and the color of the last, lingering foliage painting the ridges in the sunrise.

Camden, Belfast, Bucksport, Ellsworth. The white towns flashed by, and everywhere you could see signs announcing: "Hunters' Breakfast — 4 A.M. to 8 A.M." We saw other hunters heading toward their camps. Tomorrow, November first, was opening day, and the deer-hunting clans were on their way to rendezvous.

Beyond Ellsworth, the road traversed the shore of Tunk Lake, with Tunk Mountain to the north. Then the magic turnoff toward Sprague's Falls, the end of blacktop, then narrow, rutted gravel. Jake's Rangers' headquarters is the last farmhouse at the dead end of the Sprague Falls Road. There, Uncle George, in his tattered checked shirt, greeted us from thirty feet in the air. He was prancing along the ridgepole of the house, where he had been examining a chimney for smoke leaks. I held my breath while Uncle George, all the time waving at us, danced down an intricate system of ladders to the ground.

"I was scared you'd fall, Uncle George," I said.

"Five, ten years ago," he said, "I'd of jumped. Once, in a shipyard in East Boothbay, I jumped sixty feet from the topmast of a—"

"Never mind, Uncle George," Bentley said. "How's the firewood supply?"

Uncle George gave Bent an outraged look.

"Firewood? When that chimney might leak flame? Burn us all to a cinder? Would *you* of cut any?"

Uncle George was in splendid form. So was the chimney. And I had a newly filed bucksaw and an axe in the wagon. While we unloaded the supplies, Uncle George told of new enemies he had made during the past months and of his plans for disposing of them. He had done in quite a few of them, when Bentley interrupted with The Great Hardy Perennial Hunters' Question:

"Are there many deer around, Uncle George?"

"Not a one. No deer at all."

Bent and I looked at each other in a flood of relief. Uncle George's reply was a surefire omen that whitetails were plentiful. So eager were we to relay the glad tidings that we could hardly wait for the arrival of the rest of the Rangers. But the time went fast, and with the thunder of Sprague's Falls familiar in our ears, we went to work cutting wood, policing camp, and stacking supplies on the shelves.

The smell of your hunting camp, as you step across the threshold for the first time in a year, is as familiar as the palm of your hand. There's the smoke of old fires, oilcloth, coffee, kerosene, soap, gun oil, cedar kindling, and, on rainy days, the steam of damp wool and leather and rubber.

That first noon, while we were eating the lunch our wives had prepared for us at home, Bent and I noticed a new, strange odor in camp. Uncle George had loftily disdained to share our lunch and, instead, opened the door to his iceless, wooden icebox. The box contained nothing save a fragment of dried pollock, and the new scent emanated from the pollock. I don't know how long Uncle George had been nourishing himself from this item, but it had a perfume definitely redolent of an old Model pollock. The old-timer shaved off a portion with his jack-knife, chewed it with relish, and closed the icebox door, lest the remainder escape under its own power. The scent of mink bait vanished with the closing of the box, and we were at peace again — until Uncle George fired us up with the one burning rumor that can galvanize any hunting camp.

"I hear," he said, "that there's a white buck around."

Even if the rumor was one of Uncle George's invention, the Rangers' hunt was made. All of us would be buoyant with the individual dream of at least a running shot at the white buck.

Jake Day and Mac drove into the dooryard at midafternoon. Before they had their rifles in the rack, Bent had told them of the rumored prize. They asked Uncle George if he had seen the great white creature.

At the outset, Uncle George had just heard. Now, it developed, he had seen.

"How many points?" asked Jake.

"Where was he?" asked Mac.

Uncle George waved a hand toward the wilderness stretching northward. His gesture was wide enough to include Tunk, Bog, McCabe, and Spring River Mountains, together with a fifty-degree segment of the Great Barrens — in all, roughly seventy square miles.

"Right there," said Uncle George, "is where I saw him."

By the time Jack Glidden, Eddie Pierce, Dr. Sam, and Bud Haugland arrived, it was dark. The night was still, except for the hollow rumble of Sprague's Falls — a sound that is built into the rafters of the old house. In a matter of a few hours, the white buck had ceased being a rumor. He was real. He was somewhere. He was everyone's goal, the substance of everyone's wakeful dreams that first night in camp.

Which rifle in the full gun rack would have the honor? Would any of them? I lay in my sleeping bag, wondering and visualizing the gleaming barrels. Most of the guns had names: "Cosmic Ray," a couple of "Betsys," and "Old Meat in the Pot" — and then there was Mac Day's .243, which came to be known as "Little Evil."

Bent and I cooked opening-day breakfast by lamplight, while, by custom, Dr. Sam made the toast and prepared the noonday sandwiches with his camp buddy, Eddie Pierce.

"Where you going to hunt today?"

That's the breakfast question. You hear it a dozen times every morning for the hunt's duration. A good question. If you know where your people are working, you avoid accidents. If a man gets lost, you know where to start looking.

Bent and Jack Glidden headed for the "Bowl," Bud for the "River Trail," Dr. Sam and Eddie for "Split Rock." These are landmark names first coined by Jake's Rangers. They are not on any map but our own. Other hunters range the same places, knowing them by different names.

Jake, Mac, and I took our rifles from the rack, crossed the decaying wooden bridge at the Falls, and started out toward the Barrens. This vast, boulder-strewn area is grown to scrub oak, small beech, and other hardwoods, with occasional "islands" of spruce and fir. Its high plateau fans off for miles. In the past, millions of feet of pine logs have been harvested from this reach and, latterly, millions of bushels of blueberries. An ancient tote road makes the gradual ascent to the plateau.

Mac left us and struck out alone into the woods to the westward. We watched him go. You could see his red shirt and cap and the yellow glow of his *Fire-Glo* vest. You saw a good woodsman in action — hand instinctively fending the sharp twig and eyes focused yards ahead, channeling the way the foot would travel, estimating the slant of ledge or boulder, testing by sight and memory the traction of the trail, and the rifle — Little Evil — cradled in his elbow, a part of the man. It has a peculiar grace and is a nice thing to see.

When Jake and I reached the Barrens, the wind had picked up to a half-gale. We heard voices, and a group of four hunters emerged from a thicket — three boys, and an older man who bore the stamp of experience. His name was Grant, and he told us they hadn't seen even a track since daylight. The younger boys looked discouraged. They were pulling out for new territory.

When they had gone, Jake and I sat behind a huge boulder, out of the chill wind. Jake told of his experience of the previous year — how he was walking along the Barrens' trail and a buck crossed ten yards in front of him, how he put his rifle to his shoulder, and then how a partridge boomed right up into his face between him and the deer.

"That buck should have credited the partridge with an assist," Jake said — and then we heard a shot.

Shots always fill you full of excited speculations. They have tremendous mystery — even the far ones that sound like someone whispering "Pow" in your ear. Each one can mean drama or climax or both. The shot we'd just heard sounded sharp, and there wasn't a second shot. Just that single, powerful "Cr-rack!"

"That could be Mac and Little Evil," I said.

Jake was on his feet, and we hurried off down the trail over which we'd just come. Two minutes later, we froze in our tracks. Three or four rifles were blazing away. You couldn't count the shots. You could tell the "Bat-bat-bat —" of an automatic. The slower cadence of a lever action. Then came silence, except for the wind hollering in our ears.

We went on cautiously around a couple of bends in the trail. Ahead of us, standing in a group, we saw six hunters. Two of them were Mac Day and Dr. Sam Belknap; the other four were the Grant party — the discouraged ones. But they weren't discouraged now. They were dressing out a handsome doe. Mac had sighted the doe, and his shot had driven the animal up to the Grant boys.

When Jake and I joined the group, the tall Grant brother — the experienced one — was giving his boys a stern lecture on too much shooting. You couldn't blame the kids for their excitement. But it was a sound lecture, just the same.

"We had the doe after the first shot," said the older Grant. "All the other shots did was ruin good meat. You kids think of that, next time. You want to have some respect for your deer."

That was a good speech, and as we started back toward camp, I thought how those boys would remember it, and someday tell their own boys the same thing.

None of the other Rangers was at camp when Jake and I got back. But Uncle George was there, and he was in a cold, trembling fury, his eyes flaming like a blow-torch. The object of his wrath was a group of Connecticut hunters who had just parked their car in our dooryard and were standing around it with their rifles. Our dooryard is the customary parking place for hunters in this vicinity, simply because there is no other place. Uncle George now stated that they ought to pay a parking fee, and that Connecticut hunters owed him for two years, besides this one. He would take it out of their hides.

We watched while Uncle George, picking up a stout cudgel, went out to assault the army from Connecticut. This is what we saw:

Uncle George crossing the yard to the car under the apple tree, eagerly and companionably shaking hands with all four hunters; smiles of welcome and goodwill on all faces; a tall, red-coated Connecticut man handing Uncle George a bill; Uncle George waving the billed hand away in austere refusal.

And then we heard Uncle George say:

"You boys park here any time you want, day or night. Always glad to see you coming back."

I don't know whether it's more fun to hunt the daylight hours to the full or to spend an afternoon in camp looking up the trail, watching the Rangers come in one by one or two by two, and listening to their individual stories as they arrive at the door, unload their rifles, place them in the gun rack, take off their wet boots, and stretch their weary feet toward the fireplace fire. But this first afternoon after Jake and Mac left for The Big Pine, I decided to stay in and nurse a toe blister.

Bud Haugland came in about three o'clock.

"Any excitement, Bud?"

Bud grinned.

"An open, running shot — not twenty yards away. It was just now, a couple of hundred yards from camp."

"I didn't hear the shot — and I've been listening hard."

"There wasn't any shot," Bud said. "The safety was on."

"The shadows got long. Bud cleaned lamp chimneys and filled lamps. Together we worked up a woodpile and stacked it on the back porch.

Mac and Jake came in. No story. Dr. Sam and Eddie Pierce came in. No story.

"You boys don't seem to be very good hunters," remarked Uncle George. "I always had my buck—a big one—hung up before seven o'clock in the morning on opening day. Sixty years running."

Bud got up and lighted the big lamp over the dining table. It was twilight outside, with full dark beginning to hover down. There was that moment of anxiety so well known to any hunting camp, that strange dread of a hunter lost, of darkness. Two men were missing.

"Where did Bentley and Jack go?" Jake asked.

"The Bowl," said Dr. Sam, who has a way of keeping track of such things.

"Maybe they got on the white buck's track," Eddie said. "That could keep them out late."

Jake began to pace up and down in front of the fireplace. Mac looked at his compass and at the framed map on the long table.

Then came the familiar voices just outside the front door. There also came a heavy thud, a groan—as in relief at dropping a heavy burden after a long, rugged haul. We grabbed flashlights and rushed outside. Bentley and Jack, their backs steaming in the chill air, stood beside the eight-pointer they had shot on the edge of the Bowl and lugged in over that rough terrain on a pole. First buck! First blood! Opening day.

"I was sitting there on a stump," said Bentley, "and Jack sitting right near me, when I saw this deer come sneaking along—"

Both the boys had fired. Both had connected. The buck had dropped instantly. Supper that night was liver and bacon.

The things you remember about the days and nights in camp—the things that keep coming back! The sounds of going to bed, the bunk springs twanging, the boots thudding on the floor; the penny-ante poker game with Uncle George standing by, telling of the times he had risked a thousand dollars on a single turn of a card; the chain-reaction coffee that Jack Glidden made; the day Bentley saw the black bear; the reshuffling of the contents of duffle bags, choosing the proper clothes against the probabilities of weather; the Sundays in camp—no hunting, but visiting with other hunters. And had anyone caught a glimpse of the white buck?

One afternoon it rained hard. That morning Uncle George had told me of two mongrel dogs belonging to a neighbor, and how he planned to do away with them. They stole his food, he said, which was why he kept his dried pollock in the iceless icebox. He had decided to pinch off the animals' head with own hands, but only after inflicting tortures of a surgical nature.

When the rain started that afternoon, and I came back from hunting the river, I stepped into the clearing and saw Uncle George and the dogs on the back steps. He was feeding the creatures choice scraps and speaking to them in words of endearment, all the while fondling their ears. To save Uncle George the shame and guilt of being caught red-handed in an act of tenderness, I remained hidden till the scene broke up.

That was the afternoon that Jake tagged an eight-pointer in the rain. He and Mac lugged it in and hung it alongside the Glidden boys' in the cellar under the farmhouse. It was a perfect mate for Jack's and Bentley's.

"I had just stepped over a little knoll," said Jake, "and I heard this noise, and I stopped still, and—"

A clean shot high on the backbone. No spoilage.

Through the years, Jake's Rangers have had a high of nine deer, which was one apiece for that year. The low was three. This trip was about average, with a total of four. Dr. Sam tagged a fat and highly edible spikehorn near Wasse's beaver dam on about the fifth or sixth day.

I remember it was the day I left camp late in the morning, because I saw the Rural Delivery mailman stop at Uncle George's mailbox—the last mailbox on the Sprague Falls Road. Uncle George sprang hopefully from the front door and opened the box. Whatever was in it was for the Smith Camp across the river. The old-timer shook his head dejectedly.

"Nothing for me again," he said.

"Were you expecting a letter?" I asked.

"It's a long time," he said, with a sigh, "since I've heard from Theda Bara."

Jake's Rangers are a bunch of hardworking, resourceful hunters, and most of them are on the go from daylight till dark. I am content with a few hours. Maybe it's middle age, or a slight lameness in my back. Or maybe it's just that I can get as big a heart bump out of someone else shooting a deer as if I did it myself. That's probably a false statement, but on this particular day it wasn't.

Mac Day and Jake came in from their hunting on "The Mountain," a wild, rocky nubble on the west side of the river. Excitement was all over them like flame, and it caught me in its contagion. Mac drew his hunting knife and showed me the blade. It had a yellow-white coating.

"What's that, Mac?"

"It's not candle wax!"

"You got the white buck!"

"Yes—me and Little Evil. We need help hauling him in."

Then Mac told it. He had been cat-footing near the top of the mountain, Jake right behind him with his camera. He had stepped up on a rock, and there in a little draw, not sixty feet away, stood the white buck. The deer dropped with Mac's first shot, lifted its head once, then slowly sank back, still.

It turned out that the famous buck wasn't pure white, but calico. But it was an experience Mac and Jake will never forget, nor will I as I saw and heard them tell the story. As I write this, soon after the Rangers' return home, the four deer are hanging in the big walk-in freezer in Eddie Pierce's grocery store. Hometown people go in for a look now and then, and anytime you happen to meet Jake, or Jack, or Bentley, or Dr. Sam, or Mac on Main Street, you can ask for the story, and it will begin with minor variations on deer hunting's immortal and forever original opening line:

"I was standing on a little spruce knoll, when I heard this deer coming..."

As for Uncle George Whitehouse, I feel it just and proper that he should have the last word. There is a moment of something like sadness when you stand at the camp door and say good-bye for a year. It was particularly so when I said good-bye to Uncle George. As I looked around over the land and forest, I thought of the snow that would come inevitably, the road closed in drifts that would cover the mailbox, the smoke from the chimney lonely and torn in the winter wind, and the old man huddled by the fire.

"Are you going to winter here?" I asked, as we shook hands.

"No," said Uncle George, nibbling the last of his dried pollock, "I've been thinking some of the French Riviera."

# The Jinx
# and Uncle George

What with years of hunting over the same terrain, encamped in the same old place with pretty much the same cast of characters, you'd think there'd be a sameness to the annual deer hunts of Jake's Rangers. That such is not the case may be attributable to a strong streak of originality in the Rangers themselves; but, more likely, it is due to the agility, invention, and flashing eccentricity of our resident caretaker at hunting headquarters, Uncle George Whitehouse. One of the more analytical Rangers, possibly Dr. Sam Belknap, has endeavored to isolate, in proportion, the elements comprising Uncle George's weight, as follows:

> Imagination, 22 lbs.
> Pride, 25 lbs.
> Dramatic talent, 29 lbs.
> Rebellion, 30 lbs.
> X factor

With Uncle George it's the X factor that you have to watch out for. This factor is the mysterious, outside stimulus, or catalyst, that churns up his other ingredients and causes him to ricochet from his course — a course which, even in normalcy, is refreshingly erratic.

The X factor has always been very hard to identify. For example, what caused Uncle George to resign his caretaker's post in mid-deer-season a couple of years back? At first, we had blamed Bentley Glidden. Bent had put a live mouse in one of Uncle George's hunting boots. It seemed clear that Bent was the X factor. Not so.

Colonel Jake Day later discovered the mouse under Uncle George's bunk. Uncle George had billeted the little creature in a dried-codfish box covered with window glass. He had equipped the box with a small sleeping bag of absorbent cotton and an extensive larder of fig newtons, bacon rind, and Hershey almond bars. You'd think no mouse ever had it so good. But Uncle George thought otherwise. In fact, he figured his mouse had been insulted. Sighing as he packed his satchel for departure, he muttered:

"No cheese. No cheese. This is the end."

You see what I mean about the X factor's elusiveness? In this case it turned out to be Mac Day. Mac didn't have anything to do with the mouse. He was miles away from the whole thing. It just happened that he had made out the grub list that fall and it hadn't included cheese, so Mac was to blame for the mouse having nothing to eat but fig newtons and the other stuff.

Uncle George started for the door, his satchel in one hand and his mouse in its box in the other. Pausing in the doorway, he announced that he couldn't remain longer under the same roof with a man who left cheese off the grub list.

"A matter of principle," he said. "Good-bye — forever."

Uncle George reconsidered and unpacked only when Jack Glidden volunteered to drive in to Cherryfield for a load of cheddar.

There are countless similar episodes involving Uncle George and his tribulations with the Rangers, but none, I believe, so bizarre as the one which enlivened last year's deer hunt. It was a weird hunt in other respects, too.

In the first place, Colonel Jake wasn't with us. The United States Supreme Court was to blame for this. Jake had to make up for time lost from his other occupations while he was on the Justice Bill Douglas expedition to Katahdin, just a few weeks before.

Second, it was on the previous fall's trip that Mac Day and Little Evil (his .243 rifle) had brought down the prized white buck. According to an old Indian named Tom Compus Mentis, the shooting of a white buck puts the jinx on the shooter for seven years. So Mac, one of our most skillful hunters, had the sign on him. Would he, or wouldn't he, beat the jinx?

Finally, there was the case of Bentley Glidden and one of the cleanest, clearest, and most heart-stopping lessons in caution with firearms that you ever heard of. You shall be the judge of that, presently. But first comes the scene of the Rangers' arrival in camp.

It was a straggling rendezvous last year. The season opened November first but since this fell on a Sunday, you couldn't hunt till Monday, the second. So the Rangers showed up at the Sprague's Falls farmhouse in twos and singles all over the weekend. Louis Doe drifted in Saturday from Bangor, where he was engaged in expert sheet-metal work. Mac and Jack Glidden drove in the same day. Dr. Sam and his camp buddy, Eddie Pierce, showed up that night. So did Bill Fraser. Bill is a cabinet-maker, as well as being our town's authority on the care, feeding, and training of power lawn mowers of all sizes and descriptions.

Bentley came in Sunday from Quebec, where he had been vacationing for a few days with his wife, Doris, and their two boys, Bob and Dave. I drove up Sunday afternoon in the rain with Bentley's gear and his 8 mm rifle with the scope sight in the back of my wagon.

I was the last one in, and as I drove over the terminal stretch of dirt road, the rain had let up and all the Rangers were out in the dooryard by the old apple tree. I pulled in alongside Bill Fraser's car and yelled a large greeting. There was no response from my fellow Rangers. They seemed preoccupied. Something was screwy. In fact, several things.

Before joining the group, now augmented by several visiting hunters gathering under the apple tree, I took a look around. Things had changed. It wasn't just the fact that the old wooden bridge across the river had vanished in last spring's flood, and that a temporary footbridge had been installed down by our spring. The farmhouse itself looked different. Both chimneys had been topped off handsomely with new brick. And a commodious, glassed-in front entry had mysteriously come into being. The old place had had a fancy face-lifting. What had got into Uncle George? What, indeed!

While I was wondering, the old-timer himself appeared majestically at the apple tree. At his approach, the group opened up respectfully to admit him. Uncle George was a changed man. His black eyes blazed invincibly behind his thick-lensed glasses. A new set of teeth gave his smile a touch of the debonair. Gone were his old hat and the elbowless, checkered-flannel shirt of yesteryear. Instead, he was wearing the garb of the classic English sports-car driver—a flat skillet of a cap with a leather strap around it, a shirt of theatrical colors and surpassing elegance, and trousers that could have been tweed by Harris.

I eased into the group, hand outstretched to clasp Uncle George's.

"Hello, old-timer!" I said. "What's come over you?"

With an imperious gesture, he waved my hand aside. It was as though I had interrupted him in the performance of some kind of rite. The rite seemed to involve a Connecticut hunter who was holding a magazine and a fountain pen toward him.

"You wish my autograph, son?" said Uncle George.

"Yes, please, Mr. Whitehouse," said the hunter.

It was Bentley Glidden who explained the spectacular doings. Jarring my ribs with his elbow and pointing to the magazine which Uncle George had signed with a flourish, Bent whispered.

"There's your X factor — that magazine."

The magazine was the previous October's issue of *Field & Stream*. It carried the account of our deer hunt of the preceding year; and in the story, Uncle George Whitehouse was the featured character. It was now November 1. The magazine had been in circulation a full month or more, and it had changed Uncle George's life, costume, and demeanor. He was a famous man.

Of the fifty-odd deer hunters in various camps and cabins in the Sprague's Falls area, at least forty-five had read the story; and of these, about twenty had brought their copies of *Field & Stream* for Uncle George to autograph. He was the cynosure of all eyes, basking in the sweet steam of recognition richly deserved if long delayed. Hitherto, Cherryfield's leading celebrity had been Carlton Willey, now pitching for the New York Mets. Carlton was running a lame second. Uncle George Whitehouse was "Mr. Prestige," and he played the role with a brilliance and aplomb unmatched since the days of John Drew and Joe Jefferson.

That evening before opening day, the rain clouds moved on and the sun sank in a sky of glacial blue. You could feel the cold front moving in. Light showed in the windows of Steve Smith's camp directly across the river. One of Steve's dogs barked at the evening star — a wild, clean sound echoing over the forest. Out in the night the sad song of the river made you feel lonely, but in the front room of the Rangers' headquarters there was cheer and companionship.

A big chunk of dry beech burned in the fireplace. Its fragrance blended with the aromas of Eddie Pierce's cigar and Dr. Sam's pipe. Mellow light shone from the hanging lamp; but when Mac Day crossed to the gun rack to replace his can of gun oil, he whacked his head on the lamp. Shaking his fist at it, then rubbing his head, Mac said:

"I'll never learn."

"It's the jinx getting in a reminder," Jack Glidden said to Mac.

And Louis Doe said: "Mac'll wish he'd never even seen that white buck last year."

As Mac moved about the room, Louis and Bill Fraser made a show of avoiding him. They didn't, they said, want any of the jinx to rub off on them. From a wooden bench, where he sat enthroned, Uncle George Whitehouse muttered sepulchrally:

"Seven years bad luck."

Grinning at his tormentors, Mac said:

"Beginning tomorrow, we shall see." And he glanced confidently at Little Evil, which stood third from the left in the full gun rack.

With their new, super-duper flash equipment, Dr. Sam and Eddie Pierce were taking what they called "posterity pictures" of Uncle George, who cooperated with poses that would have shamed a professional model. At intervals, in somber, studied tones, Uncle George would state:

"My glass is empty."

We all vied to correct this deficiency, and at supper — a huge turkey stuffed and roasted by Bentley — we fought for the privilege of waiting on our changed caretaker. The previous year he had been content with eating nothing but hardtack and dried pollock. That era was gone. The white-meat era had begun.

"And slice it thin, Bentley — if you will, please," said Uncle George.

Inevitably the conversation shifted to hunting plans for early morning. Dr. Sam and Eddie would hunt the Beaver Dam. Bentley and Jack, the Middle Ground. Bill Fraser and Louis leaned toward staking out near camp at French's Field. Mac, studying hard, was undecided.

"I've got a jinx to beat," he said. "It'll take some figuring. I may give the Barrens a whirl!"

Just why a hunter selects a certain terrain for his opening-day hunt is a mystery — unless, of course, he has cruised the country beforehand and has seen sign. If not, you play a hunch. Or you remember getting a good shot the year before at Split Rock, or in the Big Pine country, or The Nubble, and you think it will happen again. But it almost never does.

Opening day — crack of dawn. The old farmhouse pulsed with excitement.

"Where's my flashlight?"

"Who stole my compass?"

"Hand me those heavy socks."

"You snored all night."

"It was yourself you heard snoring."

*"Come and get it!"*

Bentley had the bacon and eggs ready; Dr. Sam, the toast; and Jack Glidden had made an immense pot of his famous coffee, which the Rangers call "Black-Leaf 40." It has been the cause of at least two of Uncle George's resignations as caretaker, but it would bring a dead horse to life and is fine stuff for opening-day breakfast.

The lamplight turned pale. It was daylight outside, and cold. You could see frost on the parked cars and on the canoes—and a coating on the Rangers' brand-new, unchristened deer carrier. Whose deer would christen it?

Out in the dooryard, we gave each other the traditional inspection. Fire-Glo vests, a must. Red caps. Compass. Map. Sandwich lunch. Red handkerchiefs. Nothing white showing. Nothing white in any pocket. By kindness of a New York friend who has our welfare at heart we were even equipped with red toilet tissue, and many were the bright comments concerning it.

You could hear the oily click of metal as the boys loaded their rifles. There was but one slight mishap. While loading Little Evil, Mac Day dropped a cartridge! Another jinx, if you're superstitious. And what deer hunter isn't?

"Boys," said Mac, picking up the offending .243. "I've had it. See you tonight." And he took off, long-striding down the riverbank and across the footbridge toward the forest.

Two minutes later the camp was empty, the dooryard deserted— except for Uncle George. As I hunted the dense fir and pine growth along the river below camp, I pictured the old-timer standing out by the mailbox greeting late-arriving hunters from out of state, and perhaps conferring an autograph now and then. This pleasing thought was interrupted by four rifle shots from the direction of French's Field, less than a half mile from where I stood. After a moment there were three more shots. Then, a minute later, a single. By my watch, it was 6:32.

Louis and Bill Fraser were hunting French's Field; and at the last minute Bentley and Jack Glidden had decided to make it a foursome. What was the story of those shots? Guessing is part of the fun. But, outside of hunting itself, the best fun is hearing the hunters' nightly tales.

I had a tale of my own that day—commonplace enough to be in the "That-happened-to-me, too" category. A few minutes after the final shot from French's Field, I heard a deer blow—"Whoosh-sh!" Then, through the heavy growth, I saw two small deer running, their tails flashing white against the dark firs. It was a better than fair chance, a crossing shot, right to left, about forty yards. The deer had undoubtedly been scared my way by the foursome at French's Field.

My rifle was up and swinging on the second deer. It was a fine, smooth swing developed through years of skeet shooting, and I was pretty proud of it. It felt just perfect, and the lead was just right—and then my rifle barrel snubbed up solidly against a standing dead spruce. That tree was right there beside me, a bit to my left, and I never even saw it. Another unlearned lesson. Some fine, smooth swing!

I got back to camp empty-handed and early, so as not to miss the first-hand stories of the other Rangers. It was about three in the afternoon, and the first thing I noticed was that the new deer carrier was gone.

"Who connected?" I asked Uncle George.

The old-timer placed a cedar-chip bookmark between the worn pages of the October *Field & Stream,* which he had been rereading in the privacy of the deserted farmhouse, and said:

"Louis Doe."

"Where? French's Field? I heard eight shots from up there early in the morning."

Just then, glancing through a back window, I saw three of the Rangers coming in along the winding tote road that led to the Barrens. I recognized Bentley, even in the distance. He was handling the rear end of the deer carrier. I went out to meet them, while Uncle George reached for his magazine, removed the cedar bookmark, and resumed reading.

I met the boys as they wheeled the deer carrier and its cargo across the footbridge, Louis on the head end, Bentley on the rear, and Jack alongside, carrying their rifles.

Louis's story: After leaving French's Field about eight in the morning, he had walked up the Barrens trail. The crisp, dead leaves, frozen after the rain, made so much noise that he sat on a rock and listened to the red squirrels and bluejays. Snuggled down out of the wind, the sun warmed him and he dozed off. He had been wakened by the sound of someone hurrying along through the dead leaves of the trail. The "someone" turned out to be a handsome spikehorn.

"Fifteen yards away, at the most," said Louis. "I couldn't miss."

Moments after Louis had shot the spikehorn, Bentley and Jack arrived on the scene. They had been walking down the same trail from Split Rock, and had driven the buck right into Louis's lap. The new deer carrier, which they had subsequently picked up at camp, had proved a tremendous boon.

"To think," said Bent, "of all the deer I've lugged the hard way."

The French's Field story came after we'd hung Louis's deer in the barn cellar and were seated by the fireplace. I was curious about those eight shots. It turned out that the first seven had been fired by other hunters, unknown.

"Who fired that single?" I asked.

"I did—in anger," Bentley said.

Bentley's story: He had separated from Jack, Bill, and Louis. He had come around a clump of head-high spruce bushes, and there, standing looking at him, was an eight-point buck. Seventy yards for a guess, just its back and head showing in a tangle of blowdowns. The deer's head went down, out of sight. Bent had a clean shot high on the deer's backbone, and he could see the critter's gray hairs in his scope. With his finger squeezing and his breath held, he thought: *Where are the other boys?*

Were they up ahead, the deer in line with them? He was shaking when he took his finger off the trigger. The deer ran with a snort and thudding hooves, the underbrush crashing. Moments later, Jack, Bill, and Louis showed up—*behind him!* He would have been safe in firing, after all.

"But you *did* fire," I said. "I heard that single shot."

"Yes. I fired one into an old pine stump to let off steam."

Dr. Sam and Eddie Pierce had had a long, empty day. No luck at the Beaver Dam. They had separated, agreeing to meet at the Big Pine. Eddie—of all people and all things—hadn't been able to locate the Big Pine.

"I was all off compass—can't understand it," Eddie said.

They had spent half the day hunting for each other, but were now reunited, drying their socks and warming their toes at the fire, ever and anon sipping from their respective cans of beer.

It was an inch before black dark when Mac Day came in. He was bone weary.

"It's more than first-day lameness, too," said Mac. "I've been lugging a jinx on my back."

"Any luck?"

Mac ran an oily rag over Little Evil and racked it. "Whitetails," he said. "Whitetails in the sunset. Whitetails. That's all—except miles. Please pass the rum."

Expertly ducking his head as he passed under the swinging lamp, Mac reached the long bench and sat down with a groan.

"You should have stayed in camp reading, as I did," said Uncle George. "Improve your mind."

"Yes—but how did I know?" Mac asked.

"I told you—seven years bad luck."

"Well," said Mac, "one day of it's just passed."

Bentley's experience with the big buck in French's Field was really just the kickoff of a series. The third or fourth day, he and Jack were hunting The Middle Ground—the Rangers' name for a big stretch of country between two forks of the river. He passed up a good running shot at a spikehorn because he wasn't quite certain just where his brother was. It happened—as at French's Field—that Jack was safe as a church, and a good quarter mile away with plenty of timber between them. And Jack got the spikehorn!

Bentley and Mac were drawn together by their mutual woes—Mac's jinx, and Bent's hard luck. Mac hunted all his old haunts in rain, cold, heat, and bright sun. Whitetails. Missed shots. Whitetails.

One windy afternoon Bentley had a "bushes-moving" shot. He'd been following a big doe, catching a flash of her now and then, her track plain. His instinct, mounted on top of his two other experiences, told him to shoot. All his training said *no*. The bushes moved again. He didn't shoot. The doe came from the bushes on the dead run and vanished for good in a cover of gigantic glacial boulders. Bent wondered if he was being overcautious. He couldn't sleep. He kept seeing deer behind bushes. Sometimes they snorted down his neck.

And then, toward the end of the encampment, and after what is now called "The Shooting Gallery Episode," Bent figured his luck had changed. Bent, Dr. Sam, and Eddie Pierce had gone four miles upriver to the Rolling Dam by canoe. Here the terrain is oak ridges, and the three were hunting parallel, within sight of each other, when a small buck flashed into view, running left to right parallel to the hunters' line. Being on the left, Bentley had the first shot. He fired twice, but he was certain his first bullet had done the trick. But the deer didn't drop, and Dr. Sam — midway of the line — opened up with his .30 '06. Wham-wham-wham. The deer miraculously kept running and dropped only after three fast shots from Eddie's .243.

"I had the first and the best chance," said Bentley. "That deer was mine. I was positive."

But Dr. Sam and Eddie Pierce are scientists. Hearsay evidence is not for them. And they carry scientific equipment with them at all times while hunting. With a probe and a surgically keen hunting knife, Dr. Sam removed two bullets from the deer. There were *only* two. While Bentley stood by dejectedly, Eddie Pierce took out his micrometer and indisputably proved that one bullet was a .30 '06, and the other a .243. There wasn't even a ghost of an 8 mm. Moreover, Dr. Sam's medical training gave credence and authority to his statement that the .243 bullet was the fatal one. So the deer was Eddie Pierce's.

That night Bentley felt an even stronger bond with Mac Day, who showed up after dark with another "whitetails-and-weary-miles" report. It had got to the point where jinx jokes and hard-luck gibes weren't funny anymore. It had been years since either Bent or Mac had been skunked, a fact which seemed to give their jinx and hard luck more horsepower. That Dr. Sam and Bill Fraser were still scoreless was but small consolation — especially when, on the last day in camp, they both connected.

Dr. Sam's story: He had gone alone to his favorite haunt — The Beaver Dam. Across the dam was a slope of scattered white birches, and on the near side was a comfortable sitting place on a sun-warmed log; here the doctor settled himself. The squirrels and chickadees quieted after a bit, and the beaver pond was glassy still. Suddenly Dr. Sam's eyes caught a motion on the far side among the birches. Five or six deer — Dr. Sam isn't certain — appeared walking along fast through the birches. He jumped from the log, ran a few steps to get a better view of them, dropped to one knee and fired. One shot. His deer dropped two hundred yards from where Sam knelt; it was another spikehorn. Bentley was not near enough the scene to get a crack at any of the other four or five deer.

"I was just near enough," said Bent, "to help lug Sam's deer out on the carrier."

Bill Fraser's story: Much later in the day (midafternoon) Bill had been drawn by hunter's hunch to French's Field, the scene of his first early morning hunt. He wondered, he said, if Bentley's buck might still be around — the buck that Bent had held his fire on. The buck *was!* Bill got a rearview, running shot, wounded the buck, and came straight back to camp for help. In the failing light, the tracks and the blood signs were hard to detect. But when the boys came to the river, there was the deer — swimming across to the far side. Dr. Sam and Eddie walked up to camp and brought the canoe down through the rapids. They ferried Bent and Bill across, and just before dark, Bill found his buck and fired the needed shot. It was a handsome eight-pointer, the only large deer in the Rangers' bag.

This was our last night in camp, with Dr. Sam and Bill climaxing the final day. Mac was jinxed for sure, and Bentley likewise. So, properly, the story should end right here. In this case, no. For there is a dramatic aftermath, the dart of double climax that has often characterized the Rangers' adventures.

In the morning we packed up and left, after saying good-bye to Uncle George. The old-timer was out in the yard with hammer and nails and paintbrush putting up signs to welcome late hunting parties to his kingdom. He was using last year's signs, but he had crossed out last year's messages — those that said: STAY OUT OF HERE, NO PARKING, and HUNTERS GO HOME. And there were others, even less cordial in their greeting. But now, on the reverse sides of the signs, Uncle George, mellowed by fame, had painted: GREETINGS BOYS! WELCOME TO SPRAGUE'S FALLS, and FREE COFFEE FOR ALL. And all the signs were autographed: GEORGE WHITEHOUSE, CARETAKER. It was an enduring memorial to a changed heart, and a nice thing to remember.

And so is the scene in the kitchen of Eddie Pierce's home in Damariscotta, some weeks later, on the night of the last day of open deer season. Eddie and his wife were in the brightly lighted kitchen getting supper for their two children when the door opened, and in stepped Mac Day, with Bentley right behind him. Obviously, both were elated.

"Oh-oh," Eddie said. "Let's hear it."

Mac took a bulging red cellophane bag from the rear of his hunting coat and placed it carefully in the kitchen sink.

"In that bag," said Mac, "is the jinx — or call it the end of the jinx."

The bag held a fresh deer liver.

Mac's story: Ever since returning from the Cherryfield encampment, in any time they could spare from work, Mac and Bentley had been hunting the home territory. And there is a lot of it right around Damariscotta. On the season's last afternoon, the two Rangers had tried The Heater — a field and forest terrain that stretches off not far from Eddie Pierce's house. There were other hunters around, all trying to tag a buck at season's end. Along an old sled road, heavily timbered on both sides, Mac had heard a deer blow. He had waited stone still, Little Evil at ready. When the deer crossed the road, Little Evil let out a snarl, the buck dropped — and Mac's jinx was a thing of the past. The buck was a handsome six-pointer.

"That jinx had me down," Mac said now, in Eddie's kitchen. "It would have worried me all winter. Tonight, I'm going to *sleep!*"

"Same here," said Bentley. "This has been the greatest day's deer hunting I've ever had. I'll never forget it."

Bentley's story: After helping Mac dress out his buck, Bentley had hunted in the fading, last light of the last day, while Mac went out to the main road to get the deer carrier. Bent came cat footing around a boulder and into an open, grassy glade ringed with spruces and spruce tops, where someone had been cutting pulpwood. Forty yards across the glade, the branches of a spruce tree moved — the lower branches.

"Right behind those bushes was my last chance," Bentley said. "And I knew it. More than that, I knew it was a deer."

The bushes moved again. A twig snapped. Bent's rifle butt snugged his shoulder. His cheek pressed the stock. His finger curved to squeeze the trigger. Through his tension in his final moment, he had remembered all the chances he had passed up during the Cherryfield hunt. Overcaution! Not this time. He wasn't passing up anything. But he did. Maybe a half ounce more pressure on the trigger would have touched off the 8 mm cartridge. But Bent didn't fire. The frustrating misery of it made him tremble. Was he gun-shy?

With his rifle muzzle now pointing skyward, Bentley saw the bushes move again. A dry stick crackled — and out into the glade stepped Bentley's friend *Tom Sherman!* Bent and Tom have known each other a long time. Tom is a carpenter and contractor.

"What did you say to him, Bent?" Eddie Pierce asked.

"I think I said, 'Tom, I was never so happy to see a man.'"

# "Old Come-And-Get-It"

My oldest possession, if you don't count arms and legs, is a steel frying pan, the sole surviving relic of a camping outfit assembled in 1917 by Digsy Jones and me. Senior to my oldest tent, axe, gun, or fly rod this Homeric vessel, during its decades of active duty, has sautéed an estimated three thousand brook trout. Nine barrels of potatoes and six hundred rashers of bacon must have crossed its cooking surface. It has browned a galaxy of white perch, pickerel, and bass — and as many pancakes as would be required to shingle the library in Bangor.

The name of my skillet is "Old Come-and-get-it." The aromas risen from it have enchanted the nostrils and inspired the gastric juices of two generations of hungry, far-wandering men. Haunch of porcupine, deer liver and onions, venison steaks, pot hellions, slumgullions, breast of partridge and black duck, and an entire drumlin of baked beans have had the treatment in Old Come-and-get-it. Blackened, carbon-scaled, dented, warped, and sand-scoured, it is still in service — mute testimony to the durability of pressed steel and the human stomach.

Digsy Jones and I bought the frying pan for $1.45 in a hardware store in Framingham, Massachusetts. Although it is twelve inches in diameter at the bottom the outward-flaring sides make it a good fourteen inches across the top. You can lose a porterhouse steak in it.

Its trademark was Cold Handle. An outer layer of pressed metal covered the main core of the handle, which allowed cooling air to circulate. But the handle assembly, altogether, was over a foot long, which made the frying pan awkward to pack in a knapsack. So Digsy Jones and I invented a new type of cold handle, good to this day.

We took our new skillet to Paradise's Blacksmith Shop, and John Paradise postponed shoeing a horse to attend to our more urgent needs. At our instruction, he cut off the handle, leaving about four inches of the base. To the top side of this stub, he riveted two iron loops rectangular in shape. It would be a welding job today but John Paradise's copper rivets still hold fast.

For a really cold handle, you cut a two-foot length of maple sapling and hew the big end square, then shove it through the iron loops, driving it in snugly. You cut a new handle at each campsite. The pan packs well. You never burn your fingers.

To break the pan in, Digsy and I scrubbed it with a mildly abrasive soap, dried it carefully, filled it half full of cooking oil, and left it on Digsy's mother's wood stove for two days. Mrs. Jones sewed a muslin bag to fit the pan, so it wouldn't sooty up other items in our knapsack. Through the years, several such bags have been worn out and replaced.

Old Come-and-get-it is big enough to serve as its own grate. You build your fire between two flat-topped stones, or a couple of green logs, and rest the pan a-straddle of them. It does not, however, conduct heat as evenly as an iron or aluminum pan; and, before we learned its vagaries, there were times when the bacon came out chilled at one end and cindered at the other. On exposure to the fire, its bottom expanded eccentrically. Sometimes it bulged; sometimes it dished. In either case, it made startling sounds. But, despite these foibles — or because of the abundant memories that rise from it like savory smoke — I declare that Old Come-and-get-it is the most distinguished frying pan in existence.

One of the first scenes featuring Digsy's and my new pan occurred in the barn of a Framingham neighbor named Carl Robbins. We were about to leave for Maine's Machias Lakes and River on the first big canoe trip of our lives. We were teenagers, and Carl Robbins was an adult — a hero in our eyes. For he had been to Hudson Bay. He spoke familiarly of romantic-sounding rivers: the Rat, the Ogoki, the Severn. He mentioned the Height of Land and Moose Factory.

We had spread our outfit on Carl's barn floor, and Carl examined it with an expert's eye. It was a thrilling moment as he began shooting questions:

"Matches? Maps? Fly dope? Salt? Axe? Fishing tackle? Canoe glue? First-aid kit? Compass? Whetstone?"

It was to be a trip of several weeks, and Carl went over our grub list carefully. Then he asked about cooking equipment. Digsy opened the muslin bag, disclosing among other things, Old Come-and-get-it.

"Boys," said Carl, "there's the pan I should have had on the Ogoki."

Feeling as though we had been knighted, we packed up our stuff and started to leave. But Carl said:

"Wait a minute."

The minute turned out to be an hour, during which Carl Robbins gave us a talk I have remembered for over forty years. It had to do, not with grub lists and outfits, but with human relations on a long canoe trip, or any other kind of wilderness trip where two people are thrown close together, day by day, night by night.

You offered the other guy first drink at the spring. If there was only one pair of dry socks, you gave them to your pal. If you spilled the coffee, your partner should make a joke of it. You were dependent on each other. If one partner broke a paddle or nicked the ax, you didn't heap blame on him. You thought of his likes and dislikes, and he of yours, and this attitude was to be a constant thing. It was nothing more than The Golden Rule, but something in the way Carl expounded it brought it sharply into focus on that canoe trip so long ago.

Digsy Jones and I often talked about it afterward. Digsy told how my habit of whistling through my teeth in time to our paddle stroke drove him nuts. On Fourth Machias Lake, he had almost thrown his paddle at me, then remembered Carl's advice. On the dead water on Fifth Machias Stream my whistling so annoyed him that he was going to jump out of the bow, but checked himself in time.

"After a week," said Digsy, "I got to *like* your whistling. When the wind blew, and I couldn't hear it, I *missed* it."

What irritated me on that Machias Lakes and River trip was the back of Digsy's neck. I sat in the stern, paddling, and looking at it. Digsy's neck got redder and redder with sunburn. I thought it was the homeliest neck in the world. But then it began to peel and got homelier, and I sat there glaring at it. I felt myself getting sullen, then remembered Carl's talk and got cheerful. A few days more and Digsy's neck turned brown as an old moccasin.

"Digsy," I said, on about the tenth day, "you've got the prettiest neck I ever saw, except Grace Barnes's."

That made Digsy happy, because Grace Barnes was his girl at that time. Digsy's neck bothered me no more.

At Rollerford Dam, on that same trip, we cooked lunch — beans — in Old Come-and-get-it in the rain. As I passed Digsy a plateful, rainwater that had gathered in my hat brim cascaded in Digsy's beans. Our eyes weren't a foot apart, and Digsy's looked savage. Then they softened and he smiled.

"I'm sorry, Digsy," I said. "I should have known better. Here — take my plate."

"No," Digsy said. "I like water in my beans."

While Old Come-and-get-it has implemented open-fire meals on lake-shores and riverbanks from Massachusetts to Michigan, and in many of the provinces of Canada, it has done its greatest work in the State of Maine on the Penobscot, St. Croix, and Machias watersheds. It was in residence at Dennison's Camp on Dobsis Stream — known as "The Lock" — for over twenty years. Three of the late Harry Dennison's resident caretakers "borrowed" Old Come-and-get-it for use either at the main camp, or on numerous hunting, fishing, and camping trips.

To me, as a young and aspiring woodsman, it was flattering to have my frying pan, with its proven cold-handle arrangement, coveted by such outstanding Maine guides as Roy Bailey, Harley Fitch, Bill Sprague, Pappy Thornton, and others. It was also embarrassing. At least one of these famous men regarded my frying pan as his own. Pappy Thornton, in fact, concocted a scheme for stealing it — legally.

When there was a change in caretakers at the Dennison place, the new caretaker succeeded to the entire camp inventory. When Pappy Thornton took over, he fixed it so "one large, steel frying pan" appeared on the list. When I showed up at camp the following spring, there was Old Come-and-get-it on the camp wood stove, laden with a mess of white perch and fried potatoes — Pappy's noonday meal.

"I'll need my pan tomorrow, Pappy," I said. "I'm going to Fifth Machias Stream for trout."

"That pan's mine," said Pappy, his long jaw getting longer.

He showed me the inventory.

"Who put my pan on that list?" I asked, indignantly.

"Mr. Dennison did — so now it's *my* pan. I've always wanted it, ever since I first saw it. Now I've got it."

Since Henry Dennison was then my father-in-law, and since I had use of the Dobsis camp solely by reason of his generosity, I had little to say about the frying pan swindle.

So I said: "Okay, Pappy, can I *borrow* Old Come-and-get-it for a few days on Fifth Machias?"

"Nope," he said, "you can't. I don't want to let that pan out of my sight."

"All right—then come with me on the trip."

This is what Pappy had wanted all along; and that trip was one of forty-five I have made to Fifth Machias Stream, all of them duly recorded in the Dobsis Camp diary. Old Come-and-get-it went on every one of them.

Within the past year or so, a road has been bulldozed to the shore of Fourth Machias Lake. You can drive there from Grand Lake Stream. But in Old Come-and-get-it's early days, you lugged your canoe on your neck from the west shore of Dobsis. Then you paddled six miles up Fourth Lake to Cy Gulch, where Fifth Machias Stream comes in after nine miles of meandering and cascading through dead waters, rips, falls, and fast elbow turns, down through its wilderness from remote Fifth Lake.

We call it "The Little River," and I have no greater love for any stream. Its dark pools and quick water unfailingly produced trout, and the trout were dark-backed and brilliant-hued along the sides.

Once The Little River almost failed. It looked as though Old Come-and-get-it would go empty. Jim Dennison and I had poled up to Night Dam and set up a couple of flat rocks on the East wing of the dam. We laid a fire with birch bark, cedar twigs, and a few sticks of bone-hard, dry, split maple. We cut a green alder stick for a cold handle, and rested the frying pan athwart the rocks. We didn't light the fire. We rigged our fly rods and went fishing above the dam.

It was a hot, still, stifling July day. We hadn't been able to raise a trout on the fast water below the dam, so we waded the dead water above. None of the deep pools produced. One o'clock came, then two. Jim's stomach ached from hunger, and mine was making the odd sounds of famine. We had no grub with us except a chunk of salt pork, salt, and pepper. It was a tradition to count on The Little River for trout on the long day's trip from Dobsis to Night Dam and return.

Sweat ran from our foreheads. The blackflies clouded around our heads. Never a trout stirred. The water in which we waded was as warm as tea and the same color. Then, suddenly, as I took a step over a deep, muddy place, I felt a chill in both feet. I had walked into one of The Little River's famous hidden springs, this one in the middle of a virtual bog.

I studied the current, which was very slow. It broke along a bend into an alder-shaded pool, black with depth. I got that shaky feeling. It's half premonition, half the IBM of your brain adding up facts and scores. I knew there were trout in that pool by the alders. There had to be, because of the cold water.

I reeled in, snipped the Wickham's Fancy from my leader, and attached a Pale Evening Dun. Why a Pale Evening Dun? Because it's one of the most beautiful names I ever heard applied to a trout fly, or anything else.

Greenwell's Glory has a nice sound. Lady of the Lake is pretty, too. But for pure beauty, you can't beat Pale Evening Dun.

The one I used that day was a number fourteen. I dropped it in the alder leaves above the pool, whose waters had been cooled by the hidden spring. The fly slipped off the alder leaves and settled on the pool's black surface. Five or six trout came smashing for it all at once. I've never seen such a concentration or such fantastic action in a pool not over eight feet across.

I hooked and landed two — a matched pair ten inches long. Then I called to Jim Dennison. Half an hour later, we were back at Night Dam. We diced our chunk of salt pork, lit the fire under Old Come-and-get-it, and when the pork was brown, we put six trout in the hot fat. They curled, as fresh-caught trout always do. We pressed them flat in the pan with a big cedar chip some axeman had hewed from a king-post timber while building the dam. When the trout were crisp on both sides, we salted them and ate them with our fingers, like corn on the cob. This was one of Old Come-and-get-it's finest meals.

There was another fine meal on a clean gravel bar just below the Mill Race on Second Chain Stream. The three Chain Lakes, connected by enchanting streams, flow into Dobsis Lake on the west side. There's a fine, small, wooded island at the mouth of First Lake Stream, and many are the meals Old Come-and-get-it has sponsored on the white, curved sand beach of that island. But the meal four miles above, on Second Chain Stream, is the standout.

Roy Bailey, Pop Dennison, an Indian, and I had built a cabin on Third Chain Lake. It was a snug cabin, used mostly for the annual deer-hunting trip. When Pappy Thornton became caretaker at the Dennison place, he inherited the duty of provisioning Third Chain Cabin against the arrival of Henry Dennison and his hunting friends. Whenever I was on hand, which was often, I helped Pappy with this annual rite. We picked our weather carefully and always had fun, especially on the occasion of the meal on the gravel bar.

It was a bright, still, November day. The bare beech limbs had a russet hue, and the big pines and spruces were deep green. Each of us paddled a loaded canoe, and we were side by side on First Chain Lake, remembering other trips in all seasons: there was the brown rock we always mistook for a deer; there was the cove where we saw the black bear; and here, as we entered Second Chain Stream, was the patch of lily pads where Pappy had caught the immense pickerel.

At the upper end of the dead water, where the Mill Race — a brisk stretch of quick water — comes in, was one of our favorite lunch spots: a clean, dry, gravel bar. Our canoes made a faint crunching sound on the gravel as we sided in along the bar. Above us the Mill Race sang in the stillness. I stepped behind an old gray rock and found Old Come-and-get-it's cold handle, a stick of maple we must have used twenty times. It was right where we'd left it. So were the blackened flat rocks of our fireplace. And there was a stack of dry, split beech we'd cached under a cedar on our last trip.

The smoke smelled especially sweet that noon. We leaned our rifles in an alder crotch. When Old Come-and-get-it's bottom got warm, I spooned in some bacon fat, sliced some cold boiled potatoes into the fat, and alongside them placed two slices of liver from a deer I'd shot on Dobsis the day before.

To save washing dishes, we ate out of the frying pan. Pappy speared a cube of potato with his fork, and followed it with a large portion of liver.

I looked up at him to see his cheeks bulging, his long jaws chomping. Then, in mid-chomp, his jaws suddenly stopped working. A strange expression came into his blue-gray eyes. He was looking over my shoulder at something downstream along the dead water we'd just navigated. His big hand reached slowly behind him and found his rifle. I turned and saw the big buck standing in the dried grasses of the stream bank less than thirty yards downstream. Pappy fired and the deer dropped, and the echoes of the shot bounced around in the long, brown ridges—and Pappy began chewing again.

"This is mighty fine liver," he said. "But I know where there's some better."

We hung Pappy's deer high up in a birch to take out on our way back, and while we'd been at it, the fat had chilled and hardened in Old Come-and-get-it, and the fire was out. I started to clean the pan with sand, as I'd always done. But Pappy shook his head disgustedly and in a moment had the fire blazing again. So presently I learned how to clean a frying pan. You heat it just short of red-hot, and plunge it into the cold water of lake or stream. It is almost instantly steam-cleaned, free of grease and grime, and ready for the next meal.

When you reckon them up, Old Come-and-get-it has served quite a number of distinguished people, other than the Maine guides already mentioned. First, there was Henry Dennison himself. Dr. Miriam Van Waters, world-renowned for her work in prison reform, once made a blueberry pie. It fed eleven people in Old Come-and-get-it.

Back in the thirties I prepared bacon and eggs, together with some landlocked salmon filets, in Old Come-and-get-it for a young economist who had once come to Dobsis for a week's rest from his intensive studies at Harvard. This fellow was, and is, six feet and seven inches tall. Each morning, before breakfast, he took a cold dive into Dobsis Stream. We called him "Kenny the Plunger." His real name is Professor John Kenneth Galbraith; he is one of our country's brilliant men, a top economic advisor to the late President John Kennedy. And there were Doctor Otto Krauschaar, now president of Goucher College, and many more men of achievement.

These noted people would be amused to know that Old Come-and-get-it, during the miserable years of prohibition, did service as a kind of distillery or, more accurately, a vessel for blending "whiskey." You took a cup of sugar and a cup of water and scorched the mixture in Old Come-and-get-it till it was like caramel. Then you took the gallon can of Hand Brand Alcohol you'd bought from the bootlegger in the town of Lincoln, and you poured half of it into the caramel.... When thoroughly mixed, you funneled the blend into quart bottles. Then you pasted on the labels your printer friend had made up. Some of these labels read: "Old Sabre Tooth," "Old Perhaps," "Gates Ajar," "Hernando's Fiery Dagger," and "Breath in the Afternoon." The beverage was all the same, and it had high authority, as well as a strange flavor picked up from a thousand or more various meals which had left ghostly essences in Old Come-and-get-it. You could taste pickerel, onions, bacon fat, and—according to Pappy Thornton—fried eel. But after two drinks, it was straight nectar of roses.

There are cold handles waiting for Old Come-and-get-it—stashed away behind boulders or just stuck in the moss, all over Washington, Hancock, and Penobscot Counties in Maine. Roy Bailey and I found one on the beach at Unknown Lake last summer. It must have been twenty years old, and it broke in Roy's hands as he picked it up. It was a piece of maple.

"When did we cut that handle?" I asked Roy.

We both went wild with reminiscence. Was it the time we lugged Harley Fenlayson's deer across the Unknown Carry to Third Chain and cooked canned corned beef? Was it the time we mixed the three cans together—spaghetti, beans, and tomato soup? Was it the time we caught the big trout at Unknown Dam and fried it in Crisco? We never did agree, and we will argue about it everytime we meet.

There's a cold handle stuck in a hollow stump on the shore of Wabash (Wabassus) Lake. My son Jim cut that one when he was twelve years old. We were pickerel fishing. The lake was calm in our lily-padded cove, and we'd looked over the side of the canoe into the beautifully clear water and seen a pickerel down there—ten feet below us. The big fellow was lying doggo, absolutely still. Jim had a Pikie Minnow on his casting rod, and he touched the Pikie to the surface right at the side of the canoe. The ripples made by the plug destroyed the pickerel's visibility—but a second later he came up under the plug with a big smash of spray, and Jim "hossed" him right on up, over, and into the canoe. We went ashore, fileted the pickerel, cut a cold handle from a birch sapling, and fried our fish.

There's a cold handle, a cedar one, at Church Dam above Cedar Rips on West Musquash Stream. There's one on Louse Island on Mattagamon Lake in Penobscot County. There are two or three at the cabin on Third Chain Lake. I wonder if the cabin's present owner knows what they are for? Thinking of them, I remember the hunting trips and Old Come-and-get-it sizzling under its treasure of venison steaks; or the time Pop Dennison and I shot six partridges budding in a birch tree, and while congratulating each other, rifles empty, turned to see what had made a thudding sound behind us — three deer were getting out of there fast!

The next night the six partridges fried up brown and aromatic in Old Come-and-get-it, and Pop and I came in for some heavy ribbing about those deer. And, most of all, I remember the early mornings in the cabin, the smell of the cedar kindling taking flame and the bacon rind lubricating the surface of Old Come-and-get-it, and the hiss of the pancake batter as it spread and bubbled on the pan's hot surface; and then daylight, and the hunters going their separate ways, and the white, beautiful frost on the bottoms of the three canoes turned up on shore; and, later, the dull, muffled, far-off sound of a rifle shot, and wondering who had fired it, and at what, and did he connect?

It's a long, far cry from 1917, when Digsy Jones and I bought Old Come-and-get-it. Digsy and I drifted apart, and I haven't seen him for more years than I like to think about. But outside of the melancholy of the shifting tides of life, there is no sadness in the history of Old Come-and-get-it, none whatever. In fact, its history is a happy thing that at times reaches the point of hilarity.

Take, for example, the cold handle — this time fashioned of poplar — that you can find at Hewes Brook if you are of a mind to walk in a mile or more across the old burn from Penniman Cove on Fourth Machias Lake. How this cold handle came into being belongs to one of the zaniest true legends of the region.

When Pappy Thornton, as caretaker at Dobsis, inherited "ownership" of Old Come-and-get-it, he also inherited by way of the inventory list an item he didn't like so much. To wit, "one horse." This horse was named "Mose," and Mose had been handed down through three or four successive caretakers. He looked it, too. The old creature must have seen close to thirty summers at the time of the Hewes Brook adventure. He hung around day after day nibbling grass, bark, and sticks in the Dobsis clearing.

The reason for having Mose in a remote camp like Dobsis was the cow, Irma. The Dennison family liked fresh milk and butter, hence Irma. And

Mose was required to haul the mowing machine that cut the meadow hay that sustained Irma — and himself — during the long winter. Mose was also required to haul the single-horse hayrack on which the hay was loaded and carried to the barn haymow.

Now, on the July day that led us deviously to Hewes Brook, Mose got sleepy and lay down while hauling the empty hayrack out to the back clearing to pick up the cured hay. In lying down, he broke both wagon thills. A thill is one-half of a set of shafts.

Pappy looked down at Mose and the broken thills. Mose looked up at Pappy and me. He also looked at Bill Sprague, who had come up from Grand Lake in his canoe to help with the detested haying operation. Mose and Pappy shook their heads in despair. Then Pappy smiled dreamfully.

"Mose," he said, "looks like I got to make some new thills."

"I know where there's some nice black ash," said Bill Sprague.

"So do I," I said. "Down on Pocumpus Lake."

Anything was better than haying, and since Pappy and Bill Sprague are both superb craftsmen with edged tools, an expedition was immediately organized. After we got Mose upright and unharnessed, Pappy took thill measurements, and we got axes, a draw knife, some carriage bolts, and other equipment. We loaded these into Bill Sprague's big canoe, one of the many such canoes that Bill has built himself and sold to grateful sportsmen.

Next we made a batch of "Gates Ajar Whiskey" in Old Come-and-get-it, bottled the brew, and took off down the long thoroughfare and on into Pocumpus Lake — Pappy passing the Gates Ajar back to me amidships, I passing it on back to Bill in the stern, and then working it along back up to Pappy in the bow.

At the mouth of Wabash Stream, which flows in near the foot of Pocumpus, we met an old friend named Zeke Brackitt. Zeke was tenting out with a revenue officer from the Canadian border, and they craved company. It happened that the revenue officer, Brick Conway, had come by two forty-ounce bottles of genuine Canadian Club whiskey following a recent raid. Since our Gates Ajar was about gone, we accepted Brick Conway's hospitality.

Along about sundown, when we were working out some wonderful chords on "I want a gal, just like the gal —" Pappy happened to think about Mose and the wagon thills. Then he thought about his wife, Kate, back at Dobsis.

"Katie'll be all right," he said, "with her sister there, and her nephew. She won't worry."

"Neither will Mose," said Bill Sprague.

Zeke Brackitt said:

"I wanna gal-l-l — just like the gal that —"

All five of us hit it: "Married dear-r-r ole Da-a-a-ad."

I know it was a terrific chord, because it set the loons to hollering in the moonlight.

Brick Conway mentioned that the pickerel fishing in Wabash Stream had been fine, but that he and Zeke really craved to catch and eat some trout. That's when Bill Sprague mentioned Hewes Brook, which you reach via Penniman Cove in Fourth Machias Lake. In order to reach Fourth Lake, we had to go back via Dobsis Stream and Dennison's Camp.

Pappy shook his head dejectedly.

"Katie would see us, and she wouldn't let me go."

"So why don't we go right now, by night, when she'll be asleep?" said Bill.

"My thought exactly," said Pappy.

And I said: "I know where there's a stand of nice ash on Fourth Lake."

That justified the trip on moral and practical grounds, and we struck Zeke's tent and put for Fourth Lake in our two canoes in the moonlight. We got across into Dobsis Lake without arousing Katie and reached Penniman Cove on Fourth Machias at sunrise. A mile or so later, across the big burn, and we were on Hewes Brook — a strange, isolated, silent, dead water meandering through an immense heath ground where you see moose and deer frequently. You cast from the brushy bank, and the trout run uniform in size, mostly nine inches, with an occasional one-pounder.

Brick Conway, the revenue officer, was delighted. By eight o'clock in the morning, we had all we could eat. I cut a cold handle from a poplar sapling, Bill Sprague moved a couple of rocks into position, and we had a memorable meal, saddened only by Pappy's sudden recollection of Mose, the horse.

"Those wagon thills!" he said.

We said elaborate farewells to Zeke Brackitt and Brick Conway, who decided to camp on Fourth Lake for a few days. We found the stand of black ash I'd remembered and spent the next five hours shaping the thills for the hayrack. In the late afternoon, we lugged back across Fourth Lake Carry into Dobsis, thills and all. On the Dobsis shore, Pappy and Bill bolted the thills to the cross member and laid the skillfully shaped finished product athwart Bill's canoe.

"Katie'll see what a fine job we've done," Pappy said. "She'll know how hard we worked all this time."

"There's five trout left," I said. "I'll say how I caught them just for her, while you and Bill were working so hard."

We shoved offshore with our load. Bill started his motor and we crossed through the gut below Big Island, and then started the straight run to Dobsis Camp on the stream.

Half a mile from home, we could see Katie Thornton on the dock, and her sister and nephew, too. As the distance closed, we could tell they were distressed about something. You could feel it. When we got close, we could see Katie dabbing at her eyes with her apron. Pappy thought her tears were those of accusation, so as the canoe touched the dock, he immediately went into his pitch.

"Honey," he said, "we been all over hunting after nice ash for the thills. We found it, too. See? Mose never had better shafts in his life."

Katie sobbed. Her sister caught it, and put a handkerchief to her eyes. The nephew sniffled damply.

"Katie," I said, "while Pappy and Bill worked — in the hot sun — I caught you some nice trout. Here."

She shook her head and moaned, without looking at the trout.

"What's the matter with you?" Pappy said, glaring at Katie. "Is there something wrong with these wagon thills?"

"No! Oh, no. Only — just that — I —"

"Now, doggonnit, old lady," Pappy said, affectionately. "Quit wheezin' and croakin', and tell me what's wrong with these thills."

"Nothing," said Katie. "Nothing at all — except that —"

"Except what?"

"Mose — is — *dead*."

I think it was Mark Twain who said, "Let us draw the curtain of charity over the rest of the scene," and I am not one to try to improve a classic. Poor old Mose had died in his sleep, probably about the time we were perfecting chords on "I want a gal —." But the beautifully shaped wagon thills were not entirely wasted. A few days later, Pappy cut the curved, slender end from one of them, and from it fashioned a splendid cold handle for Old Come-and-get-it for home use.

After Pappy left the Dobsis job, Old Come-and-get-it reverted back to me. Now and then I get sentimental, remove it from its current muslin bag, and decide to cook a meal in it here at home. You'll be glad to know I've never done it. Why not? Because it would be a desecration to expose its ancient bottom to the coils of an electric stove. Old Come-and-get-it is for wood smoke only.

# The Magic Woodsman

I first met the old woodsman more than twenty years ago. Then in his fifties, he had hired on as caretaker of Dennison's remote camp on Dobsis Lake in Maine, where I had come to recover from a long illness.

The camp and its extraordinary caretaker proved a healing combination. If Pop Thornton didn't actually cure me, the unique medicine of his artfully contrived canoe trip lifted my heart and dispelled the gloom of slow convalescence, so that I heard my own laughter for the first time in weeks. And one tragic day, years later – the year the little boy drowned – he did the same tender thing in the same gifted way for my two small children, and I heard them laugh again.

His full name is Charles Elmer Thornton, but he is Pop to everyone who visited the Dobsis camp during his caretakership. He is Pop to the young couples who honeymooned there, and to the families who came for summer vacations. He is Pop to the numberless children – including my own – whom he taught and told so much, and who felt the radiation of his enchanted personality.

When Pop came to Dobsis he brought with him his beloved and devout wife, Kate; his gleaming carpenter's tools; his woodsman's skills so essential to the job. And he also brought the strange, elusive element of his charm — the quicksilver imagination which beguiled children and adults alike, and which created among many other things The Legend of the Red Bee Bird, The Long Torture of Billy Gaines, and — above all — The Magic Carpet Canoe Trip.

Each fall, before the arrival of the Dennison hunting party, it had been my duty to provision an out-cabin we had built far back on Third Chain Lake. It was a long, hard trip by canoe, with two rough portages. But this particular fall, when I was convalescing, I'd been excused. I supposed that Pop Thornton, whom I had known only a few days, was going to make the trip alone. I was wholly unaware that he had other plans.

One noon Pop's wife, Kate, asked me to call Pop in to dinner. I found him out in his workshop. He sat on a bench, the fragrant wood shavings curled at his feet, and in his pale, blue eyes the scheme light I learned to recognize as the forerunner of fantasy.

"Kate says dinner's ready," I said.

"I can't come. I'm not hungry."

"Why not?"

In his seamed and eloquent hands he held a canoe paddle he had just made. It was a work of art.

"I want to set here alone an' feel the wood of my paddle, an' look at it," he said. "It's lovely to touch and behold. If I feast my eyes on it, that's dinner enough."

He was a gaunt poet, rereading a sonnet he had written with a broad axe and crooked knife. He reached behind him and picked up another new paddle, which he handed to me.

"That's yours," he said, "to use on our trip to Third Chain Lake, tomorrow."

"Thanks," I said. "But I haven't got the heart for the trip."

"How do you know that, when you've never been on it?"

Counting summer trips, I'd been to Third Chain twenty times, and Pop knew it. But he rose up slowly from the bench, standing tall and imperious, as he said:

"You've never been there in your life, till you've been there with me."

It was true. I began to realize it early the next morning when we beached our loaded canoes at First Cabin Carry and Pop took his hand axe and stalked mysteriously into the spruces. He spent an hour fabricating an elaborate cache in a forked tree. In this secret and superfluous nest he concealed dry matches, tobacco, a junk of salt pork, and a pint of whiskey. You thought of a benign and bony king lining a chest with treasure.

"What's the idea?" I asked. "We don't need a cache."

He looked hurt and misunderstood.

"Cache?" he said. "This ain't a cache at all. It's kind of a shinin' goal — a jewill to look forward to on our way back, tomorrow. If a big storm comes, an' we get cold an' wet, we can dream ahead to this hideout, an' jest the thought of it will bring stren'th to our tired bodies over the perilous miles."

Right about then, I began to forget my own troubles in wonder at my lean, long-jawed companion. His "shining goal," his "jewel to look forward to," his disarming byplay were of the stuff of dreams. Yet they were born of reality, for Pop used his imagination as an instrument to embellish life and baffle hardship. Eventually, I learned how and why he did it. But now, as we poled up Second Chain Stream, he was unfurling the original blueprint of the Third Chain canoe trip we both knew was whole cloth a mile wide.

Leaning on his canoe pole, Pop raised his head and stared at the chill, gray sky.

"Game wardens will carry our packs on the portages," he began. "We'll put a layer of rocks in each pack. You an' me will be reclinin' at ease on stretchers carried by four guides apiece. We shall be pavillioned in splendor, canopies over us, with tassils all around. Silk cushions under our heads."

"More likely a cedar root or a cold stone," I said.

He gave me a look of patient reproof, and went on:

"These cushions I speak of will be sprinkled with Evenin' In Paris perfumery, an' will smell han'some. Squaws with palm leaf fans will fan the blackflies off us."

"It's fall," I said, "no blackflies."

"We got to have blackflies to bite the game wardens," said Pop, "so's we'll get extry pleasure from their misery. A trip like ours, you got to plan it careful."

"Okay. I suppose the squaws will feed us shelled walnuts?"

"No. They'll feed us lady fingers dipped in port wine."

I laughed, and it felt good; and as we poled up the Mill Race and lugged the loads across the portage into Third Chain Lake, I was lost in the game of make-believe. We bickered happily over the exotic luxuries and personnel of the trip, and before I knew it, we had arrived at the cabin.

Our supper consisted of canned beans and hardtack, but an imaginary Indian maid named Susan Brown Blanket washed the dishes. We turned in; and presently in the wind-moaning dark I was listening to the first of the many prayers I have heard Pop speak aloud from the kitchen bunk in that cabin in the wilderness.

What strange, sweet, touching, human, merry prayers were his! I can't remember any of them word for word—except the one he spoke the night he brought my children on the Magic Carpet Trip. That prayer we know by heart, and always will. There is a reason why.

But on my first night in the cabin with Pop, his prayer went something like this:

"Lord, I am grateful for all the blessings You gave us today, an' please help my friend to show a little gratitude, too, because this trip has almost made him well again. Also, will You keep the porcupines away from our hideout on First Chain Carry, an' keep human vandils—especially my enemy, Billy Gaines—from findin' our pint of whiskey? An' one more thing: Lord, please make my wife, Kate, miss me while I'm gone, an' make her lonesome, so's I can have the joy of soothin' an' comfortin' her when I get home, tomorrow. Amen."

I wanted to ask Pop about his enemy, Billy Gaines, but the time wasn't appropriate. Billy was to become folklore. But at the moment, I lay smiling in the darkness, thinking how my children would some day know and love the magic woodsman.

Pop was born seventy-odd years ago in a weathered farmhouse on a hill near Topsfield, Maine. Bleak, barren, untenable hilltop, snowswept in winter, wind-raw in spring, benevolent for a few weeks only in summer when the hay leaned in the breath of evening and the fireflies deified the dusk with their supernal glow.

Pop is the third of seventeen children by the same father and mother. He acquired his skill with edged tools while making wooden toys for his younger brothers and sisters. Ever since he can remember, he told them tales at night by the kitchen stove.

"It made spring come quicker," Pop said to me, "an' it made us forget how hungry an' cold we was, some nights."

Salt pork, dried codfish, and potatoes came forth as roast turkey and angel food cake under Pop's touch. The whisper of snow was the hiss of gilded steam radiators. The wagons and sleds he contrived for his little brothers became chariots, and the chickens huddling in the icy barnyard turned into peacocks.

"Or maybe sometimes albatrosses," said Pop.

He learned his superb axemanship in lumber camps, his boatmanship in bateaus on the spring log drives. Eventually, he became a master carpenter, and worked at his trade for many years near Boston. But the high wages didn't satisfy him. He was lonely and homesick for the lake and forest country of his boyhood.

"When I heard about the Dobsis job," Pop told me, "I came pretty near jumpin' off a high stagin' I was workin' from. I packed up my tools, bought Kate a new dress, an' here I am."

It was a wonderful arrangement for everyone concerned. The Dennison camp flourished as never before. Sometimes as many as ten children and their parents came up at the same time. Pop showed the kids how to build fires, and how to put them out. He showed them how to use tools, how to set up tents, how to light a kerosene lamp. And in fair weather, he took them on evening picnics in the big boat.

On one of these, he built the fire on a sand beach near a cold spring. A scarlet tanager flashed from the forest, lighted on a hazel bush by the spring, and the next instant flew away, a streak of crimson in the twilight. It was a startling and dramatic incident, and the children cried out with joy — and in Pop's eyes I saw the scheme light.

"Boys and girls," he said, in his solemn voice. "You have just seen The Red Bee Bird. He has never been seen before, excep' by an old, tired man, who was dying of thirst in the forrist."

I am convinced that Pop created the legend on the spur of the moment. While the smoke of the fire drifted like blue veils in the spruce tops, the children listened wide-eyed.

The old, tired man, Pop told them, came after three days into a glade in the deep, still woods. There were four bubbling springs, one at each corner of the glade, and in the middle of the glade a fifth spring boiled from white sand. The old man crawled with crusted lips toward the middle spring, and right then a red bird came darting, and alighted with feathery feet atop an alder beside the middle spring.

While the old man watched, the red bird lifted one foot and thrust up the feathers of its neck on that side. Then, resting this foot on the alder branch, the bird lifted its other foot and thrust up the feathers on that side.

"Them red feathers was like the petals of a lovely rose," said Pop, "and the yellow bill of the red bird was like the center of the rose.

"So then came the bees. They saw the rose by the spring, and they flew to it for rose nectar, but they suffered terrible dismay. The red bird opened its yellow bill, and a bee disappeared an' was devoured. Finally just a few bees were left, and they hummed off into the woods in great sorrow. Then The Red Bee Bird pushed its feathers down on one side, and then on the other side, and he flew away forever into the forrist an' was never seen again till you children saw him by our spring tonight."

Pop must have told this tale with variations a hundred times. It always left the children thoughtful and entranced. But, after a moment, one would ask:

"What happened to the old, tired man?"

Pop had three different answers:

"Why, he forgot his thirst," or, "he went home to tell his grandchildren," or, "ever afterwards, the old man thirsted jest for knowledge, which was harder to find than water."

The Long Torture of Billy Gaines is in sharp contrast to the mystic quality of The Red Bee Bird. At an uncertain time in Pop's past, a man named Billy Gaines borrowed his broad axe and returned it with a nick in the blade as big as two thumbnails. It must be forty years since Pop has seen Billy Gaines.

"But I still get revenge on him," Pop told me one afternoon, when he had been hewing a sill in the clearing, "an' I still make him work for me."

"Well — how?" I asked. "What do you mean?"

"Take today," Pop explained. "It was hot out there, hewin', an' my arms got lame, so I thought how every blow with my axe might be strikin' Billy Gaines, hip an' thigh. Pretty quick, my arms quit achin', an' my blows got powerful again, an' first thing I knew, the sill was all hewed, an' I heard Kate callin' me in to supper."

Billy Gaines became a very useful tradition at Dobsis. I don't know what the psychiatrists would say about him, but when the children got overtired and turbulence broke out, Pop would stalk between two combatants and hand them each a stick.

"Now, then," he'd say, "take these clubs an' go an' hit Billy Gaines a few belts. You'll feel better."

"Where is he?" the kids would ask.

Pop would aim one child toward a tree, the other toward a rock in the opposite direction. One child would whack the tree, the other the stone, until Billy Gaines — and their own tempers — were subdued. Billy gave vent to the furies of the very young, and averted small warfare, and no one got hurt, least of all Billy.

Most of Pop's creations were expressly for children, but The Magic Carpet Canoe Trip was for everyone. Children heard about it, and dreamed of the time they'd be old enough to go. Adults went, and told other adults, until it became the main event of a Dobsis visit.

The year we came up for a family vacation, my children — except for Jim, who was ten — were still not old enough. Joan was six, and the little boy, Denny, was three. The ill-starred vacation began happily; the children greeting Pop with joyous "Hi's," the long trip down to camp in the big boat, changing feverishly into outdoor clothes, meeting other members of the family who were already at camp, and the oft-repeated question:

"What'll we do tomorrow?"

That unforgettable tomorrow is many yesterdays ago. Joanie, Jimmy, and I took our lunch and went fishing. Their mother, her sister, and other relatives stayed at camp.

Early in the afternoon the weather turned damp and misty, and I headed back with the children. We came around a point within sight of the camp buildings. I heard someone cry out piercingly, and saw people running toward the dock, and knew I was about a minute behind a tragedy. Any tragedy that happened there would be close to me, and mine.

How the little boy, Denny, fell off the dock and drowned none of us knows. He had been playing with older children. He must have veered off secretly on some impulsive mission of his own. To recover a toy on the dock? We found one there. To peer at a school of perch just off the dock? The school of perch was there.

His mother and his aunt saw him lying on bottom in five feet of water, and they had jumped in and brought him up. They were trying to bring him to when I arrived.

The first shock hit us all. I saw it strike in Joan's and Jimmy's eyes, saw their faces whiten.

The gray mist hovered wet and cold over the dock, as we worked in shifts at artificial respiration. The nearest pulmotor, the nearest oxygen, was probably ninety miles away in Bangor. But we had all had first aid training; and Bill and Florence Sprague, and a young girl who had come to help Kate in the kitchen, were experts. After six hours, we knew no chance of life remained. There was no spark to revive. The child was dead.

During the nightmare of the next day—getting word out by boat to officials and loved ones, making arrangements to have Denny's body taken back to Cambridge, trying to comfort one another—Pop was constantly with Jim and Joanie. We saw him sitting under the apple tree with one on each side of him, or walking through the back clearing, each great hand holding one of their small ones, stilling the wretchedness in their hearts.

When at last we were ready to go home, Pop came into the camp alone, and I saw once more the scheme light in his eyes, but was scarcely aware of it.

"Guess we're all set, Pop," I said. "Are you ready with the boat?"

"Yes—and I've got two canoes ready, too. For when you get back. Will you—?"

He hesitated, looked away, then looked again at my wife and me, his eyes imploring.

"Will you let me take Joanie and Jimmy on the Third Chain trip? And you come, too—Ed? Leave the kids here with us, till you come back, after the services. Will you, please?"

We stared at Pop, incredulous. His proposal seemed incongruous, astonishing. Didn't he realize that Dobsis, for us, was no more? That the thought of it would haunt us as long as we lived? Yes. He knew. And he also knew how we dreaded having Joanie and Jimmy go through the ordeal of their brother's funeral, when they were both so young and overwrought. He had either sensed this, or overheard us talking about it.

And now his slow, thoughtful voice brought us out of ourselves, and made my return for the Third Chain Cabin trip seem sensible, and profoundly important in our lives.

"You could be back by Wednesday," Pop said to me. "Kate and I will care for the kids. Bill and Florence Sprague will stay, too—till you come."

We couldn't leave our children in more able and comforting care. But a return to Dobsis and the Third Chain trip rose up before me like a black and barbarous obstacle—till Pop finished what he had to say.

"This trip is for Joanie and Jimmy," he said. "And it will help you, too. I want you to come. If you don't come back and make it, you'll never come to Dobsis again. I can see it in your face, and the kids' faces are like yours."

He looked off through the window toward the apple tree, and added:

"Besides that—I've promised them."

"Pop's right!" my wife said, suddenly. "You'll do it, won't you? I'll be all right. I'll stay with my family. It will mean everything to the children—and you. I know."

So do I—now. I think the trip was a kind of salvation. I know it restored the love of the Dobsis camp for all of us.

We beached our loaded canoes in the morning sunshine at First Chain Carry and Pop crept stealthily into the spruces with his hand axe, Joan and Jimmy at his heels. In a new, elaborate cache—like the one he had fashioned for me so many years before—he stored for my children some pieces of spruce gum, six molasses cookies, and a Peter Paul's Almond Joy.

"Why do we leave them here?" asked Joanie.

"To think about. To look forward to on our way back."

"Are we really going to see Third Chain Cabin, at last?" Jimmy asked.

"If we can struggle up through the rapids an' triumph over the perils an' hardships, we'll be there before dark," said Pop.

He had made small knapsacks for them, and he strapped them on. The carry seemed long and hard. Once, Jimmy said:

"My pack's pretty heavy."

"Heavy?" said Pop, his forehead wrinkling. "Why, Jimmy, it don't weigh a thing. Billy Gaines is carryin' it, his legs painin' him, an' the sweat jest rollin' off him."

Before we got to Second Chain Lake, Joanie had become a spotted fawn, lifting her head, flaring her nostrils. Pop had told her how deer traveled the carry every day, and had shown her tiny hoofprints beside the mother's larger ones.

I could see the magic woodsman's light getting between my children and the dark loneliness of their sorrow. It was a strange and moving experience.

Paddling down Third Chain Lake toward the cabin, I heard Joanie's laughter drifting back from Pop's canoe, where she was seated in the bow. And Jim said to me:

"Let's go faster, so we can hear what Pop is saying."

We came alongside after a time. Pop was saying:

"Now, that rock on the carry, where you hit your knee. Tonight, when I say my prayers, I'll ask the Lord to remove that rock, an' fill in the hole with silk cushions, an' gum drops underneath."

And Jim said:

"Pop, ask Him to let me catch a pickerel, will you?"

"I'll take it up with Him. Tommy Anderson had me put in a claim for two pickerel one time, an' he caught three."

"And you made him put one back," Jim said. "I heard about that. I know all about it."

" 'Course I made Tommy put the third one back. He only had me ask for two. You have to be fair with the Lord."

We opened the cabin door in the dusk, and you could smell the tar smell of the oakum chinking, and the smoke of long-ago fires. Pop showed Jim how to whittle a cedar tinder stick and start the fire in the stove. After the supper, he told them the story of The Red Bee Bird once more. Joanie came to him afterwards, walking gingerly, a spotted fawn again. She kissed his cheek, whirled, and pranced away to her bunk.

We turned in, and Pop took the lamp into the kitchen, turned it low, and got into his bunk. I could see him lie back, and close his eyes, and I saw the tears squeeze from his eyelids. He reached out and turned the lamp lower, and blew it out, and the dark settled around us. The night was still, and starlit, and when Pop began his prayer it seemed beautiful beyond understanding, and there was an ache and an elation, as the old man, in his low, kind voice, spoke the ageless words:

"Our Father Who art in heaven...."

# Death of a Haunted Tent

When Johnny Towers and Red Atwood came to the house to borrow my tent for their spring canoe-and-camping trip, I figured it was safe to let them have it. Not that I cherished the tent or feared for its safety in their able hands. Don't get me wrong on that. It was Johnny's and Red's safety I feared for. They could get hurt in that tent. They could even get killed. I almost had myself, at least twice.

I am convinced it was accident-prone, doubtless a rare thing in tents. Or it was like a beautiful horse that kicks you without warning, or a fine car with a built-in tendency to dump you over a cliff. There had been times when it had me spooked.

I didn't tell Johnny Towers and Red Atwood any of this. I didn't tell them I never wanted to see the tent again, or why. It would have ruined their trip before they started. Besides, they were expressing their gratitude and giving me all kinds of credit for being a generous, kindhearted guy.

"Not at all," I said. "The pleasure is mine."

I meant it literally.

The tent was a haunted house. But it had been in my attic, unused for a long time, and I figured its ghosts were laid or at least nontransferable, which — probably — made it a safe shelter for my young friends on their trip.

So, with only a slight shudder, I got the tent out of the darkest corner of the attic, brought it down to the back lawn, and shook it out, half expecting to dodge a shower of black widow spiders. Almost everything else had shared the tent with me. Why not a black widow?

"Say!" Johnny said. "What a tent — Explorer's model, hey? She's a beaut."

"Yuh. She's a beaut, all right."

Red Atwood was looking at the monster with open admiration.

"Ground cloth sewed in," he said. "Bobbinet front — with slider fastener. The works."

"Sure," I said, "the works. Everything but free liquor and separate thermostat."

They had begun to notice the tent's patches. There were quite a few. I suppose to Johnny and Red they were picturesque, romantic. To me they resembled the scars on the face of a sadistic Prussian duelist. At any rate, the patches were all weatherproof and sound. The tent was a beautifully constructed bit of fabric. On that sunny afternoon in May you couldn't see its black soul or remember its nightmares.

"You've been places in that old tent, hey, Ed?" Red asked, examining the long, curving, ribbon-narrow patch that slashed the back wall.

"Yup," I said. "Quite a few places."

"You're sure — really sure you want to let us have it?"

"I'm not only sure. I'm positive."

"You'll get it back just as it is. We'll take the best of care of it."

I was going to say, "I was afraid of that," but it would have made them curious. So I said:

"I know the old rag is in good hands. Keep it as long as you like. And good luck and good weather on your trip."

Johnny stowed the tent carefully in the back of their ranch wagon, on top of which was fastened their canoe, and they took off, starry-eyed. Which left me alone with my thoughts.

The first thoughts were of vague concern for the two young men heading north in their wagon for the upper reaches of Maine's Penobscot River, East Branch. They were strong, capable men in their middle twenties, experienced campers and canoemen. So why should I worry about them just because they had my tent along? Was it because, in effect, I was encouraging them to do something I shrank from doing myself? To wit, sleep under that tent? Or was it simple, primitive superstition? If so, it was ridiculous. Hell with it. I put it out of mind. But it came back in through a kind of rear door.

Why hadn't I gotten rid of the tent years ago? I would never have any fun sleeping under it — or trying to sleep — under it again. I suppose I'd hung onto it for a souvenir, or because a Yankee hates to throw anything away, while a Yankee's wife simply won't. My wife and I had discussed the disposal of the tent several times. It had always gone about like this:

"Let's burn it."

"Idiotic!"

"Let's give it to the Salvation Army, or someone like that."

"No. It might come in handy some day."

"All right. Put it where I'll seldom see it."

"Aren't you being foolish — investing this tent with diabolical qualities?"

"Yes. I mean, no."

My wife had stored the tent in the attic, and I hadn't seen it for a long spell, until the day when "it came in handy" for Johnny and Red. Superstition, spooks, jitters, hunches, or voodoo, I was more than half certain that something would happen with, to, or in that tent before the boys got back from their trip. What would happen wouldn't be nice.

It had all started the first time Digsy Jones and I pitched it, brand new, on the bank of the Peabody River in New Hampshire. There's a peculiar thrill in putting up a new tent, tightening its ropes, staking it down till the walls are smooth. You walk around it. You tap the taut fabric. Night comes. The river has a lonely sound. But inside the tent, the bobbinet front open, the firelight flickers on the walls, and there is a sense of security.

Digsy and I lost our sense of security late that night when we woke up to find a couple of porcupines shacked up with us. We knew they were porcupines because of the smell. And because of the sound, too — the busy, gnawing sound as they chewed on the leather straps of my pack and on Digsy's camera case.

Digsy reached for his flashlight, got it, and snapped it on. He also got the full, sweeping slap of a porcupine's tail across his naked forearm. He dropped the light. I picked it up and got a wrist full of quills for my pains. We finally got the creatures outside. I reached for the slide fastener to close the front. It stuck. I gave it a yank downward, and its sharp, inner edges laid open the back of my forefinger.

In the morning, Digsy's forearm was puffed and swollen. So were my finger and wrist. It had also begun to rain — very hard. We ate a watery breakfast, hiked out to our car, and drove in to Gorham to Dr. Chandler's. The doctor was delivering a baby somewhere out on a farm. We waited five hours, and all the time it was raining a steady downpour.

The doctor finally arrived and patched us up. When we got back to our campsite, the river was out of its banks with the fast runoff from the surrounding mountains. Our fine, new tent had washed away and snagged itself in the debris lodged on a bend in the river. Our fireplace and cooking equipment had vanished in the freshet. We retrieved the tent and drove home.

Digsy was sick with blood poisoning for two weeks. This was before sulfa drugs, which came in around 1934–35. We sent the tent back to the maker to have patches sewed over the two holes chafed by rocks and snags.

Those patches were on the right wall about two feet above the groundcloth seam. I remembered that Red Atwood had examined them with interest. When Red and Johnny came back, maybe I'd tell them the origin of *all* the patches, especially the long slash in the back wall. But that came later, much later.

Johnny and Red had been gone a couple of days, during which I had frequently listened to weather reports from the northern part of Maine. They sounded pretty good. I knew the part of the river the boys were on and wondered where they had pitched camp their first night. There was a nice spot under the trees just above the bridge on the Grand Lake Road. Another, downriver a piece on a high bank on the east side. But no! Not a bank, boys — please.

There was another bank I remembered on the Pere Marquette in Michigan, where Charley Winter and I made camp on a fishing trip for brown trout. A lovely campsite under a big white pine that grew atop the sheer, enticing, sandy bluff. We had suspended the tent by its short ridgepole from an overhanging limb of the great pine, thus obviating shear poles.

We'd had a long day on the river and went to sleep right away after a trout supper. Just before dozing off, I remember hearing the soft wind in the pine boughs above our tent.

Charley's voice woke me up.

"The ground's trembling," he said. "There must be an earthquake."

"My eye! Not in Michigan."

Then I felt it. But it wasn't exactly a tremor. Under us, under the tent's ground cloth, the earth was moving, writhing, slipping away from beneath us. We could hear stones and pebbles splashing into the river ten feet below.

"I'm getting out of here," said Charley.

We both dived for the tent door on hands and knees. But beyond the door, in the darkness, our hands touched nothing. Where once had been sod at the bank's edge, there was now *space!* At that moment the entire bank gave way and dropped into the Pere Marquette in an avalanche. Everything went out from under us. But the big pine held.

Like puppies in a sack, Charley and I hung inside the tent, suspended by our fragile ridgepole, which was tied to the limb of the pine. We couldn't get out. Our weight, dragging the tent downward, sealed us together in a standing position. We swung back and forth, struggling, elbowing each other unintentionally about the head and face.

And then the stick we'd used for the ridgepole snapped, and we dropped into the river. We surfaced downstream a few yards, rolled ashore, and fumbled our way out of the tent, soaked through, dismayed, still scared, but not quite half drowned. I still go through that one in occasional nightmares. There's no sensation quite like it.

Our weight, during our midair suspension struggles, had pulled a seam near the tent's peak. The patch would be directly over the heads of Johnny and Red as they slept — wherever they were camped. In the morning light, it would show as a dark rectangle.

In certain lights, from inside the tent, you could also see the narrow patch on the back wall. It made a long, shallow curve, like the blade of a scythe — the same type of scythe you see in imaginative pictures of the Grim Reaper.

The weather reports from northern Maine continued fair. The boys were having it pretty good. They'd been gone four or five days, with only one day of light rain. The forest-fire hazard was Class Three — not dangerous. The news reports were happily free of canoe accidents or other mishaps that might involve my friends, so I began to relax.

My apprehensions were probably unfounded and overweening. Maybe my "Charles Addams" tent wasn't so ghoulish after all. All the nights I'd spent under it weren't disastrous. Some of them had been pretty idyllic. But not the one on the Machias River when lightning struck the old spruce tree we'd camped under; not the one in the dry creek bed in Montana when an upcreek cloudburst created a flash flood and we got out, tent and all, a few yards ahead of a wall of water; and not the time on Caribou Pond in Maine when — in broad daylight — a heavy dead maple limb fell. Alex Payson and I had been boiling the noonday kettle at the time, the fire six feet from the tent door. We didn't know there was any dead limb on the maple. It was concealed in the tree's upper foliage. It crashed down through without warning and flattened the tent. Some of its fragments knocked over our tea can; the boiling water scalded Alex's knees. He'd been kneeling beside the fire.

The limb broke the fabric high on the left wall of the tent, where it sloped in toward the ridge. The hole was covered by a round, bull's-eye patch six inches in diameter. I imagined Johnny and Red looking at it and wondering.

All these events, a good many of them recorded in the tent's patches, occurred at fairly wide intervals over a period of years. The effect was slowly cumulative, and somewhere along the way I became certain the tent had the mark on it, the hex. You don't believe in such voodoo? Neither do I—yet there it was.

For example, this tent seemed to bring out the worst in animals. Raccoons, chipmunks, red squirrels, dropping in for a crust of bread or some peanuts, frequently bit the hands that fed them. At one campsite near Kingman, Maine, on the Mattawamkeag River, a stray dog wandered in for a handout. Tony Kochek gave the pooch a chop bone. The dog lifted its leg and wet down the side of the tent. Tony, naturally outraged at this type of gratitude, rushed at the mongrel with a switch, and the creature bit him on the shin. Antirabies shots for Tony.

A cow moose and her calf once almost knocked the tent flat. Al Foster and I were inside it reading a map by a big dry-cell light, the kind you can hang on a peg. From outside, the tent must have looked odd to the moose—like a greenish incandescence. The fabric, except the ground cloth, was green and translucent. Moose are prone to be curious about light. This one was. She and her calf came along and seemed to lean against the tent. We drove them off, but not before they'd stepped into our grub box and flattened out some of our aluminum cooking utensils. When you are kneeling in a tent door, with a flashlight, a moose looks twenty feet tall. Or maybe it's the terrifying, gigantic shadows that the creature casts against the surrounding forest. However, the moose invasion didn't damage the tent. No patches to show for the visit. Johnny Towers and Red Atwood would have to take my word for it. Or possibly they'd have had an experience that would make mine pale by comparison. They'd have to go some to beat the ghastly night Burke Whitman and I put in on Shaver's Fork in the West Virginia mountains one summer. But no, they couldn't match that night, because it couldn't happen in Maine. It could only happen where there are rattlesnakes.

That campsite on Shaver's was one of the prettiest I ever saw—the wild, mountain stream talking among its boulders, the firelight flickering in the black, sultry night, the bobbinet front fastened against mosquitoes. But at the bottom, where the bobbinet met the ground cloth, there was a break in the netting. It was no bigger than a jelly glass cover—just the right size to admit the visitor of the evening.

Burke Whitman woke me up with a nudge in the ribs.

"Something's crawling over my feet," he said, and I could tell by his voice he was scared stiff.

"Where's the flashlight?" I said.

"I don't know. Don't move. *It's a rattler!*"

Sweat broke out all over me. The beads on my forehead felt as big as grapes.

"How do you know it's a rattlesnake?" I asked, hoping Burke might be mistaken. He wasn't. He was a West Virginia hillbilly, and he knew his stuff.

"The smell," he whispered. "Like cucumbers. Smell it?"

I did, plainly, and I began to shake as I heard the dry rustle of the reptile's rattles. It wasn't the warning rattle, just the faint rustling as he moved slowly over our feet, one thickness of blanket between our flesh and the snake's belly.

We were boxed for fair. Groping with my hand, slowly, an inch at a time, I found the flash and pressed its button just once. I'll never forget what the brief brilliance revealed: the three-foot, fat-bodied snake moving in loops across our feet; the flat, vicious, triangular head raised, so that we saw the whitish-yellow underbelly; the beady eyes bright and sinister; and the ghastly shadow magnified on the tent wall to the right of the bobbinet door.

To get out, we would have to reach over the snake and down to the slide-fastener key. One of us, to do this, would practically have to touch the rattler. It was unthinkable for either of us, and fear grew, lengthened in time, sickening and without predictable end.

How long does a rattlesnake stay in your tent if he has his way — as certainly this one did? An hour? A day or two? There wasn't anything about it in Ditmars' or other herpetologists' books I'd read. It wasn't a subject that I had seen treated anywhere.

Supposing the snake wanted to stay, and you wanted to go? This was how it was with our snake, and Burke Whitman, and me. But how could we go out that bobbinet door, even if we could manage to unfasten it, without insulting the snake and getting a fang full of deadly poison in the face, hands, or legs, while we crawled over and around him?

Remember that scene in the movie *Lives of a Bengal Lancer?* There's a hooded cobra on Franchot Tone's chest — up there swaying back and forth — and Franchot had heard how they are charmed by music. With the sweat beads popping out of his face, he is tootling on a flute, hoping he will keep the cobra in a friendly frame of mind, but he is not really pleasing the cobra with his effort on the wind instrument. Just as the cobra is about to strike, someone — Gary Cooper, I think — shoots the reptile's head off with a nicely timed shot from a pistol. But Coop and his pistol were not around anywhere in my tent that night on Shaver's Fork. I didn't even have a flute. Besides, it was pitch-black dark.

The tent was the smallest room I have ever been in. In effect, it was the size of a coffin. There was, I felt, hardly enough room for the snake, let alone Burke and me. And it smelled alarmingly of cucumber.

The rattlesnake moved slowly upward toward our knees. Something had to be done, and quickly. I slid my hand out toward my hat, which was upside down near my head. I used it at night for a receptacle for my match safe, compass, loose change, and sheath knife. I got my fingers on the knife and slipped it from the sheath.

"I'm going out the back way," I said. "I'm going to cut the tent open. Be ready."

I rolled up, drove the knife blade through the back wall, and raked downward. It made a strange, sharp, ripping sound. Burke and I shot out through the slit in the fastest tandem action ever seen on Shaver's Fork, and just behind us we heard the deadly, never-to-be-forgotten metallic sound of the rattlesnake sounding off. The *business* rattle!

Once out of the tent, we got our courage back. But we were still shaking and weak. Burke got a big fire started in the fireplace. By its light, he cut a sapling. After a time, the rattling inside the tent ceased. The flat head of the snake and a foot or more of its body oozed out through the aperture at the bottom of the bobbinet door. Burke let fly with the sapling, and that was the end of the snake.

So now you know the origin of the scythe-shaped, ribbon-narrow patch on the back wall of my tent that Johnny Towers and Red Atwood had borrowed for their Upper Penobscot, East Branch, trip. And you know why my spook about the tent is perhaps justifiable, even if it isn't sound in logic.

Johnny and Red were due back on a Sunday afternoon. They didn't show up. They didn't show up on Monday. On Tuesday morning, I decided to call bush pilot Elmer Wilson at Shin Pond and ask him to fly the river and spot the boys. But before I did, Johnny Towers showed up at the house. It was just before noon. I was never so glad to see anyone in my life.

"Where's Red?" I asked.

"Home, asleep," Johnny said. "We got home very late last night."

"You needn't have bothered to bring the tent back so soon," I said.

"I — I *didn't* bring it back," Johnny said, uncomfortably.

I could see he was embarrassed and upset.

"I shouldn't have done it," he said, referring apparently to something done on their trip.

"Done what? Did someone steal the tent?" I asked, hopefully.

"No."

"Where is it now?"

"I – uh – don't know. That is, it's a lot of places."

"How can a tent, or anything else, be in more than one place?"

"*Your* tent is," said Johnny, forlornly.

Reaching for his checkbook, he said, "I know money can't replace an old tent, like yours – with all the wonderful associations you've had with it, all the nights under it, firelight and shadows – but – how much do I owe you, Ed?"

"Nothing!" I said, quickly. "Not a plastic nickel."

I was thinking how it was I who owed Johnny Towers money, if the tent were really gone forever, permanently lost.

"I'm sorry," Johnny said. "Sorry as hell."

"Get over it, Johnny. Just tell me how it is that my tent is not in one place, but a lot of places."

They had set up camp the fifth night, explained Johnny, on a gravel bar somewhere above Grand Pitch. I knew the spot well. The river winds down following the great, rolling slopes of Traveller Mountain. On their map, the boys had spotted Traveller Pond, high up on Traveller's east shoulder. It's an isolated, lonely pond. They had got the itch to see the pond and fish it. On the map, it hadn't looked so far.

"Listen, Johnny," I interrupted. "The way to get to Traveller Pond is from –"

"Yes, from Wayne Chapman's Camps, three miles below Grand Pitch. I know it, now. We got lost. We lay out a night on the mountain. And when we got back –" He paused, and I prompted him:

"When you got back?"

"Yes – to our campsite. The gravel bar was gone. The tent was gone. The river had come up four feet. There was nothing left – nothing."

The East Branch can do just that around the middle of May. The melting and melted snows fill the immense water basins above – Telos, Webster, Chamberlain, the Grand Lakes, and the vast Trout Brook drainage. That water has to go somewhere, and with the gates of Telos and Grand Lake dams open, it goes right down the East Branch. It can't go anywhere else. In this case, I couldn't have been happier about where all that water went.

"Ah!" I said.

"I know what you're going to say," Johnny said, rubbing his forehead. "'Only fools pitch tents on sandbars!'"

"I didn't say it – and I won't."

I was thinking of that first night with the porcupines and Digsy Jones so long ago on the bank on the Peabody River in New Hampshire. It was full circle.

"Did the tent go downriver, Johnny?" I asked.

"Some of it. It's pretty well scattered around. Some of it's strung on the jagged rocks below Grand Pitch."

"That's just swell," I said, thinking of the thirty-foot drop.

"Don't be sarcastic, Ed."

"I'm not. But tell me this: Did pieces of the tent get well down below Grand Pitch?"

"Yes. We found bits, here and there."

"Did the remains get down into the Hulling Machine?"

"Yes. We followed them all the way down to Chapman's Camps."

I smiled inwardly—perhaps even outwardly. The thought of my fabric haunted house getting chewed to hell in the Hulling Machine rapids was just beautiful.

"So there's nothing left of it, Johnny? She's a goner?"

"A goner is right. Nothing left bigger than a postage stamp. A heck of a thing."

"No—a fine thing."

Johnny looked mystified.

"You mean you're *glad?*" he said.

"It goes a good deal deeper than that," I said. "I'm not only glad. I'm overwhelmed with joy. I am also flooded with relief."

"I don't get it."

"All right. It's two minutes past the yardarm. Let's have us a tall bourbon—and I'll tell you about that tent."

And I told Johnny Towers the story, pretty much as I've told it here.

# Jake's Rangers

## vs.

# Spring Fever

As a sprightly epic of Spring Fever, its contagion, witchery, horse power, and high jinks, I offer herewith the case history of Jake's Rangers, of Damariscotta, Maine, and the handful of magic pine shavings which lured us, one and all, through the core of New England's last wilderness in quest of trout. The enchanted expedition took place during an unforgettable week in May 1958. But before it ever got off the launching pad, many strange things came to pass.

At the outset, I must explain that Jake's Rangers are a group of seven normally sane business and professional men. Our roster includes Damariscotta's postmaster, its veterinary surgeon, a leading physician, grocer, artist, and insurance man. A nonmilitary and nonbelligerent organization, we are called "rangers" only because we range far and wide throughout our home state in search of trout and the blue horizon.

Dedicated to the outdoors, open water, and fishing, I suspect we are representative of sportsmen groups in small towns all across our land. We have no bylaws, no regular meetings, no dues, and no headquarters unless you count Perley Waltz's drugstore on Main Street, or the Post

Office next door. Our claim to distinction is our leader, the man for whom the Rangers are named. He is Maurice "Jake" Day, artist, naturalist, long-time explorer of Maine's wilderness region — and shrewd alchemist of the Rites of Spring.

In 1958, it seemed to us that spring was deliberately avoiding Maine. Just when you were about to inventory your trout flies or paint your canoe, another blizzard wrecked your dream. Six or seven of them pasted us in March. The most detested object in town was the snow shovel. Jokes about the weather wore out and fell flat, and by late March the morale of Jake's Rangers hit a deplorable, all-time low.

But, unbeknownst to the rest of us, Jake himself had taken on the task of reviving our hope of spring and sun-warmed brook banks. Secretly and single-handedly, he had been at work on this problem through many consecutive snowstorms.

The first inkling I had that Jake was making Medicine came one dismal, ice-gray morning when I walked into Perley Waltz's drugstore for coffee. Three of the Rangers were already entrenched at the marble counter — Dr. Sam Belknap; Eddie Pierce, whose Yellow Front Grocery is a Damariscotta landmark; and Jack Glidden, our insurance man. They were talking with an animation long subdued. Dr. Sam and Eddie wore wide smiles, while Jack Glidden was laughing right out loud — a sound I hadn't heard since the Winter Solstice.

"What right have you guys got to be happy?" I asked. "Don't you know it's snowing again?"

They exchanged secretive glances, and immediately clammed up. After a moment, Dr. Sam said:

"Stop at Jake's on your way home."

"What gives?"

"Obey orders, and you'll find out," said Jack.

I left them and went into the Post Office, next door. Dr. McClure Day, our veterinary surgeon and Jake's son, was in the act of plucking his mail from his box. He held up a fishing tackle catalog he'd just received, waved it like a banner, and said, "Hurray!"

"Hurray for what?" I asked. "Who do you think is going fishing?"

"You are," said Mac, mysteriously, and went out into the snow.

I stepped up to the mail window. Behind it showed the round, merry face of Bentley Glidden. Bentley, Jack's younger brother, is Damariscotta's postmaster. He seemed to be shining like a portly, human sun as he slid my mail under the wicket. My mail consisted solely of a seed catalog.

"That's a personal affront," I said. "I refuse to accept it."

"It's for your wife, not you," said Bent, gayly. "And there's two cents postage due. Drop in at Jake's on your way home."

Jake Day's house, up near the Baptist Church, is one of those solid, four-square, white colonials. Mellow with age, it was built by Jake's great-grandfather, and the door has seldom been locked in a hundred sixty-one years.

I let myself in, scowled at the snowshoes stacked in the front entry, and went up the stairway to Jake's studio. It isn't the kind of artist's studio you read about. No skylights, plate glass, or folderol. It's just a big, cluttered, upstairs, corner room. Nor does Jake himself resemble the standard concept of an artist. He doesn't wear sandals. He wears moccasins. His smock is an old flannel shirt, and instead of a beret his head is adorned with a vagabond felt hat, abused by countless rains and suns, its band a beat-up leather strap.

At sixty-seven, Jake is lean, wiry, and feather-light on his feet. On mountain fishing trips, he can walk the ankles off his Rangers, all of whom — except me — are his juniors by about thirty years. This gifted man has the spirit of youth and the genius for embellishing life. Perhaps they are the same. Both seemed to beam from his deep-set, hazel eyes as he met me at the doorway of his studio, a corncob pipe between his teeth.

"There was an emergency meeting of the Rangers last night," he said, removing the corncob. "We tried to reach you."

"I was in Portland," I said. "What happened? The boys appear to be strolling in green pastures."

By way of answer, Jake stepped aside from his doorway; and — with a magician's gesture — waved me into the room. Suddenly, to all intents and purposes, I found myself in the wilds of Maine's immense Baxter State Park in the green benediction of spring. The impact, and the scene itself, in contrast with the bleak reality of the March day, are indescribable. But I'll try.

Flanking me on either side of the room were twenty or more of Jake's wonderfully realistic watercolors of the unpeopled Katahdin wilderness we loved and knew so well. Some were from his old portfolios and sketchbooks. Others he had painted for the occasion. They haunted me with ghosts of old campfires and inspired the promise of new ones. I saw Russell Pond under a blue sky, a pair of wood ducks near shore. I saw South Branch Pond, its fringe of birches misted with green. There was a lone canoeman on Wassataquoik Lake, and Traveller Mountain, and an old black bear and her cub on Pinnacle Ridge. Trout were rising in Six Pond, a kingfisher riding on a cedar frond, and there was a tiny, flickering campfire with its smoke skeining through the spruces. You could smell it! The total effect was uncanny — as if Jake somehow had been working hand in glove with the Vernal Equinox.

I had seen many springs in this wild country — but never a one without being there, till now. No one but Jake Day would ever have dreamed of such a mystic spread, let alone possess the talent to execute it.

"Jake," I said, "you've broken up a hard winter with a paintbrush. I shall go home and burn my snow shovel."

"Wait!"

Jake stepped to an easel which stood between the two aisles of paintings. The easel was veiled — with the cover of an old sleeping bag. Sweeping this cogent shield to one side, Jake disclosed the Katahdin and Traveller Mountain quadrangles of the U.S. Geological Survey. He had mounted the maps on cardboard, and in red pencil scored the seventeen-mile foot trail which traverses the wildest part of Baxter State Park, from Roaring Brook Campground at the southern border, to South Branch Ponds Campground near the northern extremity. About midway of this trail, in the heart of the park, and accessible only on foot, is Russell Pond Campground. This mountain solitude, in Jake's lettering, was tagged:

"Base Camp, Jake's Rangers, Spring, 1958!"

"Does this mean we're going to fish those hidden ponds this year — at long last?"

"It does. Take-off day is May eighteenth."

"How are we going to sustain life, till then?"

From his shirt pocket, Jake ceremoniously removed a small cardboard box. He rubbed the box lovingly, which somehow made it resemble Pandora's — or maybe Aladdin's Lamp.

"I have here," he said, "life-giving medicine — the smelling salts of the wilderness."

He opened the box and held it under my nose, and the scent of clean, sun-dried pine pervaded me. Resinous, pungent, supreme. It seemed to put a kind of hex on me. I thought I heard the song of a white-throat sparrow proclaiming life from a spruce top, a loon calling from a sequestered deadwater. Wind seemed to whisper in young leaves, and the full trance and heartache of spring were upon me.

"Jake!" I said. "This is alchemy."

"No," he said, tapping his Pandora's box, "it's just a handful of pine shavings. I whittled them from that old stump above Trout Brook Crossing in the park last fall. I've been sniffing them for weeks. I call them 'Old Doctor Jake's Golden Spring Medical Discovery.'"

What with his wilderness watercolors, his maps, and his siren pine shavings, Jake had deliberately created the worst case of Spring Fever since the Song of Solomon. The Rangers — including Jake himself — were smitten to the point of frenzy. And in April, when wild geese, green grass, and lilac buds began to show, we had reached a state of euphoria. We could talk, think, or dream of nothing but May 18th and our expedition.

The rigors of the trail to Russell Pond were reduced to ashes in the fires of anticipation. The inner core of the park is a hundred square miles of jumbled peaks, ravines, glacial boulders, forests, ruffian watercourses — and isolated ponds, many of them rarely fished, a few of them *never!*

Only two of the Rangers had experienced this rugged terrain in spring, but in our zeal for a try at the far-back ponds we forgot the facts of life on a hard trail and all fell into The Old Map Trap, or The Pitfall of the Contours. The trail looked easy — on paper. We simply leveled off the mountains. The congested contour lines were nice, artistic arrangements of brown curves. The streams we would have to cross were innocuous ribbons of blue. Trout seemed to be breaking up through the surface of the paper. We had breathed the giddy incense of Old Doctor Jake's Golden Spring Medical Discovery, and were all infected with invincibility and lightheadedness.

Whenever two Rangers met, even in the middle of Main Street, we would snap to attention and salute. On some occasions traffic was obstructed. Bob Turner, the town cop, threatened to lock a couple of us in the pokey as an example to the young. The saluting, prompted by Bentley Glidden, was but one manifestation of Spring Fever's lunacy and the perfume of the pine shavings.

On the back of his pack, as a challenge to the Russell Pond Trail, Bentley stenciled the words U.S. DOMESTIC AIR MAIL. Jack, during his day's travels, stopped at any convenient field or bit of open water and practiced fly casting. Jake and Mac drew up the trip's supply list and submitted it one evening to the full roster of Rangers at Dr. Sam's house. This meeting was called a "Survival Seminar." The supply list was as lovely as a sonnet. Not a single item had been forgotten — except dry matches and salt. For this crucial oversight, we reduced Jake in rank. But we acclaimed him full Colonel the next morning, shortly after Bentley handed him a letter from Mr. Helon Taylor, who is Supervisor of Baxter State Park, and a longtime friend of Jake's.

Unbeknownst to the rest of us, Jake had written Mr. Taylor of our expedition. And Mr. Taylor was intensely interested. He was eager for a report on the park's remote trout fishing. There had never been one, a fact which would make our survey the first. The supervisor concluded by saying that he had personally invoked Pamola, the legendary Indian god of the Katahdin wilderness, to watch over us. Our trip was now not only blessed by high authority, but by legend as well.

And all this was climaxed by a second letter. Addressed to Jake and me, this letter simply wished us godspeed, good fishing, and fine weather. It was signed by no other than the Honorable Percival P. Baxter, Mr. Maine himself—the man who, singlehanded, bought and gave Baxter State Park's two hundred thousand acres and fifty mountain peaks, to us and all men, "to be forever held ... forever left in its natural, wild state."

The cheers, boasting, and self-esteem inspired by these gilt-edged documents can't be imagined. It has to be endured; and it was endured by the citizens of Damariscotta, and by the seven long-suffering wives of Jake's Rangers.

Perley Waltz, after threatening to bar us from his coffee counter, said: "Why don't you characters buy something—or else pay rent?"

Skip Freeman, presiding behind the fishing tackle counter at Wickstrom & French's Hardware, was even more forthright. Skip said: "Hurry up and get the hell out of town."

With equal vehemence—and in many cases verbatim—Skip's sentiment was echoed by the wives of the Rangers. The wives had had enough of palaver, of houses strewn with fishing gear and apparel, of forsaken children asking, "Why is Daddy going to another Rangers' meeting?"

In their homes, at night, some of the more earnest Rangers had taken to sleeping in their sleeping bags for practice. This form of training was finally outlawed by their wives as being irrelevant, uncomfortable, and unfriendly.

On May 8th, Jack Glidden started the countdown to our take-off day by yelling "TEN!" at the top of his lungs, right on the Main Street sidewalk. It startled the seagulls from their perch on the ridgepole of the Gay Block. Rangers within hearing took up the cry, as did many sympathetic bystanders. Thereafter, any morning at coffee time, you could hear the current countdown resounding anywhere from a point near the town library clear down to the Newcastle Bridge: "Nine!" ... "Eight!" ... "Seven!"....

Suspense mounted daily. Sleep, fitful at best, was disturbed by dreams of fishing the mysterious waters of our destination. The substance of these dreams was unwittingly, but publicly, recorded by Eddie Pierce on the morning of the six-count. While chalking the day's offerings on the big front windows of his grocery store, Eddie somehow went adrift—and between a bargain in soap powders and another in ready-mix flour, he marked up this eye-catching Special Sale item:

TROUT 59¢ a Peck

Eager purchasers filed into Eddie's store and filed out again in disappointment when Eddie, reorienting himself, explained that he had meant "potatoes."

Our revered and venerable leader, Jake, severely stricken by his own alchemy, went into Don & Bob's Barber Shop on the afternoon of countdown four, and, half an hour later, emerged — with a *crew cut!* His first hairdo of this dashing type since his army hitch at the Mexican border.

That same afternoon, Dr. Sam's charming wife, Lucy, sailed into the drugstore and asked to buy some camera film. Didn't she know, asked Perley, that her husband had already purchased a large supply? Lucy knew all about it. It was Sam's afternoon off, and the Belknap children were all scrubbed and dressed to be photographed by their father. But the films were packed for the Rangers' trip.

"Why don't you unpack them?" asked Perley.

"I can't. Sam's mowing the lawn."

"What's that got to do with it?"

"The pack is on his *back!*"

It was a fact. Dr. Sam, with his full pack — and a pedometer affixed to his belt — was mowing his spacious lawn as a kind of dry run for the Russell Pond Trail. At the conclusion of this training exercise, the pedometer registered slightly more than five miles. Sam, who had stood up well under the effort, was now confident and ready to face the real thing.

Count-down, "ONE!" Late Saturday afternoon, with take-off coming early Sunday morning, all seven Rangers gathered in the alley back of Eddie Pierce's store for the ceremony of loading the packed supplies into my station wagon.

Dr. Sam and Dr. Mac had arranged with colleagues to care for their patients, both human and animal, beginning tomorrow. Freedom was at hand, and the car-loading proceeding jubilantly, when a tall, sorrowful man appeared in the alley, and said:

"Is Dr. McClure Day here?"

Mac's face fell a mile. A serious emergency involving horse, cow, or dog would scratch him from the trip. To judge by the sadness in the stranger's face, this was it.

"What can I do for you?" said Mac, balancing a carton of flour and bacon on the wagon's tailgate.

"My white cat, Snuggles," said the man, "has got mats in her fur — and she won't let me cut them out."

Mac looked at the man with infinite relief, gratitude, and mercy. He said:

"You bring Snuggles to my office before eight o'clock tonight, because tomorrow, I'm going to be hard to find."

Next morning, in deceptively beautiful weather we were on our way, rolling up the seacoast, then swinging northwestward, inland, to Maine's mountain region. That afternoon, with two hundred miles behind us, we entered Baxter State Park and halted for the night at the bunkhouse at Roaring Brook Campground. We stood fair in the shadow of the great, gaunt mountain, Katahdin — majestic, lonely, its ravines and higher elevations wearing the white scars of snow.

In the camp clearing, a sign said:

### RUSSELL POND CAMPGROUND 7 MILES

"That means us," said Jake.

He pointed to the wilderness stretching to the north, then to the log bridge which spanned Roaring Brook.

"The trail," he said, "starts right there at the bridge."

There it was. The trail. We were looking at it. Anticipation was over. Realization was at hand. But "reality" is the truer word. On the bunkhouse roof that night came the deafening drumfire of rain — an all-night, four-alarm downpour. In the morning, Roaring Brook was in flood, and our bridge had vanished. First baptism in ice water occured right there and then. Soaked to the waist, chilled to the marrow, but with spirits never so high, we were feeling with the soles of our feet the trail we had been dreaming about for six weeks.

Some trail!

Less than a mile, and snowdrifts loomed. Blowdowns barred the way. Laughter and bright banter tapered away to silence. You heard only the tinkle of the tin cup suspended from Jack Glidden's belt, the scuff of boots on rock, a groan as someone made a misstep or sank to the hips in a ridge of snow, and always the pounding of your own heart.

Shoulders lunged into packstraps on a steep ascent. Sweat trickled. Breath steamed. The pace slowed and steadied for the long pull. This was the shakedown of Jake's Rangers on the Russell Pond Trail. Not a Ranger will ever forget that seven-mile trek.

In August, it's an easy two hours or so. In an ordinary spring, you'd make it in three. But in the spring of '58, with three-foot drifts, blowdowns, bridges washed away, and rivers in flood, it was seven and a half hours of heartbreak and hazard.

Eddie Pierce went in all over fording the iced rapids of the South Branch of Wassataquoik Stream. On the Main Wassataquoik crossing, we thought Bentley was a goner. Bent stumbled, plunged through the last ten yards of whitewater, finally made land with helping hands yanking him ashore. Each crossing was a point of no return. You wouldn't dare cross back again. You couldn't. So you went on.

If the trek is unforgettable for its bone-wearying, all-out effort, it is even more so for the sweet, last turn in the trail, and the triumphant, heart-lifting moment of stepping into the clearing at the Russell Pond Campground. There were the log lean-tos; the log cabin bunkhouse; the encircling mountains; the blue, sunlit expanse of Russell Pond — and trout breaking the surface. And, above all, the solitude.

"I'm dreaming," said Jack Glidden, dropping his pack. "Don't wake me."

Merle Scott, the big, able, redheaded park ranger came from his cabin to greet us. Merle had been in there alone for two weeks. He said he was gladder to see us than we were to see him.

"We have just heard the misstatement of the year," said Mac Day.

It was Bentley Glidden who summed up both the trail's anguish and the sense of rest and achievement that now pervaded us. Bent had his boots and socks off and was gazing in open wonder at his bare feet. He wiggled his chubby toes. Admiration mounted in his eyes as he reckoned up what his pinkies had just been through. In an awed voice, he said:

"They ought to be buried in Westminster Abbey."

In the isolated ponds of Baxter Park, the best time for trout, if not for men, is mid-May through June. In all ponds the limit is five fish per day. The trout are exclusively *salvelinus fontinalis,* variously called brook trout, speckled trout, natives, or squaretails. These inner waters have never been stocked. Neither the trout you catch nor their ancestors ever heard of a hatchery or rearing pool. Their color is sunset-brilliant, their flesh pink and firm, their flavor matchless.

The fishing began that afternoon right at Russell Pond after a rum ration and an hour's rest for all hands. We fished from canoes, which you can rent at Russell. No one carried those canoes over the trail. They were flown in on the pontoons of bush pilot Elmer Wilson's "Jet Cub" airplane.

Eddie Pierce scored first with a beautifully colored fourteen-incher. In that first hour's fishing, the Rangers caught and released thirty-two trout. We kept a dozen more ranging in size from eight inches up to Eddie's fourteen-incher. They came to standard flies and to gold-bodied spinning lures, and they were strong and jet-propelled.

A large moose wandered out of the forest and stepped into the pond to view proceedings. He seemed to take a special liking to Mac Day, wading in a leisurely manner toward the veterinarian's canoe.

"My office is closed, fellah," said Mac to the creature. "Snuggles was my last case. But I'll take your photograph."

Mac did. So did Eddie, Jake, and Dr. Sam.

At sunset we gathered in the bunkhouse and started a fire in the stove. When the cabin warmed up, the little spiders that had wintered there came creeping from their cracks in the wall logs to see what was cooking. The answer was native trout.

We were in our sleeping bags at dark, too tired for chatter or wisecracks. You could hear bone-limbering sighs of comfort, the "tap" and "hiss" as the drops from someone's wet socks on the line above the stove fell on the still hot lids.

A whippoorwill tuned up, and from 'way back in the forest an owl hooted. That was all—except for the distant roar of rapids reechoing from the walled valley of Wassataquoik Stream. It couldn't touch us now.

There are miles of Wassataquoik Stream that are seldom, if ever, fished. They are too far and too hard to reach from either approach, upstream or down. We had "map-fished" these enticing reaches back home, but now unanimously abandoned the idea. The ponds were our real objective, and besides, we were on the outs with the Wassataquoik after what it had almost done to Bentley.

From the Russell Pond base camp, within a day's round-trip, you can fish approximately fifteen ponds—not all of them in a single day, by any means. Wassataquoik, Draper, Six Ponds (there are six of them), Deep, Long, Pogy, Weed, Bell, Russell itself, and a couple which are unnamed. We fished all but two or three of these ponds. Mac Day and the Glidden boys caught fifty-odd trout in Bell Pond. They were the first to fish it within the memory of man. The trout ran uniform in size—eight to ten inches.

The fastest fishing was at Deep and Six Ponds, where four of us landed and released over a hundred fifty fish. The largest was Jack Glidden's fifteen-incher. Back at camp that evening, Dr. Sam Belknap treated Jack and Bent Glidden for an ailment he, or any of us, had never seen before. To wit, multiple, tiny lacerations on the patients' forefingers caused by the teeth of countless trout as the anglers released them to the waters of Deep and Six Ponds.

But no report—this first one, or any that may follow on the park's wilderness fishing—can pin itself to trout alone. Climb to the Lookout, a high crag two miles from Russell Pond, and you know why. The view from the Lookout, as described by an unidentified observer, is this:

"—from here you sense the full power and grandeur of the wilderness into which you have penetrated. You feel that right here is the place man has gone too far away from in his search for something he has never clearly defined. You feel that whatever you have longed for is here, around you, a full three-hundred-and-sixty degrees of mountains, streams, lakes and ponds, named, unnamed, solitary."

As you stand on the Lookout, you can see, near at hand, the spindles of the young spruces, silent and steady in the still air, aspiring to the sun, and aloof to the inquiry and presence of man. Then, lifting your eyes to the northward distance, you see the rolling, thoughtful peaks of the Traveller Range and the valley where the Pogy Notch Trail leads to South Branch Ponds Campground. That was our trail out, and it was time to go. With hardened muscles and lightened packs, it was a lark compared to the Russell Pond Trail.

We had arranged to have our cars driven from Roaring Brook around the park's peripheral road to meet us at South Branch Ponds. This campground, with its two clearwater ponds lying blue between the steep crags and faces of Traveller and South Branch Mountains, is one of the most beautiful on our continent. Here Jake's Rangers spent the last night of the expedition. And it was here we realized that something had happened to us, over and above our adventure. Our Spring Fever had been cured! But you don't actually cure it, like a disease. Recovery is a little like falling out of love. Suddenly it is there no more, and you can hardly remember its yearning and heartache.

But there was one among us who didn't treat it so lightly. On the start home, just after we left South Branch Ponds, a white-throat sparrow sang. It sang as I had imagined I heard it in Jake's studio that bleak March day so long ago. It may be that Jake heard the White Throat, too. Because down near Trout Brook Crossing, just before you get to the main park road, Jake stopped his car and got out, and approached an old pine stump, drawing his sheath knife as he went. He came back presently with a handful of rich, yellow, resinous shavings tied in his handkerchief.

"We'll be needing these next spring," he said. "Now—home we go."

# Part TWO

*It is the blight man was born for*

Gerard Manley Hopkins

# *Appointment With Death*

A faint sound in the night outside his cabin — a step, a rustle, a sound that didn't belong to the November storm — made Web Martin lift his head from his cupped hands and listen intently.

The rain drummed on the roof. Wind moaned in the spruces. A loose pane rattled in a window. Nothing more. Web had begun to think his ears had tricked him, when he heard the soft, rustling sound again, and knew that someone was feeling his way in the dark along the log wall of the cabin, outside.

Web sat motionless at the wooden table. The lamp, its flame uneasy in the creeping drafts, stood at his right elbow. On the other side of the table a bench rested along the wall. In the wall was a window. Something moved in the window, moved again, and steadied.

When Web first saw the girl's face, he thought it was hallucination. He thought it was about time for that sort of thing to catch up with him. His nerves were worn raw. He was hollow-eyed with exhaustion. He hadn't had a night's sleep since the hunting accident — since that still, October morning five weeks before, when, sick at heart, he had walked out of the woods to the sheriff's office, and said: "Gill, I shot a man."

"No, Web! You didn't. You don't mean it."

"I'm telling you, I shot a man."

"Where is he?"

"On the edge of the Littlefield Burn."

"Is he hurt bad?"

"He's dead."

The thing Web Martin dreaded more than anything on earth had happened to him in one blinding, nightmarish instant. It crushed against his reason and instinct, against his life training as a woodsman and guide. Its horror was violent in his mind.

With Gill, the coroner, the game warden, and the state policeman, he had gone back in to the Littlefield Burn to where the man lay in the red leaves. They had found Web's tracks, the tracks of the man, and the tracks of the deer that had drawn Web's rifle shot. From the tracks, they had reconstructed what had happened.

"Accident — pure and simple," Gill had said; and the others had nodded agreement.

It didn't help any. It didn't help the man, his wife, or his family and friends. It didn't help Web Martin. Accident or not, the agony pounded in his heart. He felt his hands shaking, but when he looked at them, they were steady. The trembling didn't show. It was inside, and unceasing...

Now, on this night weeks later, when he saw the girl's face in his cabin window, Web thought his nerves had snapped. Beyond the black, misty glass, the face seemed unreal. The dark eyes, dazed and staring, haunted him — a reflection of his own panic.

But when one hand came up, and her white knuckles tapped the windowpane, he knew the girl was real. He recognized the desperate expression in her eyes. He had seen it half a dozen times in the eyes of men lost in the woods.

Web stood up, motioned toward the cabin door, stepped over and opened it. For an instant he saw the girl framed in the doorway. Then a gust of wind poured into the cabin, and the lamp flared out.

In the dense blackness after the light, she seemed to have vanished. Yet Web still saw her with startling vividness: her bronze-colored hair under the hood of a yellow parka, the brown flannel shirt showing at her throat, the rain-wet, high-boned face, the dark eyes, wild and staring.

He remembered the strange behavior of lost people — how, sometimes, they ran at sight of the search party, even fled from warmth and shelter. But the girl was still in the doorway. Through the darkness, he could feel her near him—a warmth, a radiation.

"If you'll come inside," he said, "I'll close the door and light the lamp again."

In the dark, as she stepped across the threshold, her shoulder touched his. He closed the door, struck a match, and lit the lamp on the table. Then he turned and got a good look at her.

She was twenty-three or -four, taller than he had thought—taller and more beautiful. Her lips were parted, and she breathed in long, aching gasps, as if she had been running. In one hand, close to her breast as though for protection, she clutched a green handbag. Web thought of a lost child, clinging to security by hugging a toy.

"You're going to be all right in a minute," he said gently. "You're not lost any more."

"I'm not lost—any more?" she asked. "How do you know?"

Her voice, hungering for reassurance, wrung Web's heart. He knew what it was like to be lost. He was lost himself.

"You're safe here," he said. "Nothing can hurt you."

Her breathing quieted. Her grip on the green bag relaxed, and she held it guardedly at her side. The desperate look faded from her eyes, and in its place came one of intense curiosity. Web thought it was like watching someone awakening in a strange room.

"You're in my cabin," he said, "and my name is Web Martin."

"Are you sure?"

"Positive. Where are you staying? Marcy's Lodge?"

She nodded.

"You're only two miles from Marcy's," Web said. "You took a wrong trail by the lake. It doesn't lead anywhere."

"Maybe it did lead somewhere," she said. "Maybe it wasn't a wrong turn. Because—I saw the lamp in your window."

"I'm glad you did. I'm glad you're here."

She stood up and walked slowly, trancelike around the cabin, looking at everything—the stove, the woodbox, the traps hanging by their chains, the cedar stretchers for mink and otter skins, the canned goods glinting on the shelves.

Every now and then she turned to look at him, as if getting her bearings, or studying him against his background, and the curiosity burned incessantly in her eyes.

After a while, her steps soft on the wooden floor, she came back to the table and sat down. Her lips formed to speak, but a sharp thrust of wind rattled the stovepipe in its guy wires, and a falling branch struck the roof with a sound like a shot. Alarmed, her face white, she clutched the green bag in both hands.

"You're still upset," Web said.

"Yes — I guess I am."

"Let me get you something to eat."

"I couldn't eat anything — not now. I'm too —"

In answer to her hesitation, Web said, "Sure. I know."

"What? What do you know?"

"How you feel."

*"No!"* Her eyes were full on his, the wildness flaring again, her lips trembling. "You *couldn't* know!"

"Take it easy," Web said, softly. "It's all over."

"Yes — I suppose it is."

He wondered at the tone of finality in her voice. Could she be talking of something other than being lost in the woods at night?

She was sitting on the bench opposite him, her hands on the table. The rain battered the window behind her, and she shrank from it, her hands moving out along the table, toward him. Web looked down at her hands — at the fourth finger of her left hand. A white band showed where a ring had been.

"You were married?" Web asked.

"Yes. I was."

"But not now?"

"No — it's finished, for good."

"Maybe it isn't. Maybe you'll get together again."

"I doubt it. I'm afraid it's too late."

"That's too bad. I'm sorry."

She shrugged her shoulders. Tears glistened in her eyes, and she blinked them away.

Web got up and put a chunk of dry beech in the stove. He could feel her eyes following every move he made. When he came back and sat across from her, she said:

"Do you live here all alone?"

"Yes."

"What do you do?"

"I haven't done anything at all," Web said, "for about five weeks."

Her glance shifted to the metal badge on his left shirt pocket — his guide's license, now a symbol of nothing, automatically revoked for life in any fatal hunting accident, whether or not you were found guilty of criminal carelessness.

"You're a registered guide?" she asked, still gazing at the badge. "And you're not doing anything, right at the height of hunting season?"

"No," he said. "I'm not doing anything—anymore. My license is void."

Reaching up, Web unpinned his badge and laid it on the table. He knew, then, that he was going to tell her what had happened to him. He didn't know why, or how. It was just that he felt a curious relationship to the girl, an intimacy of trouble, of night, and the storm.

"What do you think about?" the girl asked, as if leading him on. "What do you think about, all alone here, not doing anything?"

"I think about just one thing."

"What?"

"What it means to kill a man."

He felt the words dry as ashes in his mouth, and saw his own anguish mirrored in the girl's eyes. She sat rigid, motionless, the light changing over her face in the flickering of the lamp.

"What *does* it mean?" she asked. "Maybe it's something I ought to know. Maybe you'd better tell me."

"You're a stranger," Web said, hollowly.

"That makes it better. You have to tell someone. Tell me."

Web's hand closed tight over the guide's badge. Its edges bit into his palm. Then, losing all sense of time, he began to talk. He didn't know the silences between his words, or between the girl's sensitive questions and his faltering answers. He didn't feel the night wearing on.

"It isn't like in war," he said. "It isn't like in anything. You're just out there in the woods you've known all your life—hunting deer."

He looked across at her, wondering if what he said meant anything, searching her eyes for understanding and encouragement.

"Your heart is beating," he went on. "You're happy in the still, cool morning. You're alive, and kind of smiling, inside."

"Yes," she said, quietly. "I know. And then—"

"And then you see a deer, running through a clump of spruces. You bring up your rifle. The recoil of the shot jars your shoulder. You hear the deer fall, hidden in the spruces. You walk up to the spot, and—"

Web hesitated, as the girl's face grew tense. He took tobacco and papers from his pocket. He began to roll a cigarette. He said: "He lay there in the leaves, still. Not full of life. Not happy. Not anything. He was dead. He was a man. I killed him."

The cigarette paper broke in Web's fingers. He looked at his hands, and they were shaking.

"If I'd had one cup of coffee instead of two that morning," he said, "it wouldn't have happened. The deer, the man, and I would all have been in different positions. I keep trying to hold onto that. There's nothing to hold. It's no good."

"No," she said, "it's no good."

"He was hidden, out of sight behind the spruces," Web said. "The deer ran between us."

"Did you know the man?"

"I'd never seen him before in my life — or his."

Web fumbled for another cigarette paper. The girl took the green bag from the table, held it down close to her on the bench, opened it and took out a pack of cigarettes. She lighted one and passed it to Web, and it steadied in his fingers.

"What did you do," she asked, "when you first saw him?"

"There was a big spruce tree beside him. I leaned against it, and shut my eyes — my forehead was against the bark of the tree."

"Then you opened your eyes? You had to look — some time?"

Web took a deep pull on the cigarette. "I had to look some time. There was his blood on the leaves. The bullet hit him in the heart. He never even heard the shot. But *I* did. It was my shot, and it was my heart. I could feel it. I can now."

Web swung up and paced in the cabin. He stopped at the stove, feeling the girl's eyes on him. He said: "I kneeled down beside him and read what it said on the non-resident hunting license that was pinned to his jacket."

"What did it say?" she asked.

"It said: 'Robert Chadson, Mill Falls, Pennsylvania; age, twenty-six; height, five eleven; color of eyes, blue; color of hair, light.'"

"It didn't really say anything," the girl said, her voice almost inaudible. "It didn't talk to you — and the man couldn't."

Struck by the sense that she had read his own thought, reached into his mind and heart, Web turned swiftly toward her.

"That's just what it was like," he said. "It was only names and numbers."

A feeling of terrible emptiness had come over Web. It had come from knowing nothing about the man he had killed, and from being alone with him in the still forest, so near him, so immeasurably far from him. Who was he, really? What were his hopes, his plans, his work? How fine a thing had Web killed? What had Robert Chadson thought about in the night time? What were his memories? Did he have a brother, a family, a father and mother, a wife, a home?

"Did he have a family?" the girl asked.

"Yes, he did. I learned about them later."

Web told how he had come out of the woods and reported to Gill Bowden, the sheriff; how Gill had telephoned long distance, and Robert Chadson's father had arrived that night. But Chadson's wife hadn't come. She had been stunned by the tragedy.

Chadson's father looked just like his son, Web went on. The likeness had torn at him. Mr. Chadson, listening to the details of the accident, had been quiet, and kind.

"His son must have been like that, too," Web said. "It made what I had done seem worse. It helped to talk things over with Mr. Chadson. But most of all I wanted to talk to Chadson's wife. I wanted to go to Mill Falls, out in Pennsylvania, and see her."

"Why didn't you?" the girl asked.

Web leaned on the table, the lamplight accentuating the hollows in his cheeks.

"She didn't want to see me," he said.

"How do you know she didn't?"

"Chadson's father told me. She was suffering from shock. She was half out of her mind, and under a doctor's care. If she saw me, they didn't know what would happen to her."

The girl nodded, and Web searched the shadows in her deep-feeling eyes.

"They had been married only a little while," he said. "She would have bitterness and hatred. But if I saw her, if she knew what I was like, and how I felt, maybe it wouldn't be that way. Maybe, somehow, I could help her."

"Did you tell Robert Chadson's father that?" the girl asked.

"Yes. And I asked him to tell her — tell Chadson's wife — how I felt. And Mr. Chadson said: 'Well, how *do* you feel?'"

"What did you answer?"

"I couldn't answer. It's a thing no one can answer. It's like a terrible secret that you can't share."

"You're sharing it now," she said, and Web's heart seem to lift its beat.

At his trial in the county courthouse, the jury had found him not guilty of criminal carelessness.

"That was just day before yesterday," Web said. "Only there's another jury — the one in me."

"But it was an accident," she told him. "They all said so — the court, everyone. You can't feel guilt, after that."

"It isn't guilt," Web answered, struggling for his words. "It's kind of like fate — fate, and failure — in the place I loved best, the woods, where I was confident where I belonged, and worked and lived."

While he spoke, a subtle change had come over her. She seemed to have gathered a kind of strength, a resolution. He heard it in her voice, felt it reaching him in the swift touch of her fingers on the back of his hand, as she said: "The woods still belong to you. You've got to believe it. Then you'll believe in yourself again."

"Yes," said Web, "maybe I will. But — what about Robert Chadson's wife?"

"Some time," she answered, "a month from now, or two months, you could go out to Pennsylvania, and see Mrs. Chadson, and talk to her."

"Tell me," said Web, his voice taut, "you're a woman — you were married. Do you think it might help? Would it do her any good?"

"Yes — I think it would."

The lamplight had paled in the first hint of day. They both noticed it at the same time. They both noticed that the storm had died. But it was a mouse that broke the tension. The tiny creature, bright-eyed and merry, scurried along a log, stopped, and examined them.

"I better set a trap," said Web. "No — I don't want to hurt anything."

They smiled at each other, and Web felt an overwhelming gratitude. As far as it ever could, the horror had gone out of him.

"I'll go back to the spring and get some water for coffee," he said. "Then I'll go down the trail with you to Marcy's Lodge."

"Don't bother. I'll find it easily."

"It's no bother," Web said. "It's a thing I want to do."

"But I know my way — now."

Web built up the fire, took the water pail from the low shelf, and went to the door.

"I'll be back," he said.

He was away from the cabin less than five minutes, but when he came back, the girl was gone. He stood stone still, listening to the cold, slow drip from the eaves, and the mounting throb of his pulse.

Fear and loneliness crept into him again. She wasn't there! Had she ever been — in reality? Was she hallucination? Had he been talking to himself? He saw his guide's badge lying on the table, and it seemed to mock him.

Yet she had been so vivid, so real in her understanding! Could that be an invention of his own mind? No! He would follow her down to Marcy's, look in the lodge register, and find her name. But even as he turned toward the door, Web knew he would only prove himself deranged. She had no name, no being. She was nothing ... a fantasy ...

*

The knock on the cabin door had repeated twice before Web actually heard it. Had she come back? Had he found the lost girl again?

He rushed to the door and flung it wide. Gill Bowden, the sheriff, stood outside. They faced each other in silence for a moment, Gill Bowden reading Web's eyes, Web trying to conceal what lay behind them.

"Are you all right, Web?" the big man asked.

"Sure, Gill—okay. Come in. I was just going to make some coffee."

Gill stepped in and looked around, his eyes troubled. "You all alone, Web? No visitors?"

"All alone."

Web poured some water from the pail into the teakettle, and put the kettle on the stove.

"You're up early, Gill," he said. His voice was steady, and so were his hands.

The sheriff said: "Yes, I am. I'm sorry, but this business isn't finished yet. Chadson's father telephoned from Pennsylvania—not two hours ago to tell me. He's flying up."

Web stood facing the table. "Chadson's father is a nice guy," he said.

The sheriff acted as if he hadn't heard. He said: "Chadson's wife is missing. She got out of the sanitarium where she's been since the accident. Do you hear me, Web?"

Web didn't answer.

"Listen, Web! Try to understand. There's an alarm out for her. She's hysterical, wild, out of her mind. She's got a gun—old man Chadson's revolver. And she's after you."

"I don't believe it," said Web.

He had moved a little to his right, and he was looking at the long bench beneath the window, his eyes entranced.

"Web," the sheriff said, "this is serious. You're crazy not to take it that way."

"I'm not crazy—not anymore."

"Then you better come to town with me—just to play safe."

"No. I belong here—in the woods. And the woods belong to me, Gill— like always."

Remembering the lost girl, Web felt a strange peace ranging through him. Some time, a month from now, or two months, he could go out to Pennsylvania and see Mrs. Chadson. The girl had told him that. He would do as she had said. For below the window, where he had first seen the girl's white, dazed face, he saw the bench where she had sat. On the bench her green handbag lay half open. He knew she had left it for him— deliberately—so that he would identify her. Inside it, in the morning light, he saw the dull gleam of the gun barrel. She wanted him to know!

*

"Gill," Web said to the sheriff, "sit down, and have some coffee with me. Chadson's wife hasn't got murder in her heart — not anymore. She hasn't got a gun. If she had, she wouldn't shoot anybody."

"What makes you so sure about that, Web?"

"Because she knows what it means to kill a man. I told her."

# Weather Prophet

Once I came up in February because I had to see how the lake country looked under snow. Steve Ireland met me at Mopang, and we started for Privilege in the pung, with a northeaster building steadily behind us. Steve yelled into his turned-up collar: "Travel eight hundred miles to spend one day in a blizzard. Jesus!"

"Maybe it'll clear."

"Doc Musgrave says it'll hold northeast for two days. He don't often miss."

Whenever Steve mentioned Dr. Delirious Musgrave, there was a note in his voice of troubled fascination. I had always wanted to meet the doctor. His personality seemed to weigh on Steve's mind. I wanted to hear Steve talk about him now, but a quickened bitterness of the storm made talk an effort.

We were crossing the wake of an old burn where the blown snow towered around us, and the wind struck sharp. When at length we came into the shelter of the spruces, the wind seemed far away. You could hear it roaring in the branches, and the snow swept down like spilled veils, but the storm was at arm's length, momentarily.

Steve lifted his chin above his collar, and said:

"He claims the day he does he'll die."

"Does what?" I asked, my wits half numbed.

"Figures wrong on the weather."

"Oh, Doc Musgrave?"

"Yuh," said Steve, resettling his chin.

We put a blanket on old Chub in the Privilege stable, fed him his oats, and floundered up the hill above the lake to Steve's cabin. It was nice inside. You could smell peeled spruce, oakum chinking, and wood smoke. The wind sent the fine snow hissing against the windows, reminding us of our comfort within.

"This time of year," Steve said, as he primed the pump, "there ain't much doin', only ice fishin'."

"I don't mind. I got to dreaming about winter on the lake, and had to come and see."

"You're seein' it, all right. You better stay over a few days."

"I can't do it. I'll have to go in the morning."

I opened the bottom draft of the stove, and the fire woke up and made the chimney roar. "Maybe if the storm holds, I'll be snowbound."

"He claimed it would," Steve said. A gust rattled the stovepipe in its guy wires, and Steve added: "Listen to that."

We ate fried salt pork, pickerel, and tea. Steve inquired for all my friends he had guided. I asked about Uncle Jeff Coongate, Neilly Winslow, the Iron Duke, and Jim Scantling. Steve said they were all smart, and let it go at that, but when I mentioned Peter Deadwater, the Indian, he perked up.

"Say! Peter's wife's goin' to have a kid."

"Honest?"

"Fact, so help me. Talk about a happy Injun."

"I thought Peter and Sadie couldn't have any kids."

"Well," Steve said, "they thought there wa'nt no hope, an' so'd everyone. They been wantin' one twelve years."

"When's the baby due?"

"Peter figures apple-blossom time. He's been poundin' ash, an' got a cradle built, an' a basket, an' a doe-skin suit with pants to it, soft as silk. It's a caution, the way that Injun works. Changed his whole character. He ain't touched a drop of lemon extrac' nor essence of pep'mint, not for five-six months. Just works, an' tends Sadie, an' lays plans for that kid."

"That's wonderful, Steve."

"It's the Lord's mercy. Let's wash the dishes."

We cleaned up, and got out the ice-fishing equipment. We were ready to start for the lake, when Steve spotted a gap in the chinking. A fine spray of snow had blasted through, building a hard white mound on the floor. Steve got a mallet and caulking iron and closed the gap with a twist of oakum. "Some storm, to find a hole that small," he said.

"Steve, didn't you say you drove Doc Musgrave's buggy for him, when you were little?"

"Yuh. We was good friends in them days."

"Aren't you now?"

"It's mighty queer, but he don't care for me now, me nor anyone at all."

A moment later we were out in the blizzard, toting our fishing gear down to the lake. I was more than ever determined to meet the doctor some day; but now his prophecy of weather was of direct concern. We chiseled our holes in the lee of Genius Island, but shelter was scant. The snow gave visible shape to the turbulence in the sky, and my forehead ached with cold.

The tip-ups were active, but we couldn't hook a trout. "They're slapping it with their tails," Steve said. "You can watch 'em do it, if you lay still over a hole."

I tried it, shading my eyes with my hands. Down there in the deep clear water, you could see the togue swimming along slowly in single file. They would bump the bait with their noses, and, as they swam by, bat it with their tails.

"Can you see 'em?" Steve asked.

He was kneeling on the opposite side of the hole, facing me. I glanced toward him, but my answer froze. Just behind Steve, and to one side of him, stood Peter Deadwater, the Indian. He was wearing snowshoes — the long, narrow Cree model for open travel. Suspended from a thong in his left hand were two lake trout of about six pounds. Steve saw my astonished expression, and turned.

"You ghost," he said to the Indian.

"No." Peter made an up-and-down motion with his free hand.

"Heard us chiseling," Steve explained to me; and the Indian grunted.

I stood up and brushed off the snow. "Hear good news, Peter," I said. "Congratulations."

Peter grunted again.

"How things with Sadie?" Steve asked.

Peter shrugged. While we took up our sets, he stood perfectly still in the exact spot where we had first seen him. Steve kept glancing at him curiously, and, when we were ready to go, said:

"Peter. You come my cabin. Get warm. Tea. Pickerel chowder."

Peter declined with a headshake and held out one of the lake trout, saying: "Namaycush."

"Come help eat," Steve said, taking the trout.

"I go home. Sadie hot. Crazy talk."

Steve looked quickly at me. "He means Sadie's sick." Then he turned to Peter. "How long Sadie hot? How long talk crazy?"

"Morning."

"This morning?"

Peter Deadwater nodded, his eyes vacant.

"She got pain some place?"

Peter touched his forehead, then put his hand down over his stomach, groaned, and stared at Steve.

"You go home. Take trout to Sadie. I get doctor. See?"

Peter moved away a few steps, turned on his long webs, and came back. "Doctor cross lake to Injun Village in storm?"

"Yes."

"Tell him open water Leadmine Point. Spring-hole. Tell him very danger spring-hole."

"I know," Steve said. "I tell him."

Peter started off, the snow blowing shoulder high around him. Ten steps and he had vanished. It was six miles, due southwest across the lake to the Indian Village. In the falling dark, even with the northeast gale full on his back, it would be a bitter journey.

Steve and I hid our tackle on Genius Island and went straight in to Privilege. I had to stop behind a shed at the public landing to get out of the wind for a minute. I thought my forehead was frozen, but it wasn't. Steve drew off a mitten and blew on his knuckles. "You're goin' to get a hell of a start," he said. "Doc Musgrave talks like he wasn't there at all."

"What? How do you mean?"

The shed trembled in a gust. In the dark you could still see the snow-shapes racing. Steve said: "Well, he don't say 'I done this,' nor 'I done that.' You'll think he's talkin' about someone else that ain't anywheres around. Once, when I was a kid, he told me why. Thought I'd forget, p'raps, but I didn't. He told me it was his other self he is talkin' about—the man he might of been, he said. But all the time it's really him, because he ain't no one else. But you got to talk to him like he was."

"Are you going to drive him across the lake tonight?"

Steve put on his mitten. "You can't work a horse on the lake. Four bad reefs in the ice between Genius Island and Caribou Rock. He'll go on snowshoes."

In the back room of Sam Lurch's barbershop in Privilege, we found

Dr. Musgrave. He was a man in his early fifties. He sat on the wood box, a bottle between his knees, apparently entranced by the gleaming nickel stove rail. The air in the room was hot and foul, but Musgrave wore a heavy sheepskin coat. The lamplight showed the birthmark which spread from his right temple over his entire right cheek to his jaw. His upward glance was too swift for me to see his eyes. With no sign of recognition for Steve, whom he had known since boyhood, he resumed his staring at the nickel rail. Steve had told me what to expect, but no warning could have prepared me for talking face to face with a man who not only dreamed he wasn't there, but demanded that others honor his unreality.

"Well," Steve said to him, "he said it would hold northeast for two days."

"Yes," said Musgrave. "He is an authority on the weather, as well as on rum, axe wounds, and obstetrics."

Outside, the wind rose shrieking. You could hear the hard snow batter the walls like shot. As if at this corroboration of his prophecy, Musgrave grinned and leaned closer to the stove.

When the gust had spent itself, Steve said: "Would he cross the lake tonight to tend a sick woman in the Injun Village?"

After a long silence, Musgrave said: "He would think hard during such a trip — think himself into a stupor."

To see the man actually sitting there, yet talking of himself as if he were absent, gave me the shivers.

"He would have his coat collar up," he went on, "and his face wrapped to the eyes. He would keep the wind dead fair on his back, and — "

Steve moved toward the doctor nervously. "He would want to keep the wind heavy on his right shoulder. That would bear him inside of the open spring-hole off Leadmine Point."

Dr. Musgrave took a small drink from the bottle, replaced it between his knees, and, as if Steve had not spoken, resumed:

"— his thoughts would keep him company, and he would hum. His humming, and the cadence of his steps, would make him forget the night."

"But," said Steve, his voice rising, "he would want to keep his mind on that spring-hole. If the wind backs into the north, it would veer the doctor off course. He would walk right into *open water* in the dark."

"He stated that the wind would hold northeast," said Musgrave complacently. "And it will."

"Even so, he'll pass within two hundred yards of the spring-hole!" Steve took a radium-dialed compass from his pocket and held it out to Musgrave in his open palm. "The snow is blowing so he won't even see his feet," he went on, his voice growing unsteady. "Wouldn't he take this?"

"Does a prophet need a compass?"

The man on the wood box seemed to ignore our presence as well as his own, and, while we humored his strange conceit, the purpose of our visit had been obscured. When I could bear the suspense no longer, I began speaking to him, unnaturally, in the third person:

"Is he equipped to take a six-month's baby from the wife of Peter Deadwater? While the men discuss the weather, the Indian's woman lies out of her head with fever."

"He has performed cesareans in this country under strange conditions," Musgrave answered, "and with strange instruments. Once he cauterized an amputation with a heated abutment spike. And he did a transfusion with the quill of a goose."

"But the Indian woman has been delirious since morning," I said. "The man with Steve Ireland thinks it may be emergency."

"Ah, yes, no doubt," replied Musgrave, blandly, "but the doctor hates cold—cold and terror, they are the same." He picked up the rum bottle and held it to the light. As near as I could judge, he had drunk half the contents. He removed the cork, took another swallow, and said: "Northeast for two days."

"Maybe the Indian's woman will die," I said, "and they are all here, talking."

"Maybe," said Musgrave, rising.

In the act of buttoning his coat collar to the throat, he turned toward us, and I saw him full face in the light. I knew why Steve Ireland both feared and pitied him. Above the doctor's straight merciless mouth were the eyes of a child; and I saw in these features the evidence of a man divided. You looked into his wide child's eyes, and pitied. You remembered his mouth, and shrank from him.

Steve went to him, begging: "Would the doctor please take a friend for company tonight? The friend that used to drive the buggy for him?"

"No."

Musgrave jerked his snowshoes from a peg, and kneeled to tie their lampwick lashings. Whether Steve was driven by a superstition about putting on snowshoes indoors, or by his dread that the wind would shift, I do not know. But when Musgrave stood up, Steve clutched him by the shoulders, and shook him, saying:

"If he walks into that spring-hole, *both* of him will go under the ice together—the one he is, and that other one, too!"

For an instant, as Steve backed away, the child part dominated Musgrave's face. He seemed touched that anyone should go to such lengths to warn him away from danger; and, in the only natural sentence I heard him speak, he said: "That's all right, Stevie—I'll be there in two hours."

He put on the pack which I assumed contained his instrument bag, and we followed him out into the blizzard. At the lakeshore, he said: "He will go on from here alone." He hesitated for just a moment, then turned away, and walked off in the dark.

For two or three minutes after he had vanished, we stood looking out over the howling blackness of the lake. Then we turned wearily up the hill to Steve's cabin.

The warmth, the smell of broiling trout, and the leaky kettle's hiss could not remove the spell of Dr. Musgrave. Steve kept glancing at the black windows. It was as if he thought he might actually see the wind's direction.

"Steve," I said, "how wide is that spring-hole?"

"Better than a quarter-mile, when I last saw it."

After we had eaten, I lay in my bunk; but, despite my snow-burned face and eyes, there was no drowsiness. And there was none for Steve. He looked at his watch, and said: "It's thirty-eight minutes, now."

"Where would he be, about?"

"Mouth of Hardwood Cove."

Presently, as if Musgrave were with us in the cabin, we began to talk his way. To Steve Ireland, whom I had known fourteen years, I said: "The men lay in comfort wondering if the wind would change."

Steve got up, opened the door, and looked out into the whirlpools of the sky. He had to use his strength to close it, and the cold wind drove in a spray of snow and tore the ammunition-company calendar from its hook. "One of the men knows the wind is changing," he said.

"Where would he be now?"

Steve answered so quickly that I knew he was with Musgrave almost step for step: "Forty-three minutes — off Bear Trap Landing."

"They thought of how, in summer, they had paddled often across the six miles to Peter Deadwater's shack."

Steve got out his compass and set it on the table. He looked again at his watch. "The men couldn't rest good."

"No," I said. "They were thinking of the other man, counting on the wind to hold him on course, and the wind veering him toward the open water, and the Indian waiting, and his wife hot and crazy talking."

"For Chris' sake!" Steve cried. "I'm goin' outside and see for certain."

When Steve came in again, he face looked numb. His hair, powdered white with snow, made him seem prematurely old. He went to the stove and sat on the deacon seat, his back to the warmth. He kept looking at his watch, while the snow melted, glistening in his hair.

"Well?" I asked.

"The wind's due north — changed, with never a lull to warn him."

Steve got a lumberman's blueprint map of the lake, and spread it on the bench beside him. With a pencil he drew a straight line due southwest from Privilege six miles to the Indian Village on the far shore. Along that line he marked various points, and the times he estimated it would take Musgrave to pass them, at a speed of three miles per hour. Hardwood Cove, 38 mins. Bear Trap Landing, 43 mins.

At Caribou Rock, an hour and five mins., Steve drew a gradual curve on the map. The curve bore left—southward, as the wind veered into the north. A mile south of Caribou Rock, he drew in the spring-hole off Leadmine Point. Then he looked at his watch again, and said: "Munson Reef—an hour and twelve minutes."

"My God, Steve! How many, many times we fished that spring-hole in hot weather when the trout were deep."

Steve made a dot on the penciled line which curved and then straightened toward the open water. He sat tense, his watch under his eyes, his pencil poised.

"Sometimes," Steve said, "when we was makin' calls away out somewheres away from the villages, he was mighty nice. He was kind. He would tell me to stop the buggy by a field of daisies, or hockweed. Them things made him happy. If he saw a doe deer on the lakeshore, that would make him happy, too, or a loon callin'. It was the same with insects, any livin' thing, or anything that was pretty to look at. He could explain them things. I thought the world was flat, till he told me why it ain't. He said I was the only one he could talk to, or that could talk to him. I was eleven years old, then...." Steve's pencil point touched the map, as he checked the time. "Little Mopang Bar—hour an' eighteen minutes."

"Steve! How close is he to it—now?"

"Seven minutes."

Steve brushed his hand over his damp hair, and wiped the wet palm on his thigh. "It was when I got older that he changed toward me. But I guess he thought 'twas me that changed. He wouldn't talk to me no more, nor he didn't want me 'round. He said people was no good after they stopped bein' children. But *he* was good, them times with me, when I was a boy. There wa'nt a thing he wouldn't do for people that was ailin'. But outside of for that, he wouldn't go near no one."

Steve got up from the bench, took off a stove lid, and stirred the fire. A furious wind blast drew back down the stovepipe, and the fine ash rose in the room.

"Big Mopang Bar," Steve said, "hour an' twenty-three minutes."

"That leaves him three minutes!"

"Two.... I wonder how Peter's woman's makin' out?"

"But he knows the lake, Steve. Maybe, when he got out there alone, with the storm, and the darkness—maybe he remembered what you said, and kept the wind heavy on his right shoulder. That would save him. He would pass Leadmine Point inside the spring-hole."

Steve looked intently at his watch. I saw his lips move, as he checked over the last minutes. Then he stopped counting. He was so quiet it was as if he had stopped breathing. After a long time he folded the map, put the watch back in his pocket, and stood up.

"Well," he said, "I liked him, just the same. It's like I was with him out there tonight, right beside him the whole way, till he drowned. Only nothin' I could do to help him, like watchin' a blind man walk off a cliff, an' your voice gone."

"Steve, I can't believe it!"

"That's 'cause you don't want to, an' I don't, neither."

Steve crossed to the table and turned down the lamp. He stood there with the dim light on his face, until I had stretched out under my blankets. "All set?" he said.

"Sure — maybe he made it all right."

"Maybe." Steve blew out the lamp and we lay in the dark, listening to the long-drawn fury of the storm.

Morning broke clear with a light north wind. Steve had the bacon frying. The cabin was warm, and bright sunlight streamed through the windows. I looked out, and saw the lake stretching white and lovely below us. That view, so peaceful now, so immaculate, made the night seem unreal.

"Steve, how do you feel this morning?"

"Frisky," he said. "That was bad last night."

Yet in Steve's voice there was uncertainty. I felt it, perhaps in his very cheerfulness. When we had eaten and were on our way down to the stable, Steve said: "Would it trouble you if I got Jim Scantling to drive you to Mopang this mornin'? I want to cross the lake."

"No, Steve, of course not. I'd stay and go with you, if I could."

"Well, I just got an awful hankerin' to make it across," Steve explained.

Jim and Steve hooked up, and old Chub's breath blew white in the cold. We climbed to the seat, and I reached down to shake hands with Steve. "Let me know about things, will you?" I asked.

"Sure. I'll write you a letter. So-long."

I looked around once to see Steve striking off across the white-glaring lake toward the Indian Village.

Dere frend,
 I seen from his drifted tracks right where it begun to change on him near Caribou Rock. I followed the curve of them until I dassent go no closer the

open water, where his tracks run off I seen one of his mittens layin on the ice where he tried to claw back on but that is all so I swung back and went to the Peter Deadwater shack and the priest was there. Peter's woman was dead and the baby was dead.

Well my good frend I must close now as there is a diver comin from Eastport to dive for him and I am to lay a boom on the ice for him to work off of, but they will never find him as the currents will draw him under, as ever your frend Steve Ireland.

P.S. I told Peter how we tried to get the doctor to him and he said all right.

# *The Tenderfoot Who Wasn't*

As soon as they got off the train at the flag station, Mercer began to deride the place, its dilapidation, even its unknown inhabitants. But Mr. Reuben Usher, who at sixty had never been in the wilderness, said quietly: "The stillness doesn't frighten me. I like it."

"You wait, Reuben," Mercer said. "The real stillness is when we get in the canoe — on the lake."

"And if it were noise I liked, then would you also know where were even finer noises?" said the old man, in a most patient voice.

"Humph," growled Mercer. "Like to buzz this dump in a plane."

Mercer chuckled in his thought of startling the natives. Strident in the belief that he was a sportsman, he wore a heavily checked shirt, an exaggerated belt, and high laced boots. He was fat, bluff, permeated with his own heartiness. But on the splintered platform of the flag station, his uniform looked fake.

"Seems good to get the old woods clothes on again," he said flexing his huge arms. "I wish young Ireland would hurry up. I told him nine o'clock in the *morning*. But time means nothing to these backwoods guides."

Mr. Usher remembered that he had come here by promise of the very timelessness which Mercer now impugned. He was glad in this new and tranquil environment, even though he felt ill-equipped to comprehend it. He felt a trenchant yearning to know, and to participate; and he pointed to some swallows mustered on the telegraph wires, and said: "Look, isn't that a storm warning?" Somewhere he had read that the congregating of swallows foretold a storm, and this small knowledge would be his contribution.

"Doesn't mean a thing," said Mercer, glancing contemptuously at the sky. "Not a cloud. It's clouds that count."

"I must have been misinformed."

"Takes experience to read weather right, Reuben. Of course I've been at it a long time. Were you worried about the canoe trip on the lake?"

"Maybe — maybe I was thinking of that, deep down."

Mercer strode away along the platform, and the old man looked wonderingly at the forest. He discovered it to be both beautiful and melancholy, and he resented the railroad tracks which had cut through it. Precocious, incredible tracks! He reflected that only twelve hours ago he had been at peace in the roaring twilight of the North Station, Boston. He had felt at home, consoled, one of a myriad beings bustling under a roof. But here — he was not quite sure. He was fascinated, troubled, wary, and profoundly reverent.

He looked beyond the tracks at the slow uncoiling of the river. Somewhere in his immense talk, Mercer had mentioned a rapid named Slewgundy Heater. Mr. Usher looked up the river as far as he could see, then down, believing he might be rewarded with a glimpse of this savage-sounding place. But from one direction the river flowed deathlessly out of the forest, and in the other as deathlessly into it. He was refreshed by the supernal stillness of the river's flowing.

In front of a shack on a slope, a sequestered prophet chopped wood. The old fellow seemed vastly unannoyed with this work, and the blows of his axe belonged. Never had Reuben Usher heard the "chock" of an axe in a clearing, yet by some miracle the sound was familiar. The odors of spruce and wood smoke made him tingle, and he wished slyly for the nostrils of a hound so that he might sniff and isolate even finer ingredients.

Thinking reverently of the forest, Mr. Usher saw how little of its meaning books might convey. After sixty years he felt on the brink of a new and more beautiful kind of life. He understood people, the management of industry, toil in the cities of the world. He knew music, literature, and painting, and he felt that music alone might construe the talents of the river, the forest, and the sky.

Now from the telegraph wires, the swallows twittered and made brief nervous flights, reminding Mr. Usher of his newness here. Again came Mercer in his brown, emphatic boots. Mercer trod auspiciously and was a prophet of weather.

"Here comes Ireland!" the big man said. "He'll do anything for me. I knew his father well."

The earnest ears of a horse showed on the skyline, then horse, wagon, and man were visible on the dusty road. Mercer was stimulated by Ireland's approach. "Well, how do you like it, Reuben?"

"It's good," said Mr. Usher, softly.

"You'll catch on. Wait till you get on the lake and hook your first trout. Ever been in a canoe much?"

He had told Mercer several times that he knew nothing of canoes, but he repeated patiently: "Just once, in the park, when I was a boy."

Mercer chuckled as if his knowledge of canoes were occult and patented. "This is the real stuff." Then, lowering his voice in confidence, he said: "You ought to have bought high laced boots and woolen pants."

The old man looked gravely at his linen trousers, his new white sneakers, and his shaker sweater.

"Mark you as a tenderfoot right away," said Mercer, disapprovingly.

"I am a tenderfoot."

"Yes — but you don't want them to think so."

When the wagon drew up, Mercer gave the horse a dusty slap and was first to greet Steve Ireland.

"Hello there, Stevie. Knew your old man well, so we'll start right off with first names, eh? Mine's Al. Al Mercer."

"Yes," Steve said. "I've heard of you, Mr. Mercer."

"Brought my friend Usher — Reuben Usher. He's interested in a little rest in this country you fellows have got up here. How are the trout biting?"

"Ought to pick up a few."

They climbed into the wagon and started toward the lake, and the wheel sounds were muffled in the dust. Everywhere the sun shone on deserted fields and on the leaves of spring.

Mr. Usher noted that Steve was young, lank, and sinewy. He looked straight ahead and listened calm-faced to Mercer's outbursts of lore. Steve was not uncommunicative. He was reserved, quietly and courteously withholding his personality, as if he felt too many men had tried to get acquainted with him in seconds. As they passed a farm, Steve looked long at an old cow which lay on the grass. He looked from the cow to the sky, then straight ahead again. "Cow layin' down in the mornin'," he said. "Storm 'fore night."

"Not today, Stevie," contradicted Mercer. "Not a cloud in the sky. I was telling Reuben, it's clouds that count."

Steve nodded, and Mr. Usher felt a deep affection for his swallows.

Before they reached the lake, a buck deer cleared the road ahead of them in a single leap. Astonished, Mr. Usher rose from his seat, as if with longing to capture and suspend this flash of beauty. For him all the forest was enriched by the live, wild thing which was a part of it.

At first sight of the deer, Steve's eyes had darkened in a quick and savage joy. Steve Ireland was a native hunter; and, crouched on the wagon seat, he had gestured fiercely, saying: "God! Look at him! Look! Look!" Then he sat back, sighing, relaxed, his lips wrinkling in a dreamful smile. Damp beech leaves on a long ridge, a fire no bigger than the bottom of a tea pail, liver broiling on a stick, and that buck hanging by his gambrels from a bent sapling. Peace and plenitude were Steve's. He wanted only things which were probable of fulfillment, and he did not wonder whither he was going, or why. Here was this buck, working in his country! He looked artlessly around him, saying in his mind: "I'll hunt this ridge, come fall. I'll dump that critter on his nose before a lynx gets him. God A'mighty, I can taste the gravy now, and the drool a-gatherin' in my mouth a'ready."

"Lot of deer up around Jackman," Mercer informed. "That's the place to see deer. Ever up around Jackman, Stevie?"

"No."

"You ought to try it there some time."

Through the trees the lake shone with abrupt radiance, like daylight at the end of a tunnel. Mr. Usher climbed from the wagon and walked with boyish eagerness to the sand beach. He stood there, a silver sheen of hair curling from under his hat. He felt strangely beholden to something. He could not remember when he had felt both awe and gratitude simultaneously. Was it the long mystery of distance? The remote and dusky shores? The boulders atop themselves in trembling mirage? Or was it simply the hovering paternity of earth and sky? Oh, he would bring his children here, and show this to them, watching while it penetrated them as it penetrated him.

Beneath a dignified spruce, Mercer babbled and assembled fly rods. Steve unhooked and hung the harness on a tall gray stump. He waved to the horse, and said: "Go it, old Crawnch! Go it, boy!" The horse shook and trotted up the road, its destination private.

At the edge of the forest, Steve rolled a green canoe to his shoulder and brought it down to the beach. He thrust the bow into the water, loaded the duffel, and took a long steady look into the northwest.

"How far is it to camp?" asked Mr. Usher.

"They call it eleven miles. I guess we're all set, sir." Steve leaned on his paddle, and while he waited, stared again at the sky. The cloud was there, all right—black, and low down in the horizon.

Mr. Usher stooped and touched the gunwale of the canoe. "This is all new to me, you know," he said.

Mercer, having finished with the rods, came down in time to overhear this. "Don't worry, Reuben. A canoe'll scare you to death before it'll drown you. Right, Stevie?"

Steve nodded toward the bow, and said to Mercer: "Will you sit forward, please?"

Mercer stepped in and moved to his position. "That's a fact, though—about canoes, isn't it, Stevie?"

Steve's active eyes squinted a trifle as they focused for an instant on the low-lying cloud. "That's what they say," he said. Bending, he steadied the canoe for Mr. Usher. "Just step in the middle of her. Here, grab my shoulder. And when you set down, rest your back agin the middle thwart an' face towards me."

Carefully the old man did as he was told, and he marvelled at the grace with which Steve shoved off and jumped into the stern, his moccasins making scarcely a whisper on the cedar planking of the craft. Steve's paddle knifed into the water, and the canoe moved out into the lake.

Mr. Usher peered into the water. The sides of boulders loomed, fell away to depth and darkness. Mercer had begun casting and was making handsome predictions as to the size and number of trout he would take. But it appeared that his prophecies were delayed of fulfillment, and he grew petulant and dismayed and spoke of great catches in Moosehead Lake, and of rainbows from the Cowichan River on Vancouver Island, and of the merits of many places quite impossible to reach at the moment.

"Why don't you get the canoe out farther?" he said to Steve. "Can't you tell by this time they're not lying in close?"

"Just as you say," said Steve. He had been following the margin of an underwater bar, but he nosed the canoe outward. For a while they fished fruitlessly a quarter mile offshore, and Mercer began again: "This is too far out. I didn't mean this far. Can't you take us where they are?"

Steve angled toward shore until he picked up the shadowy outline of the bar again. It was his job to keep his sportsmen happy, and to do what they said, no matter what. It was also his job to keep an eye on the cloud which stretched long and straight across the northwest. Maybe it was just as well their backs were turned to this cloud. He rolled a cigarette, and had trouble making the paper stick. "I got the driest spit of any man I ever see," he finally remarked, tossing the cigarette away.

In the narrows between two long points, Mercer began to catch trout. He grew voluble, informative, and obstreperously happy. "See? I told you, Reuben," he said. Everything he said was loud and definite, and his voice reechoed from the point. Mr. Usher felt curiously glad of this double stating. The stillness was now hovering, oppressive, and Mercer's prattling somehow served as a contact with humanity.

"Got another!" he shouted. "A beauty. Say, how many I got now all together?"

"You got enough," said Steve. "Shall I let this one go?" Paddle balanced across his knees, Steve held the trout underwater in the net.

"Let it go?" protested Mercer. "What's the sense in catching them if you let them go?"

"He'll live. You got more'n you can eat a'ready."

"Let him go," said Mr. Usher.

A few moments later, Mr. Usher felt a violent tug on his line. He had been trying to cast, and, doing rather badly, had allowed his fly to trail in the water. As the trout struck, he had instinctively lifted his rod and hooked the fish. He sat forward, eyes sparkling with delight, his lips spread in an embarrassed smile.

"Steve! What shall I do now?"

"Reel in! Reel in!" instructed the tireless Mercer. "Keep a taut line! How do you like it now, Reuben?"

"You're doin' all right, Mr. Usher," Steve said, peering into the water. "Good fish. Go mighty near two pound."

Suddenly the old man's line went slack, and the spring of the rod whipped the fly clear of the surface.

"Gone! But I don't care, Steve — not if you don't. Really."

Steve grinned at him, and Mercer said: "What did I say about keeping a taut line? You can't catch trout unless you learn the art of keeping a taut line. Right, Steve?"

"Well, it's too bad Mr. Usher," Steve said. "Your first one, too."

"But I'm just as happy. Really, I've never been so happy."

Steve had no time to savor his wish that all men were like Mr. Usher. A puff of wind snapped out of the northwest, and a dark cat's paw fled across the water. The wind reached them all in a cold, quick pressure which put Steve's hatbrim flat against his forehead and brought the water to his eyes. His lips twitched and tightened as he reached for his hat. He was looking far away at the cloud, and he saw that its lower edge was ripped and lacy.

The canoe emerged between the two points into the widening body of the lake. Distances stretched ahead and to the right and left. Steve looked measuringly at Cardiff Point. He could duck behind it if things got bad. Or, if the sportsmen wanted to reach camp, he might try for the lee of Munson Island, three miles away. His two passengers sat with their backs to the cloud, and they had not seen it. When the time was right, he would call it to their attention. Anticipating that moment, he gave them each a sharp glance of estimate. Steve had classified them simply as the fat bastard in the bow and the old man aft of the middle thwart. You could feel the wind pretty good now, he thought — a cold one. The lake was rippling some, too, and the spruce tops waving on Cardiff Point.

Mr. Reuben Usher reeled in his line, and sat thinking, his eyes half closed. The young guide, so close to him in the stern of the eighteen-footer, had a quality which he hoped his own sons might some day possess. This quality, Mr. Usher believed, concerned the patience to remove ten thousand stones from a field and the reticence to hew in a clearing. What if one transplanted himself permanently into this environment? What would he miss first? One wanted to cry out: "I would miss nothing!" But was that true? Mightn't one long for good music, for his work, or for someone with whom to draw comparisons?

An unfamiliar rocking of the canoe disturbed him. Glancing about, he noted some remarkable changes. Everywhere was motion. The waves marched in sharp, unending echelons, and trees swayed against the sky. In any direction it was a long way to shore, but you could see the swaying of trees, distance or no. Young Steve had changed his course, so that he quartered into the waves. These waves slapped briskly against the starboard bow, and they seemed impious and direly purposeful.

Downwind came an eerie babel of laughter, and Mr. Usher thought suddenly of ghouls and glanced apprehensively at Steve.

"Loons," Steve said, serenely. "They do that sometimes when the weather's changing." He stuck his hand in the water and scooped some to his mouth. Wiping his lips, he said: "Better reel in now, Mr. Mercer."

"Reel in? Why should I reel in?" the big man asked.

Steve twitched his paddle. The canoe swung sharply, rolling in the trough of the waves. At this angle, by turning their heads slightly, all three men could see the cloud. Its forward edge was smooth, dense, jet black; and its trailing edge was torn and coppery.

"See that?"

Mr. Usher nodded. His swallows! They had been right.

"Well, what about it?" Mercer asked.

"Wind."

"So what? What's a little wind?"

Mr. Usher observed that the men were shouting, not in anger, but to make themselves heard. The wind pressed hard upon his cheek and howled in his head. He had read of squalls, but there must be a limit, a restriction somewhere on velocity. At a certain point in the wind's acceleration, it ceased its benediction, and became arrogant, menacing, and cold. It knocked the tops from selected waves, and scattered them on the back of one's neck.

"I can make Cardiff Point," yelled Steve, his shirt ballooning, "or I can try for Munson Island. Camp's on the mainland, just beyond Munson. What do you want to do?"

"It'll blow over," said Mercer, reeling in. "You're not scared of a little wind, are you Stevie? Head for Munson Island."

Steve snatched off his hat, placing it on the floor of the canoe, his knee on the brim. The wind tousled his black hair, parting it indiscriminately and showing the white scalp.

"Suit yourself," he said.

The cloud shut off the sun, and the sun's abatement did something ominous to the scenery and to the moods of the men. In the dim light the waves became black and murderous, and their crests hissed, and were dirty white. Steve began to study them steadily, not just once in a while.

Mr. Usher wished they were now about to land on Munson Island; but Munson was an imperishably far distance, and this was so of all shores, and the canoe seemed to be making no headway. He recalled two recent shouts from Mercer, and in these shouts he perceived a special significance which he had not noticed at the time.

One shout had been: "How do you like it now, Reuben?" and this had been in a kind of paper-thin voice, a voice uncertain of itself. The second shout had been directed to Steve: "Why don't you turn and run with it — *any* shore?"

"Swamp over the stern," Steve had answered.

Thereafter, Mercer had been silent, and Mr. Usher realized that Mercer was frightened, and that he himself was frightened, and that of all living men, Steven Ireland was most important. There was something very illogical about their predicament. You could step away from an onrushing train, a tiger, or a madman. But you could not step away from this.

Always Mr. Usher had regarded wind as something wild, free, and magnificent. He saw now that it was also wanton, merciless, and unpredictable. It snapped off the top of any tree at random. It filled the air with frayed leaves, and tumbled crows in their stride. Moreover, it imparted to the lake a cold, coherent lust.

The waves came close and crowding. They came on, towering, toppling, threatening Steve Ireland's precocious vigilance. And the waves applauded themselves by the hiss of their torn crests.

The canoe lurched, and a gout of spray spilled over them, spanked the bottom of the canoe, and cascaded toward the stern. Steve steadied her with his knees, and yelled to Mercer: "Lay down! Lay down! They don't get no smaller if you rise up an' look at 'em. I said lay *down!*"

Mr. Usher's stolen glances toward Munson Island brought nothing but a sickening sight of power beyond belief. They would never make it. And if there were no progress, why continue this teetering, this hypocritical effort to keep the bow of a canoe in one direction? Munson Island was a bait designed by experts in irony. It was a thing toward which to struggle in vain. They had all been very cunningly trapped.

The old man felt that his fear was degrading and shameful; and he wondered how long a human being could live in its concentrated misery. Many times in life he had been startled, momentarily filled with terror. Time was the element which differentiated between fear and fright. Mr. Usher knew that his wish to pray was weak and pitiful, because he knew it was merely the wish to live. But he said in his mind:

"God, please wait a minute if You can. God, what is a minute to You?" He knew it was his finest prayer.

He was wet clear through, and when the canoe heaved under him, he seemed to compress, growing inferior in stature and great in circumference. Whereupon, the canoe pitching downward over a crest, he became a being of only vertical dimension, and all his width was evaporated. He could anticipate these mad sequences by the crackling antagonism in Steve's eyes. Steven Ireland knew exactly how to look at a wave, and the look was not scornful.

The old man began arranging sincere objections to his own drowning. There was too much work left undone. A man should be duly warned and prepared for such a climax as his own death. He should be permitted to order his larger work of life, so that it could be entrusted to an able successor. But it didn't work out that way. Had he actually believed that he would lie down some day in a quiet place and say: "Now I am ready to die"? If so, he had been guilty of false thinking, for it was apparent that one could prepare only for life. In fact much of life was nothing else. Death had its own incalculable volition, and anyone who thought it might procrastinate in his favor was a fool. Munson Island was undoubtedly a beautiful place where men could walk or lean gratefully against trees and stare out at this cold compendium of hell. What did it matter, now?

Mercer, who had been so boisterous, so braggart in the placid wilderness, lay in the bow, eyes shut, face slack and ugly in its terror.

Steven Ireland knelt in the stern, working. Mr. Usher believed him possessed of all knowledge useful on earth, as well as an amazing sense of balance. Steve must also have an unswerving egotism to engage these waves. His hair was whipped and stringy with spray. Water spilled from him and was blown to vapor. When Mercer moved, a victim of his own panic, Steve yelled, "Lay down!" He yelled so that the cords in his neck strung tight, but his voice was reduced to a whisper in the howl of wind and crashing of the seas.

Without realizing what had happened to him, Mr. Usher had buried his fear in his admiration for Steve. The situation itself belonged to Steven Ireland. He alone was useful and articulate. His patience was an enduring attribute, proof against this wave, the next, and all others. Steve was here against his own judgment, the only judgment which counted. But he wasted no time in thinking he would soon be dead. He did not appear enraged at anyone for getting him into this, yet each paddlestroke must have drawn achingly of his strength. His shirt was a wet skin plastered over his chest. Under it the muscles showed lean and live. He was incurably busy. No sooner would he defeat one wave, than he would be about the outrageous problem of the next. He took no time for triumph, breathing, or oration.

Of a sudden Mr. Reuben Usher came aware of his own returning courage. Winning this fight no longer seemed grievously important — if only he could help Steve. The old man's eyes glowed with his new excitement. He leaned forward, crying out through his numbed mouth: "I want to help!"

Steve's lips curled briefly from his teeth. Without taking his eyes from the waves, without missing a stroke, he reached behind him and tossed an empty lard pail into Mr. Usher's lap.

"*Bail her!*"

Working joyfully with his lard can, Mr. Usher bailed. In time he developed a great pride in his technique. He found that he could plan his awkward scooping when the canoe was tipped, and thus get nearly a full pail at a scoop. On these great occasions, he would glance warily at Steve, and Steve was infallible and wordless in his gratitude. This moment, felt the old man, was very close to inspiration ... when one fears nothing, when everything at once seems fine, and in one's heart is the wholesale evidence of truth.

At length they came exhausted into the lee of Munson Island, and now that rest and security were at hand, they doubted the violence of their own adventure. No one, they felt, could have come through alive. They must have been imagining things. But on the mainland, less than half a mile distant, they saw a cluster of motionless men. Then they had had witnesses! Then it was true! Steve wigwagged with his paddle, and all the men on the mainland waved their arms at once, and moved about in a state of excitement.

Steve sided the canoe into a sheltered cove on the island, and held her steady while Mr. Usher stepped out. The old man's legs were cramped and stiff. They buckled beneath him, and he felt himself obliged to fall down. The stones upon which he lay seemed to heave, as if the waves had imparted a habit to them. Steve Ireland bent over him and lent him a hand.

"Mine won't straighten out neither," Steve said. "It's like they're wore away to a couple of danglin' cords, ain't it?"

Steve got his axe from the stern and walked off looking for a dry pine stub. When he had gone, Mercer raised his head and looked around, blinking. Mercer did not disembark from the canoe. Rather, he emerged from it, like some huge and lumpish animal. At the sound of an axe, he glanced along the beach, noting that Steve was well out of earshot.

"That was awful, Reuben," he began.

Mr. Usher scarcely heard, so intent was he upon the nearness of trees, and upon the feel of round stones and earth.

Mercer was regaining confidence and voice. "That was some blow, Reuben. Ireland had no business getting us into that, you know. It's sheer luck we weren't all drowned."

Reluctantly Mr. Usher turned his gaze away from some flies which by a method known only to themselves had congregated in numbers on the calm water.

"What did you say?" the old man asked.

Mercer began to pace the beach, to gesticulate. "I say that young fool has poor judgment. I'm going to see to it that his guide's license is revoked permanently."

"Oh, do they have to have licenses?"

"Licenses? Certainly. Take his license away, and he can't guide, see? Teach him a lesson."

Mr. Usher reached into his shirt pocket for a cigar. Sorrowfully he discovered that his supply had become a dark brown mush, which had stained his shirt. He turned his head slightly, noting that Steve had fire started between two boulders up the shore. Wood smoke. The old man's nostrils twitched, and in him there awakened strange longings.

"My fortune is considerable," he said, very soberly. "And I had wished to divide it equally among my sons. But if you should happen to have the boy's license revoked, I shall gladly spend the whole fortune reinstating it."

He knew it sounded foolish, dramatic, and pontifical, but he didn't care.

He stood up and walked to the fire which was blazing merrily. Steve knelt close beside it, drying his clothes, and melting the chill from his bones. As Mr. Usher approached, Steve jumped up and handed him an ancient coat, resplendent with elbow patches and assorted buttons.

"By God," he said, evenly, "you put this on."

Mr. Usher did as he was bid, and pointed curiously to Steve's feet. "Do you suppose you could get me a pair of moccasins exactly like yours, Steve?"

"Why, sure. Sheldeye Linton makes them, by the old Britton tan. I give three dollars an' thirty-five for these."

Mr. Usher licked his lips. He leaned against the side of a boulder and stared into the fire. "Was it really a bad blow, Steven?"

"It was real bad."

"Well — tell me this: when you see a lot of swallows together, is that a sign of a storm?"

Steve nodded affirmatively and dropped a piece of split cedar on the fire. The old man smiled, as if he knew his next question was to be boyish, but could not resist asking it.

"Was I any use to you — out there?"

Steve pushed his hat back on his head. He lowered his voice the merest trifle, then bent closer over the fire.

"I wisht they was all like you," he said. "Jesus, I do!"

# *Last Trip Together*

My old man laid there in his bunk in the cabin, an' the swamp robins never stopped singin'. First off, it hadn't seemed right for nothin' to be singin', but lookin' at it another way, I was glad of them robins goin' it. Maybe they remembered how he always loved their song an' thought he could hear it now. They was everywheres around in the woods by the lake. They made it seem like the old man might wake up pretty quick, an' say: "Web—hear them robins? Storm 'fore night. Better load me an' start."

It was twenty-eight mile to Privilege, an' I knew I ought to get a move on, but couldn't seem to. There was things of his in the cabin I couldn't bear to touch, things as much a part of the old man as his hands was: his paddle, his hewin' axe, his watch, an' the pen he wrote in the diary with.

Mr. Rogers, the New York sportsman that we built the cabin for, he wanted the diary kept regular, an' Father hadn't missed a day till this one. I went over to the table where the diary lay open with his pen in the middle of it. The date was May 21. I dipped the pen an' wrote down how it happened:

> Jim Rivers and son Web here since the ice cleared hewing sills and peeling spruce for the addition. He complained bein tired, said when we was done work he would lay abed the next morning to seven o'clock. Last nite we was all done, and this morning I couldnt raise him from sleep, as he must of past away durin the nite.
> We are leaving 8 a.m. bound for Privilege. Wind southwest, clear, temp. 58°. This entry by his son Web Rivers.

Father was heavy an' didn't handle good. I had to joggle him an' bump him 'round wrappin' him in the tarp, but I wrapped him fine'ly, an' toted him down to the shore an' laid him on the beach by my canoe.

I walked back to the cabin to close up an' get a few things. I got my tea boiler an' some tea, an' dippers for us to drink out of. I took my old man's paddle to use on the trip down. Seemed like if I used his paddle, he would be helpin' me, like all the other times.

I put everythin' inside the cabin that the porcupines might chew up. After I locked the door, I went down an' took the middle thwart out of my canoe so he could lay out straight. Then I loaded him an' started for the outlet.

It was our last trip together, an' in some ways the best we ever had. I could really be some use to him now, it seemed. All he'd ever showed me an' told me was clear in my head, an' I had to do the talkin' an' thinkin', an' make the decisions for the both of us.

Off Mink Carryin' Place, there come a blustery breeze. "Father," I says, tuggin' at his feet, "you come to the stern a little. She's bow-heavy." After he come back, she handled good in the cross-chop.

His paddle was sure a good one — thinned down at the handle an' throat, an' the blade edged so 'twould knife the water without a sound. Many's the dry doe we'd sneaked onto an' shot in closed time with him paddlin' with this very paddle, still as a cat on a cushion. He was a good woodsman, my old man was, an' he showed me everything I know.

At the outlet where the lake emptied into the Little Mopang River, I went ashore to cut a pole to set down river with. "You wait here," I says to him. "I won't be long."

I found a dry spruce, good an' springy, knotted it off smooth, an' we started again. On the quick water, I aimed to show him everything he had learned me. "Take the left channel, the way the water is," he seemed to say, an' he sure must of been proud, the way I handled her on Ellum Stump Rips, an' the Elbows, an' Hell's Gate. I was good that mornin', an' we made a fast run. I never realized how fast till we come to the long deadwater. I unwrapped the tarp an' took out his watch, an' it was only five minutes past ten. Twelve mile in two hours!

"It's too fast, Web, an' you ain't had no breakfast."

"That's so! I never thought about it. Where'll we boil her this noon, Father?"

"Same place."

"By that rock across Chancery Portage?"

"Yes, sir. That's where. It'll be out of the wind, an' we can see the lake there."

We come down lacin' the suds over the last pitch of rips, an' I throwed the pole away. It was all lake or deadwater from there, an' his paddle made the canoe jump. I lugged him across Chancery Portage, an' only set him down once when my heart got poundin' so I was scared it wouldn't hold out. But it made me 'shamed to set him down. "You used to lug me across when I was little. So now it's your turn, Father."

"But there ain't no hurry, Web. Take it easy, boy. We got all day."

When I come with him to the shore of the big lake, I looked out an' seen a black cloud in the northwest. I figured he was right about them swamp robins predictin' a storm, so I set him down comfortable agin' a big pine that would shelter him while I went back for the canoe. I had to take a little time puttin' the middle thwart back in, but she carried faster that way. The shower broke while I was on the way over, but I was dry under the canoe, an' I knowed he was all right there under the pine. I found him just as I left him.

I took my belt axe, split some kindlin' off a cedar stub, an' before I had a fire goin' the rain quit, an' it come off hot an' muggy. Flies commenced to hatch all along that shore, an' the big trout an' salmon come boilin' up two or three foot out of water. I never see such a sight in my life.

"I seen it like that just once before — on the west shore of Otter Lake." He'd told about that lots.

"Say, Father! If Mr. Rogers was here now with his friends, an' their fly rods!"

"You want to set that down in the diary. It's them things he wants set down there, Web."

The tea water boiled, an' I throwed in half a handful, let her boil up once more, an' set her to one side. I spilled in a little cold water, an' when the tea settled I poured the dippers full. I picked up my dipper, an' put it to my mouth an' said: "Wow! Jesus!"

"Hot, ain't it?"

While I was waitin' for it to cool, Father moved. I heard him, an' looked, an' he had slid a little way down the tree trunk, like somethin' had disturbed him. I looked all around to see what was wrong, an' seen my mistake. I had left his paddle layin' in the hot sun.

"Well, it was rainin' when I got the canoe over, an' I never thought," I says, an' shoved the blade in the water so it wouldn't warp.

"You want to keep them things in mind, Web."

After we'd had our tea, I took out the middle thwart again an' laid him out comfortable full length, an' shoved off for the last eight mile down lake.

It was a wonderful time durin' that last stretch, best we ever had. Everywheres on the shore of the big lake was places where things had happened to us, an' we got talkin' about 'em, an' laughin'.

"'Member in there back of Caribou Rock, an' us layin' quiet with a hindquarter, an'—"

"Yes, an' them two wardens in the canoe went by not two rod from us, an' never suspicioned."

Pretty quick we rounded Leadmine Point, an' there was an open place in the trees on shore. "That's where we was bark-peelin' two springs ago, an' them jeesely yellow jackets drove us to hell out, 'member?"

"Yes, an' it was right here—no, maybe farther north—where the squall hit that time. 'Member?"

"I never thought we'd make it that time, Father. Never thought we'd get ashore."

We were away offshore from Leadmine now, an' you could see just where the Injun Village was by the sun on the white cross on their church. I kep' lookin' over there a long time, till he said:

"Web, you keep clear of them young squaws boy, or you'll hate the smell of sweet grass the rest of your life."

I laughed, an' the sound set two loons to hollerin', an' then I said: "By God, Father! How'd *you* know about that?"

"You just mind what I tell you."

The loons hollered again, so I laid the paddle on the gunwales, wet my hands in the water, an' whistled to them. Then we started again, an' pretty quick the houses in Privilege come into view, dancin' a little in the distance across the water.

I leaned forward an' says: "What time is it?"

"You take my watch an' quit botherin' me."

So I took it out from his pocket, an' looked, an' it was only quarter past one. "Say, did you wind her?"

"I wound her last night. She's goin' all right."

"It ain't only quarter past one. I thought it must of stopped."

"No, time don't stop. It's the fastest we ever made it down, Web. It's too fast. You're beat out. Do like I say, now, an' slow down. There ain't no hurry."

My arms shook clear'n to the shoulders, an' my belly felt crawly, but I didn't feel played out to speak of. Still an' all, every time I give a rake with his paddle, I could hear the water sing along her bows, an' I guess we was travellin' fast.

When we got 'way down below Genius Island, I seen a man on the public landin' at Privilege. He begun to walk back up the hill, but turned an' seen our canoe comin', an' stopped in his tracks. I was maybe a quarter-mile or so away, but he stayed there watchin', like he seen somethin' queer.

There was a dog layin' in the sun on the landin', an' he stood up an' shook, an' looked, with his nose up high.

When I looked toward the hill again, the man was comin' back down to the wharf. He met another man, an' they come on down together. Some others come out of the boathouse, an' stood; an' two more that was on the dam come over an' stood.

For a minute, I couldn't figure what the trouble was. I says: "Quite a crowd gatherin' there, Father," an' never a sound from the old man.

Now, with them standin' there an' starin' on the landin', I knew. They stood there like crows around a wing-broke hawk, only they wasn't cacklin'. They was almighty still. I sided in to the landin', an' felt myself get dizzy, an' reached out an' grabbed the edge of the landin'. I got my balance, an' looked up into the faces of them God-damn devils standin' there. It was *them* made me see where he hadn't talked at all, an' how all the time it was just me answerin' my own self!

# Some Have to Get Hurt

You know how it is at a prizefight when the fighters are hitting each other hard. You can feel the blows hurting the fighters, but the blows can't hurt you. You're not fighting. It's the same at the theater. If there's a tragedy being enacted on the stage, you can feel it, but you can't get hurt except outside on your own street, in your own life. In the theater you're immune, and you're plenty safe. It's a swell feeling.

It was something like that the afternoon the squall broke over the lake. In my cabin on the shore I had a ringside seat. Before the spindrift shut out the view, I had convinced myself that the black speck off Munson Island was just a floating log, and not someone out there in a canoe in trouble, so there was nothing to worry about. My own canoe was tied to its rack. It couldn't blow loose. The power of the wind and the violence of the lake couldn't scare me, because they couldn't hurt me. They were part of the setting. So was the weird, shrieking wind-call of the loon.

The storm passed as quickly as it had come. The sky brightened. An unearthly stillness settled over the lake and the forest. And then, a little way offore, foundering in the heavy swells, I saw the canoe. So perhaps you are not safe unless those near you in your element are safe too. While they live, and while you live, there's obligation. I went down to the canoe feeling sick, knowing that the speck off Munson Island had not been a log, and knowing I was about an hour behind a tragedy.

In the canoe, which I dragged ashore, I found a fish, a whiskey bottle, and a boy. Water taken in over the gunwales had apparently revived the fish. It was still alive. The bottle was uncorked and empty. But you wouldn't have thought twice about the fish and the bottle. You would have thought only of the boy.

He was about twelve years old. He didn't quite know where he was or what had happened. He just stared like a sleepwalker, clinging to the canoe as if he thought it might perform a last, terrible gyration before annihilating him. I lifted him out and stood him on the beach.

"What happened?" I said. "Who was with you?"

His lips worked, but he couldn't speak. I kneeled beside him, and while he stared over my shoulder toward the lake, I rubbed the small of his back. His eyes had the look of twilight. You knew he was full of blurred memories. Something about him seemed to reach out. You wanted to see what his eyes had seen and feel what his heart had felt. You wanted to share the weight that seemed to be crushing him. You knew this boy had been in something bigger than a storm on a lake.

"You're safe, now," I told him. "You're all right. What's your name? Can you tell me your name?"

He answered almost inaudibly: "Chris—Christopher Blake." Then he smiled and added: "I'm Barney Blake's son."

He said this with a pride and sweetness that warmed you all the way through. You liked the boy's father, even without knowing him. Just from the tone of the son's voice, you formed a good picture of the father.

"Was your father with you today?" I asked.

"Yes."

"Where is your father, now?"

The boy's lips were all fixed to answer when, suddenly, the fish began thrashing in the water in the bottom of the canoe. It startled me, because I'd forgotten all about the fish. But the sound did something more than that to the boy. He stiffened, and memory came up darkly in his eyes, like an omen of returning dread. He pointed toward the fish and said: "Kill him. Please kill him. Kill him dead."

It was a strange thing for him to say, and he said it in a strange, dull voice. I was curious. I hesitated a moment, then picked up a piece of driftwood, stepped to the canoe, and tapped the fish on the head.

"There you are," I said. "That's a handsome bass. He's just about ready for the frying pan."

"Hit him again!" the boy cried out. His voice wasn't dull, now. It was wild. "Hit him some more! Smash him to pieces!"

I was astonished and a little bit unnerved. Brutality didn't belong in this boy. "What's the matter, Chris? I can't hit him again. He's dead. Can't you see that? He's dead."

The boy stumbled forward, and I caught him in my arms. "My father is dead, too," he wept. "My father — my father —"

"Your father, Chris? What makes you say that? What happened to him?"

He pressed his face against my chest, and his fingers twisted in my shirt. "I saw him sinking and drowning. I want him to be alive again. My father, oh, my father. It was because of the bass and the candy. Oh, that candy! I couldn't seem to help it. It was my fault."

I didn't say any more. I carried the boy up the path to my cabin and tucked him into a bunk. Pretty soon I would take him down to the village, but he seemed now to be deranged from shock. His reference to the candy and the bass didn't make any sense. They just seemed to come out of his agony.

He had quieted down a little. I felt him watching me while I whittled some tinder and started a fire in the stove. I made tea and brought it over to him. He followed every move with his twilight eyes.

Some eyes! They told so much that you didn't need to ask many questions. They shone out of the dark corner where he lay in the bunk, and they strung you so tight your imagination hummed. It was exciting just to watch him look around sizing things up and getting his bearings. He saw my traps and snowshoes hung from the rafters for the summer. Then he saw my fishing rod, and said: "It's a Landseer, isn't it?"

"That's right. How did you know? Not many people would recognize a Landseer."

He smiled, and his eyes filled with gladness. "My father knew about rods, and fishing, and everything. He showed me all about them, ever since I was little. Oh, boy. We certainly went a lot of places together."

When he talked this way about his father, you felt as if you'd inherited joy. It was easy to see the boy and his father together. You couldn't help seeing them. You followed them 'way back on one of their camping trips and heard them talking, like this:

"Dad, can I clean the fish and cook them, all myself?"

"Sure you can."

"And build the fire, too? And light it, and everything?"

"You bet. Be careful with the axe."

Then, in your mind, you saw the smoke of their fire and their white tent in a clearing. Pretty quick you saw night coming down around them, and the boy lying close to his father, and both of them staring up into the night sky.

"Dad, how high are the stars?"

"Millions and millions of miles. No one can imagine the distances to stars."

"Is Mother looking at the stars?"

"I'm pretty sure she is."

"I wonder what she's thinking about."

"I guess she's thinking about us."

"Why, Dad?"

"Because we're thinking about her. When you love people, you think about them, especially at night."

Suddenly, out of the starlight, a voice seemed to say: "If it could always be like this!" Maybe the boy said it, maybe the father. Maybe the mother said it. But maybe you just said it your own self, because when there is this kind of beauty, you want it to last forever, and all the while you know there's a shadow and a trouble waiting to spoil it. . . .

Actually, since I had lifted him from the canoe, the boy had said little. But in this other way he said so much! He set your imagination on fire, and you knew that the things you imagined were true to the lives of the father, the mother, and the boy.

Now, in the cabin, his thoughts had jumped an incredible distance from Landseer rods and fishing.

"Why does everyone have to die?" he said.

"I can't tell you, Chris. I don't know."

"My father didn't know, and my mother didn't either. I used to ask them, but they didn't know."

"There's some things no one knows."

He lay thinking for a moment, then asked: "Do you think it hurts very much to drown?"

"No Chris. I don't think so."

"Do people really have wonderful dreams when they're drowning?"

"I think they do. I think it's really true."

He was lying on his back, staring up at the rafters. All of a sudden his eyes filled with tears, and his throat began to work. "I wish I knew what my father dreamed," he said.

I couldn't say anything at all for a while after that. I went over and looked out the window, wondering just how it had happened, wondering about the bass and the candy, and what they had to do with it, and why the boy blamed himself. The lake was dead calm, peaceful in the sunset, but all I could see was the accident happening, and afterwards the boy lying alone in the canoe, the blown spray climbing around him, the waves high and white, and the canoe blowing wild.

I turned away from the window and started to put some wood in the stove. The boy was lying still, his eyes closed. I thought he was asleep, so I didn't touch the stove for fear of waking him. Instead, I got my bottle of whiskey from the shelf where it had stood untouched for three years. It wasn't a problem to me any more — the whiskey, I mean. But right now there was a hollow in me that a drink would fill. I took a little and put the bottle back. When I turned around, the boy was up on one elbow, his eyes shining and happy.

"I know what my father dreamed," he said. "I know, now! He dreamed of not wanting a drink!"

So that was the trouble waiting to spoil their happiness! I stood there as if my moccasins were nailed to the floor. I had clean forgotten the empty bottle in the canoe, and because of what I already knew of the boy's father, I couldn't believe that it had a bearing on the accident. I was to find out that it had — but not in the way you would naturally think.

What struck me now was the depth of this boy's understanding. He wanted to think of his father's having a last dream, and he wanted his father's dream to be beautiful. He knew, somehow, that to a man who is trying to stop drinking, a dream of not wanting a drink is beautiful.

I came over and sat on the bunk by his side. "Maybe that's what he dreamed," I said. "I used to dream that dream, once."

"But not any more?"

"No, not for a long time. It came true up here."

It was getting dark in the cabin, but you could still see the curiosity in his eyes. After a time he said: "Do people have to get hurt before they stop?"

"Some of them do, but it isn't their fault. It's the way they're made."

"My father said that. He said it to my mother one night in their room. I woke up and heard them talking. There was a chocolate bar beside my pillow. He always put one there when he came home late."

My mind started racing again, only this time it wasn't so much imagination. The story seemed to pour out of the boy's eyes. He kept referring to the night he had overheard his father and mother, and he gave hints of how he had first learned about his father's trouble, sticking in a name or a detail once in a while. From his voice and eyes you knew so much about his father and mother that you could almost hear them talking.

Now, out of some old corner of his memory, the boy said: "I caught a trout that day. It was a swell day by the brook. My mother had sandwiches, and we were all together."

"What day was that, Chris?" I asked him.

"The day Doc Morrison came up from the brook to see us, and my father said, 'No, thanks, Doc.'"

You didn't need to know any more than that. You had the whole scene, the mother sitting under a tree near the picnic basket and the father teaching the boy how to use a fishing rod. Orioles sang in the elms, and the brook talked among the stones of its bed. They were all happy there together, and there was no cloud until Doc Morrison waded toward them from the brook where he, too, had been fishing.

You knew all about Doc Morrison. He was like the other lucky ones — jolly, good-natured, big, and red-faced. He was full of friendship and compliments. Maybe he visited the family once a week, but he would greet them always as though he hadn't laid eyes on them in years.

"Ah! My dear girl, you're lovely as ever!" he'd say to the mother, and to the father: "Barney Blake! Barney, old pal, old pal. Certainly glad to stumble onto you folks. And little Chris, too. Some boy. Yes, sir! Tops!"

Maybe it was right then that Doc Morrison took a flask out of his fishing coat and waved it like a banner. The father and mother looked at each other, and the boy wondered why they looked that way.

"No, Doc — no, thanks," the father said.

"What's this, Barney, old pal? What's this you say to me?"

"No, thanks, Doc."

"Oh! So you can take it or leave it alone, eh?"

The father glanced quickly at the mother, and then he said to Doc Morrison: "I wish it was as simple as that."

So Doc Morrison's face got round, and serious, and full of understanding. He put his flask away. "I'm terribly sorry it's that way, Barney," he said. "All those other times I thought we were having fun together. But I didn't know how it was. I'm sorry."

Then, on that day by the brook bank, after Doc Morrison had gone, you saw the mother turn gay and sparkling as if a danger had moved back. You saw the boy looking curiously from his mother to his father, mystified by his father's danger because it was invisible, and troubled because he could not help his father by means of fists or a flung stone.

While this part of the story had been coming from the boy I had been sitting beside him in the dark. I stood up now and lit the lamp and stirred up the fire in the stove.

"Do you think you could eat a little something, Chris?"

"Yes."

"Afterwards, I guess we better go on down-lake to the village. Don't you think so, Chris?"

"Yes."

He had been dreading that trip, and so had I. He had been thinking how he would telephone to his mother, and what he would say, and the way her voice would sound after he told her.

I cut some bacon and put it in the frying pan. Pretty soon after the bacon began to sizzle, the boy got up from the bunk and walked over to the stove. He sat down on a bench I had hewed out of a spruce log. He drew up his knees and locked his elbows over them, resting his chin on his crossed arms. The lamplight carved dark hollows under his eyes, and sharpened the points of his cheekbones. He was watching me, but his mind was a long way off.

"I didn't eat the chocolate bar that night," he said. "If I wanted it, and didn't eat it, I would feel the way my father felt. He came almost home with me that night. But he let go of my hand and went back in the rain to see Jake and those other men in a place downtown."

He was referring again to the night he had listened to his father and mother talking. You didn't have to take much for granted. He said enough, in that strange way he had. He said it all.

You could see the boy and his father walking toward home in the rain. Maybe his father had stopped at a tavern — stopped just for a minute — and when he was like this, Chris was happy. There would be affection in the father's voice and the warm lift of life and confidence. His thoughts would come fast and beautifully worded, and Chris would know he could ask his father anything.

"Why did you marry Mother, Dad?"

"I fell in love with her."

"What is love like, anyway?"

"It's like having the answer to all the questions you ask yourself when you're looking at the stars. It's as if you looked into a person's eyes and asked her 'Why?', and she said to you, 'I am the answer. I am your reason for being alive and on this earth. Stop searching. You have found me, and I have found you.'"

As they walked along on the wet street of the town, the boy must have been wondering if he, too, would fall in love, and what the person would look like. And it must have been while he was wondering that some cheerful doors swung open, and a man rushed out on the sidewalk, hailing them with an avalanche of cordiality.

"Hi, Barney! Saw you through the window. Where have you been hiding these days? Come on inside out of the rain. Some great fellows in here I want you to meet."

You knew that Barney Blake drew people to him. They approached, as if to warm themselves in his warmth. But now, while the man expanded his welcome, you knew that Barney Blake was struggling. You knew that his hand closed hard over his son's hand, as he said to the man: "I guess I'd better not, Jake. Thanks a lot."

"Just one."

"I've already had one."

"One more, Barney."

"Not now, Jake. Maybe some other time. Maybe a little later."

So Jake stepped back to the doors, holding them open for an instant as he went through. There was a glimpse of a bright room and a row of pleasant men arranged at a bar. Heads turned. Faces gleamed. Inviting arms shot upward, and just before the doors swung shut, a voice called: "Hi, Barney! Where you going? What's the matter?"

As they turned into their own street, Chris must have believed for a little while that his father had won a victory, and that he, Chris, had in some way helped him. But his father was quiet. He wouldn't talk any more about love, and Chris stopped trying to make him.

Then, in the rainy dark in front of their house, Barney Blake suddenly and unexplainably let go his hold on the boy's hand.

"Go ahead into the house, Chris. Tell Mother, I'll be along. Tell her I—"

"Where are you going, Dad?"

"Downtown again."

"I thought you weren't going to do that."

"I thought so, too."

"I don't see why you have to go, Dad."

"I don't, either."

You saw them standing there, both of them bewildered. You saw the father's arm creep out hungrily and hug the boy around the shoulders. That was Barney Blake trying to tell his son that he loved him, that he didn't want to go back, but couldn't help going and didn't know why.

So Chris went on into the house and told his mother. You knew what she was like. She was already facing it straight. She was one of the cool, steady kind that would say: "Let's wait a while, dear. Supper isn't quite ready, anyway. Have you done all your homework?"

"Why don't you call him up, Mother?"

"No. I guess not. I guess I won't do that."

"Why? He's at that place by the hotel—the Shamrock."

"I think he'd rather I didn't call him."

"But we ought to help him! Something's wrong with him!"

"We are helping him—every single second."

"But how, Mother?"

"By loving him and believing in him during these times when he has lost faith in himself."

A long time later that night Chris woke up and heard his father and mother talking in their bedroom next to his. The rain had stopped, and their voices were lonely and frightened in the still night.

"Oh, Barney, how did it happen? Why did they let Jake drive the car when he was like that?"

"It might have happened anyway. The road was slippery. He couldn't make the turn."

"Was he hurt badly?"

"Yes."

"Are you sure you're not hurt, Barney?"

"I wish I was hurt. I wish I was hurt in some way that would make me stop. Why am I one of those who has to get hurt? Why can't I be like the other ones?"

"Barney, don't talk like that! I'm so frightened when you say that. You can't be hurt. I won't let you be hurt. I love you."

It must have been right after they stopped talking that Chris's hand touched the chocolate bar his father had left beside his pillow. He unwrapped the candy, put it to his lips, and then snatched it back. He lay in the dark stillness trying to multiply his longing for the candy. He multiplied by a hundred, a thousand, and a million. He wanted to feel as his father must have felt that time on the brook bank when he said to Doc Morrison: "No, Doc — no, thanks...."

You know how it is when someone you love is dead. You think of the last time you saw him, and what he said, and what you said. I guess the boy had been trying to stay away from that last moment when he saw his father in the water, but now, as we cleaned up the supper dishes in the cabin, he was getting closer to it. Perhaps he was thinking of what he would say to his mother on the telephone when we got down to the village at the foot of the lake.

"Well, Chris," I said to him. "How do you feel?"

"All right."

"I guess we better get going. What do you think?"

"I guess we better."

I got him an old jacket. It came down to his knees, and his hands disappeared in the sleeves. When I blew out the lamp he moved over close to me, and we walked down to the lake together and got in my canoe. He sat in the bow, facing me, the moonlight glowing over him, and his eyes on me every instant.

I kept close to shore, still-paddling the way the Indians do. The boy was quiet for a long time. Then, suddenly, when we were sliding past Caribou Point, he began telling me about the accident. Maybe he wanted to get it all straight in his mind for his mother, or maybe he wanted to talk it out with me because of my understanding of his father's trouble. His story came out in little bursts, and just once in a while I asked him a question.

"We always had a candy agreement on our trips," he said. "It was my idea. I thought it was a swell one, too."

"How did it work, Chris?"

"Dad said a boy ought not to eat too much candy between meals. So I agreed to eat a piece just only when I caught a fish."

They had got to Red Jackson's camps on the lake at three that afternoon, two hours before the squall. A little wind had already sprung up, but the black cloud was low down in the horizon to the northwest. They unpacked in the camp, and the boy's father took a drink of whiskey and left the bottle on the table when they went to their canoe at the wharf.

"I saw a fish swirl down there," Chris went on, "but the chocolate bars were up in the camp. Dad went to get them, and when he came back he brought the bottle with him. I guess he wanted it a million times more than I wanted the candy. Was he bad? Was my father bad because he wanted it?"

"No, Chris," I told him. "You never want to think of it like that. He was good. I know he was good."

The boy moved a little in the canoe, and some ripples spread out over the lake in the moonlight. He began talking again, his voice was young and clear.

"After we were on the lake, I thought of a plan to help my father. He took some more whiskey, and then it was time to tell him the plan. I said from now on he would get a drink out of the bottle only when I caught a fish. It was just like me with the chocolate bars. I told my father how we were both in it together, and I thought it would help him, because I didn't think there were many fish around, with the wind blowing so hard."

But pretty quick the boy and his father had come in their canoe into the lee of Munson Island. The wind quit roaring around them. The black cloud had climbed up hiding the sun, but they couldn't see the cloud. It was coming up fast behind the island, and the loons were shrieking their crazy, wild, storm call.

"All of a sudden," Chris went on, "a white perch jumped, and I was afraid I would catch him, but I got the fly away from him in time. There was a whole school of perch, and I wanted them, but I didn't catch any. They were wonderful ones, huge ones. But I could see their fins come out of water when they started for my fly, and I'd pull the fly up quick and miss them.

"Once or twice, when I almost caught one, I saw my father reaching behind him. He was doing something with the bottle. I guess he was getting ready, so he could have a drink when I caught a perch. But I didn't dare look at him much. I had to keep missing those perch; they were wonderful ones, too, but I didn't even catch one, and I guess my father thought I wasn't fishing very well. When the perch all went away into deep water, I looked at my father, and he had the strangest expression on his face. He was smiling, but his eyes were — they were —"

"They were what, Chris?" I asked him.

"Well, they were wonderful, but not happy. I never saw him look that way. I never saw anyone look that way."

Now, listening to the boy, you suddenly knew something that he didn't know. You knew what had happened inside his father. You knew that Barney Blake realized exactly what his son was trying to do. Barney Blake must have added it all up, right then — all the misery and heartbreak, all the chances he had taken with the two people who loved him most and had faith in him when he didn't have any in himself. He added it up and told himself the right answer in that instant when he saw his son giving up everything he loved in order to help him.

A few minutes after the perch had disappeared, Chris raised a big bass near some lily pads on the point of Munson Island. Just beyond the point in the open lake the waves were running white and wild, but they didn't notice it especially.

You saw them there together, each intent on the other, thinking of the other, the father with that strange look on his face, and the boy tense, fearful that he would catch the bass. You felt as Chris must have felt when the big bass came to his fly. You knew how he wanted the bass, with all his hot boy-longing. And when he snatched his fly away, his father said, "Cast again, Chris."

Chris cast again. He cast deliberately in the wrong spot, and his father said, "That isn't where he was, Chris. He was over near the lily pads. Go ahead and catch him."

"Heck, Dad. He won't come again. He was only a little one, anyway."

"He's a beauty, Chris. I never saw a better one anywhere. Go ahead and cast near the lily pads. It's all right, Chris. I want you to have him."

So Chris, not knowing what had already happened to his father, gave in to his own hot boy-longing and hooked the bass. When the canoe came around the point into the open lake, the wind hit them with a cold, quick pressure. Barney Blake couldn't hold the canoe into it, but he wanted Chris to have the bass.

It may have taken Chris ten minutes to play the bass on his light rod out there in the wind, and when his father slipped the net under the fish and flopped him into the canoe, the squall was nearly on them. But Barney Blake knew they could ride out the squall lying down in the canoe. Right now, he had something he wanted to say to his son, but he didn't get a chance to say it. All he said was, "Chris! That's a wonderful bass! Look at him, Chris! I want you to be glad you caught him. Are you glad, Chris?"

Then Chris looked miserably at his father and said: "I guess you won a drink, Dad!"

When Barney Blake reached around to get the bottle, a big wave heaved under the canoe, and the landing net rolled off the gunwale. He grabbed for the net, and another wave pitched against the canoe. He lost his balance and went overboard.

It all happened in a second, and it changed everything. He came up and caught the gunwale with his hands. Chris grabbed him by the arm, and his father said: "Don't do that! We'll upset her. Lie down, Chris. There's going to be a big wind."

"Get back in, Dad! Can't you get in?"

Barney Blake tried to climb in over the gunwale, but it was hard with the big waves knocking the canoe around. He might have done it, but he didn't want to take the chance. He couldn't hold onto the gunwale much longer, either. His weight tipped the canoe in the combers, and one of them crashed in over the gunwale, drenching the boy. Barney Blake was afraid that he might swamp the canoe.

"Chris, listen to me. Lie down flat and don't move. You'll ride it out all right."

"Dad! What are you going to do?"

Barney Blake knew what he was going to do, and he did it. He did what every man would want to think of himself as doing. He did what a man would always hope to do and dream of doing. He let his fingers slide off the gunwale, and the canoe blew free in the gale. In a second, the canoe was twenty yards away.

"Lie flat!" he yelled once more. "Don't move!"

Chris peeked over the gunwale and saw a huge wave break over his father. He saw his father come up swimming, saw him make a downward motion with his hand. Chris saw his father's lips move. He knew his father was telling him again to lie down, but he couldn't hear anything but the roaring of the wind and the crashing of the seas around him. Then the blown spray came up off the lake like a white curtain, covering his father, and that was all Chris knew or remembered till he got ashore on the beach in front of my cabin.

Now, in this still moonlit night, as I was paddling the boy down to the village, it was hard to imagine there had ever been a storm. The islands looked lonely, part of another world, and a thin mist lay along one shore.

Only when you looked at the boy's face did you remember the storm and what it had done to him. Telling about it had hurt him, and he was crying softly.

"I wish I hadn't caught that darn bass," he said. "I wanted to help my father, but I guess I didn't help him at all."

I looked away at the lights of the village for a time. Then I said: "Chris, let me tell you something. He knew what you were doing when you began missing those perch. He knew why you were doing it, and that's what helped him. He wasn't going to take a drink after you caught that bass. He had already taken his last drink, and he knew it. He was just going to show you the empty bottle. He'd poured it out in the lake. That's what he was doing when you saw him reaching around, while you were missing the perch."

"Do you think so?" the boy asked.

"I know it. The bottle I found in your canoe was uncorked and empty."

We didn't talk anymore till we got to the canoe landing at the village. But I was thinking how it is that some have to get hurt, and how it must have hurt Barney Blake when he was watching his son out there in the lee of Munson Island. And I thought how bad it was that this good man, his father, had to get hurt so hard it killed him, and how in that last moment he didn't even think once about himself, but just about his son.

At the canoe landing, Chris said, "I haven't got any money to telephone. Have you got any?"

"Sure. Don't worry about that."

"It might cost a dollar."

"That's all right."

We went up to the store where the old men were sitting. They had probably started their talk about today's storm, but now they were telling about storms that had happened forty years ago. Chris stood just outside the telephone booth, facing the door, while I put in the call for him. They had trouble getting the call through. I guess some poles had blown down.

But while I was waiting, I saw something happen that made my knees shake. I was watching the boy when suddenly his face turned ash white. He swayed, and took a half-step forward. Out of the whiteness of his face his eyes burned like a dark, blue flame, and all the old men in the store got still. I knew who the boy was looking at. It couldn't have been but one person.

My voice must have sounded crazy, like someone yelling in a library, when I said to the operator: "Never mind. Let it go. Just let it go."

They were standing looking at each other, the father in the doorway of the store and the boy by the telephone booth. They were white-faced and frightened, each thinking he had killed the other, each thinking he was maybe dead himself and in heaven with the other. They never said a word—not a word. Maybe they didn't think it was real. Maybe each was waiting for the other to vanish. Then, suddenly, the father, Barney Blake, walked slowly and kissed his son on the mouth, the way his mother would have kissed him.

The boy kept reaching out for his father and feeling of him, the long sleeves of that old jacket bothering him, because he couldn't get his hands outside where he could touch his father.

"Hi, Dad," he said, in a thin voice. He had to know if it was real, if his father was real, and if he was real.

"Hello, Chris."

"Are you okay, Dad?"

"Yes. Are you all right?"

"Sure, Dad. I'm all right."

Before I went back up to my cabin that night I found out how it happened; how Jim Blanket, the Indian, had sighted them in trouble off the point of Munson Island; how old Jim had gone in the Forest Patrol boat, holding her straight downwind when the spindrift hid everything from view, and how he had come sliding through it almost straight to the boy's father struggling in the water. Barney Blake was almost done in, and old Jim had taken him back to the Forest Service camp on the mainland. Afterwards they had gone in the boat hunting for the boy, but they hadn't seen his canoe on the beach by my cabin, because they had come onto that shore a half-mile below.

So I went back up lake that night in that wonderful calm moonlight feeling pretty good. But I wished I had got hurt like Barney Blake. I wished I could have got hurt just a little sooner, before it busted up my family. My own son would be about two years older than Chris was. I wondered what he looked like now. I hadn't seen him for three years, and I wondered if he was a swell kid, like Chris. I wondered if it was all right now for me to go back again and start over, and if they would want me. And I wondered if my son had ever wanted to help me, the way Chris wanted to help his father. I guess he had wanted to, all right.

# *The Last Hermit of the Maine Woods*

Toward nightfall of a bitter January day, while hunting bobcats on Webster Stream with his dog, Dixie Two-Spot, Fred Harrison made an unlucky step over a spruce blowdown and broke a snowshoe bow. The mishap—one that all lone woodsman dread—occurred near the mouth of Hudson Brook, a remote and desolate spot even for northern Maine.

Fred's cabin on Hudson Pond was four miles away. It would be hard going even for Dixie Two-Spot, whose four paws were webbed with winter hair. But Fred Harrison was a man with one snowshoe. He might as well have been without legs. In the zero cold, sinking to his belt at almost every step, Fred knew that the miles to his cabin would multiply to an incalculable agony.

The snow was over three feet deep, soft and drifting. Darkness had fallen over the Maine wilderness. Fred was alone. He had been alone most of his adult life. But as the northern lights began their eerie dance across the sky, he had never been lonelier.

He flipped off his mittens, untied the lampwick binding of the broken snowshoe, and dropped it in the snow. Standing one-legged on the other web, he called in his big, orange-and-black spotted hound, and said:

"Dixie girl, it's trouble."

Then, with Dixie a few steps in the lead, the hermit of Hudson Pond began a journey all but foredoomed. The single snowshoe was more hindrance than help, and he soon discarded it. Near Webster Stream, Fred caught hand holds on the slender, pick-pole spruces, pulling himself up and along. But on the beech ridge, where the wind moaned in the frozen dark, he sank, wallowing, wrenching his back and thigh muscles, squandering his strength in the white mire.

His track was a grotesque zigzag, his progress a series of contortions. At first, whenever he fell, Dixie Two-Spot came to lick his face. But as he tired, he fell more often, not really falling, but leaning, letting himself sink down to rest. It took him longer and longer to get up, and Dixie ranged farther ahead and, finally, just lay on the snow, waiting.

Halfway up the ridge, Fred stopped on a bare spot under a big pine. He decided to build a fire while he had the strength. He would rest by its warmth. If he didn't, he would fall again and again, sinking down on his knees, and there would be a final fall, the everlasting one.

Fred kicked some dry twigs together. But when he tried to unscrew his metal match safe, he found that his fingers wouldn't work. His hands were bare, his fingers numb and useless. He had left his mittens where he'd dropped them on the bank of Webster Stream! Why? Why had he made that fatal step on the blowdown? Why had he picked this ill-starred day to go cat hunting? It was a chain of errors and accidents linking toward disaster.

Fred was in a trap unwittingly contrived by himself. He knew it. He acknowledged it. The land he loved, the wilderness he had worshipped all through his hermit life, was now about the remorseless business of killing him dead.

The last half of Fred's journey was a nightmare under northern lights. I have heard him tell the story many times, and it is not fiction. It is the record of an invincible human spirit against inhuman odds.

There was always the creep of numbness, with its lethal invitation to lie down and go to sleep. He invented schemes to stay awake, goals to lure himself on. He courted hallucinations that at the time seemed lucid and life-sustaining. He imagined a pint of whiskey, amber and warm in the lamplight on the windowsill in his cabin. This goal gave him strength to reach the top of the ridge. Then, suddenly, the lamp went out and the whiskey vanished.

Why was it gone, Fred asked himself? Who took it? The theft was the work of Fred Walker, of course! And Charley Mahar! And Pat Steen! These men were his friends, but in the fantasy they became devils. They were all in his cabin, stealing his whiskey, drinking, laughing, and warm.

In reality, Fred Walker was twenty miles away in a cabin below Mattagamon Dam. Charley Mahar was at Trout Brook Farm. Pat Steen was at remote Black Brook. But Fred's hallucination bunched them all in his cabin, and a dream of vengeance drove him on, while the disillusionment of his friends turning against him was a power of itself.

When at last Fred stumbled onto his cabin porch, it was near midnight. He had been almost eight hours making the four miles. Dixie Two-Spot whined and nuzzled the cabin door. Fred kicked the door open and stood glaring at the dim, starlit interior. There was no Charley Mahar, no Fred Walker, no towering Pat Steen — no whiskey. There was nothing but the lonely vapor of his own breath.

His match supply was in a pint mason jar. He knocked the jar off its shelf and broke it. Holding a bunch of matches between his numbed fists, he managed to light them and start a fire in his stove. Life returned to his fingers. He crawled under the blankets on his bunk. Dixie Two-Spot curled up beside him, and they slept the clock around.

In the fifteen years I knew Fred — from 1946 till the time of his lonely death in 1961 — I must have walked twenty round trips with him from his cabin to the mouth of Hudson Brook, the same trail as the one of his nightmare journey. But we were on spring fishing trips to Webster Stream or bird hunting trips in October. They were joyful expeditions. On the way back to the cabin one time, Fred stopped under a big pine, and said:

"Here's where I was going to build a fire that night."

It was a spring day, still and warm. Our baskets were heavy with Webster Stream trout. Snow and cold were long gone, but Fred's eyes were haunted with the memory.

"What year was it, Fred?" I asked. "You mentioned lampwick snowshoe bindings. I haven't seen them for ages."

"It must have been the early thirties. A few of us old woods roamers were still using lampwick, even then."

Fred took a faded, age-yellowed snapshot from his wallet and handed it to me.

"There she is," he said. "Dixie Two-Spot. I think of her every time I walk this trail."

Even from the inexpert photograph, you could tell that Dixie had been a fond and able creature.

"Some old girl," he said. "She got me over thirty cats."

"What happened to her, Fred?"

As he returned the wallet to his pocket, a strange look troubled his pale, blue eyes. And he answered:

"I shot her."

"*Shot* her!" I said aghast. "Why? An accident?"

"No. She took to chasing deer."

It's the law, written and unwritten in Maine, that deer-chasing dogs must be confined or shot. It's part of a game warden's job. Had Fred elected to do the job himself, rather than let a game warden do it? In those days, he didn't see a warden twice a year. I couldn't quite understand it. I kept seeing the picture of Fred and Dixie sleeping the sleep of all-out exhaustion that night in Fred's bunk.

And now, under the big pine, there was that troubled look in Fred's eyes. It was the look of a kindly man remembering the performance of a brutal duty. In view of what finally happened to Fred, and to another dog, years later, the look in Fred's eyes may have been significant, perhaps even prophetic.

I don't know, because it's hindsight. I can only guess. And how can anyone guess the thoughts and motives of a hermit? You think you know a man. But do you, really? What makes him a hermit in the first place? And what is it like to live alone in the wilderness?

These questions are fascinating, because nearly everyone, at one time or another, has dreamed of being a hermit. Why? What is the appeal? You beat the rap of civilization. Yes. You are independent. Yes, practically. Living is cheap, and money no prime object. You live on bobcat bounties and proceeds from the fur you trap. You do a little guiding, if you happen to like the individual sportsmen who ask for your services. You make your own laws. Outside of loneliness, your only enemy is Nature, which, conversely, is your dearest friend.

"In the woods," said Emerson, "we return to reason and faith."

But most of us would lose both if we stayed there long enough. Fred Harrison lived in the woods for forty-five years. And he died there.

I first met Fred in 1946 when my wife and I were building a cabin home on the roadless, north shore of Mattagamon Lake — twelve airline miles east of Hudson Pond. One bright September afternoon we looked up from our labors with axe and crosscut to see a canoe land at our dock. A man in a black-and-white-checked shirt and moccasins stepped ashore, and we went down the path to greet him. His hair was a fringe of silver, his crinkled eyes a pale, cornflower blue. He was about five feet nine, in splendid physical condition, and he stepped over the rough ground without even noticing it.

"I'm Fred Harrison," he said, as we shook hands. "I thought I'd call and see how you're getting along."

We had already heard a lot about Fred. It was all good, and we told him so.

"You're the hermit of Hudson Pond," my wife said.

Fred looked pleased, as he said:

"That's what they call me."

We sat on the cabin porch among the yellow, sweet-smelling spruce chips. Fred rolled and lighted a cigarette; in his low, quiet voice he told us of the tame deer in his dooryard, of how the trout were biting in Hudson Pond, of the foliage changing, and of partridge and woodcock plentiful. He told of digging out his spring and walling it with rock, and building a springhouse of peeled spruce logs. He made you want to see it, and to see the wild land where he lived, wilder even than our own cabin site.

We asked Fred to stay for supper and the night. He said he couldn't, this time. He had borrowed the canoe from the Eastern Corporation Lumber Camp across the lake, and the The Birdman was meeting him at the Eastern Landing to fly him back to Hudson. The Birdman is Elmer Wilson, one of the early Maine bush pilots based at Shin Pond.

"It's sure easier with the plane," Fred said. "I used to walk it — forty miles to Patten."

We went down to the dock to see him off. His worn Duluth knapsack rested in the bottom of the canoe. He opened it and took out a pint jar of wild mushrooms, another of wild strawberry jam, and two beautiful trout wrapped in wet moosewood leaves. He had canned the mushrooms and berries himself, and the trout were from his own pond that morning. He'd caught them expressly for us.

"For your supper," he said, shoving off into the lake. "You people come and see me. Come anytime. We're neighbors."

In the years that followed, we visited back and forth four or five times a year. Fred took us on fishing trips to Webster Stream, Snake Pond, Carpenter, Coffeeloss, Telos, Haymock, and all the far-back places.

The Birdman "tended out" on both Fred and us. On his routine flights he'd make a mail drop or check in to see if we were all right. Through him, we'd trade messages with Fred. So we'd get the word:

"Fred says Webster Stream is hot. Pack up and come."

Or: "Fred reports four flocks of pa'tridge on the Webster tote road. Eight or ten to a flock. Get your gun."

And we'd take off for Fred's cabin and walk the old tote roads in the brilliant fall foliage, miles from nowhere.

The Birdman had a canoe hidden in the dense spruce on the shore of

Fourth Lake Mattagamon. Why anything needed hiding on that isolated lake I never knew. No one ever went there but Fred Harrison and us.

We would fly-cast from the canoe, sometimes Fred paddling, sometimes I. Those Fourth Lake trout were dark and fat, their meat the color of a desert sunset. Come noon we'd light a fire between two rocks, skewer the trout on black birch skewers, broil them, and eat them with our fingers.

When the weather was hot, we trolled a "beer line" astern. This was twelve feet of cuttyhunk, a bottle of beer tied in every two feet or so to cool in the depths. When one of us took a good trout, we'd haul in the line, untie the tail bottle, and pass it back and forth. It made life seem luxurious and complete.

It must have been on Fourth Lake that we first heard Fred sing his famous drinking song. I thought I'd heard them all, but this was an original; and I can see Fred's wrinkled grin, his cigarette pulled over to one side of his lips so the smoke wouldn't sting his eyes. I can hear his words, as he sang them:

> Oh, I'm canned up in the sunshine,
> I'm canned up in the rain.
> I'm canned up in the morning,
> And the nighttime just the same.
> Oh, no little can can carry
> This happy jag of mine,
> For I'm ever being canned up.
> I'm canned up all the time.

We learned words and tune, then worked up some harmony and close, blues chords; and we sang that song on our cabin porches when we were visiting one another—and on all the lakes and rivers in that part of wilderness Maine we were competition for the loons.

When friends visited at our cabin, the highlight of their stay was a fishing or bird-hunting trip with Fred. It got to be a tradition. Our longtime friend Lew Bement, from Massachusetts, must have flown in to Fred's cabin eight or nine years in a row. Returning from one of his first trips, Lew stepped out of the plane, came on up the path with a basket of trout, and, after the plane had gone, said, "What a day!"

"You had good luck," I said, counting five Hudson Brook trout lying on the green moss in Lew's basket.

"Sure," said Lew. "But I'm thinking of a story Fred told me about breaking a snowshoe bow and walking four miles one winter night. And about his dog, Dixie Two-Spot. Some story!"

"Did he tell you what happened to Dixie?"

"He did. And he showed me her picture. We were resting halfway up the ridge toward Fred's cabin. It was under a big pine."

There was something uncanny about it. I can't determine why. Maybe the old pine was a strong association with Dixie and the frozen miles through the night. Or maybe, even then, it had begun to prey on Fred's mind. No one will ever know for sure. He had a few dogs after Dixie but gave them away. There were many years when he had no dog at all. He had none while we knew him—not until the last year of his life.

One of the pleasing things Fred did was to name trout pools on Webster Stream for our friends that he particularly liked. We deemed it a considerable honor to have fishing adventures thus commemorated. There was Shumway Pool near The Freezout, where the Shumways took a limit one morning. There was Lew Bement Pool at the outlet of Webster Lake. And a couple of turns below the old Webster Dam there was a dark, foam-flecked pool where I took a two-pounder on a Fanwing Greenwell's Glory one sultry afternoon while playing host to a thousand black flies. Fred named it Ed Smith Pool, and I basked in the honor—till the spring of the big rains and high water, when Ed Smith Pool got filled with gravel and was gone forever.

Fred's cabin was built and located to the specifications of your boyhood dream of being a hermit. It nestled in heavy fir growth a few yards from a big, gray ledge on the shore of Hudson Pond. Fred built it of peeled fir and spruce. A trapdoor in the floor opened to a small, earthen cellar. The walls were chinked with moss. There were two bunks, a stove, a table, and benches. The stovepipe came up through the roof to one side of the ridgepole, and the roof itself was covered with sweet-smelling cedar shingles that Fred had split with mallet and frow.

His cabin smelled as a cabin should—of sunlight, cedar, soap, coffee, and the smoke-scent accumulated from uncounted fires in the wood stove. Fred cut and split about ten cords of rock maple each year.

"The years were B.C.," he used to say, "meaning, 'before chainsaws.'"

His traps hung on the front outside wall of the cabin under the narrow porch roof. There were cedar stretchers for fox, mink, and otter. On a sidewall you could see heavy claw marks where a bear had tried to get inside for a go at Fred's molasses supply.

The inside of the cabin reflected Fred's life and personality. On wall pegs or crotches of peeled spruce he had fashioned, you saw his fly rod, his Winchester carbine, his Luger pistol. You saw a pair of ash snowshoe bows, bent and ready for shaping and filling; his tools—axe, frow, crooked knife, crosscut saw, bits and brace; a jar of beaver castor, another of trout oil; his provisions neatly stacked on shelves; the two bunks made up with gray blankets.

Behind the cabin was Fred's garden patch, with a high fence of spruce poles to fend the deer; and beyond the garden the trail led across the clearing to the cold spring, up over the hardwood ridge and on down to Webster Stream.

Flying over Hudson, headed for Telos Dam or Chamberlain Lake, we sometimes looked down to see Fred in his canoe, or sitting alone on his ledge, fishing. When it was cold, we'd see the smoke from his stovepipe, blue and lonely over the fir tops, and we'd think of Fred down there on the bench by his stove, listening to the guy wires of his stovepipe singing in the wind. And if a white towel showed on the ledge, it was Fred's signal for The Birdman to land.

Fred was born in 1890 somewhere in Ohio and as a young man had worked in New York State apple orchards. The only two towns he ever mentioned specifically were Toledo and Elmira. We asked him what had made him choose northern Maine for his hermitage site? His answer was that he had read about it in a trapping magazine.

"Aren't the winters pretty long, Fred?"

"Yes. But in spring you forget them."

One fall, after shuttering our cabin, with Fred helping us close up for the season, we loaned him our battery radio. The next spring, he told us how he'd followed a soap opera, got acquainted with all the characters and then, in the midst of some heartrending climax, the battery had gone dead.

"I put my ear right close to the radio," he said, "trying to hear a last word, but it died out to nothing, and the light went out."

That must have been one of the loneliest moments in his life—more poignant, if not as disastrous, as the broken snowshoe bow. You can almost hear the silence of the radio, and feel it spreading through the cabin, and into the hermit's heart.

"You ought to get another dog," I said.

Fred reached for his tobacco and papers and shook his head.

"I guess I never will," he said.

But he did. Something like thirty years after Dixie Two-Spot. Three decades. A long time between dogs.

Some accredited Maine college or university should have given Fred Harrison an honorary degree—say, Doctor of Woods Lore, or an L.N.D., which would stand for Doctor of Natural Laws. He was all but self-sufficient, living off the land as completely as anyone could. He canned wild mushrooms, berries, fiddlehead ferns, his own garden produce, and trout, partridge, and venison. In fall, his earthen cellar was abundant with these Fruits of Nature.

He knew fur animals and their habits. He knew deer by constant association with them. He knew trout. He caught them generally with a fly he tied himself with partridge feathers and black thread unraveled from an old sock. We called it "Harrison's Fancy."

Sometimes it was months between his trips out to the town of Patten for supplies and companionship. He would stay a few days or a week. And one morning he would say, "It's time I took for the woods."

And then The Birdman — or, in recent years, Ray Porter — would fly him in to Hudson.

After we gave up our Mattagamon cabin and moved to southern Maine, we saw less of Fred; but we kept in touch on return trips to our old haunts and sometimes met him in Patten. There would be an avalanche of reunion and a full tide of reminiscence. And then a couple of years passed when we didn't see Fred at all.

We heard from mutual friends that he was beginning to show his age, always talking of the past. And we heard that he had got himself a dog. The Birdman's wife, Nola, told us. We decided to fly in to visit Fred and his new companion in the morning. But the weather socked in and we never did.

We never saw Fred Harrison again.

In late May of 1961, while on a fishing trip to South Branch Ponds in Baxter State Park, I crossed trails with Game Warden Sherwood Howes, an old friend. As we chatted about Fred, trading tales of woods adventures with him, neither of us knew that he lay dead in the waters of his beloved pond. No one knew it till ten days later when bush pilot Ray Porter, on a routine check flight, found him by the old, gray ledge where he had sat so many hours in the sun.

Fred had died by his own hand. Ray found the suicide note in Fred's cabin. The note stated that he had taken his own life because he had killed his dog for chasing deer. It indicated that his act was one of strange, confused atonement.

For an instant, after learning the circumstances of Fred's death, I seemed to be back under the big pine on the trail from Webster Stream, with Fred showing me the yellowed snapshot of another dog. It was an instant of loneliness and of a sense of mystery and sadness.

But there is no sadness in the Fred Harrison so many of us know and remember. He was seventy-one when he died. But still living is the spirit of a gay and talented companion of the wilderness — the last hermit of the Maine woods.

# Part THREE

*These, having not the law, are
a law unto themselves*

Romans II Fourteen

# *Old Lady in Waiting*

The old lady was a Catholic, and when she thought of the church nothing was unendurable — not even the cruelty of the wilderness before the coming of spring. As a girl she had dreamed of attending services in the cathedral of Notre Dame, in Paris. She knew all about Notre Dame. It was said to be on an island in the river Seine. The ceiling arched to unguessable heights, mystic in the twilight of stained glass, dusky with the smoke of candles, and haunted with the yearning of ancient prayers.

Realizing as she grew older that she would not see Notre Dame, she had reefed her vision for the nearer view — the shrine in the province of Quebec. But when she knew she was never to set foot in St. Anne de Beaupré, she found consolation in a postcard showing the lighted cross on Mount Royal, farther south.

Now that the old lady had come so late in life to this wild, merciless land, she could worship only at rare intervals. Thus the thing she loved most was all but denied her. At sixty-seven, there remained for old Sarah, wife of Zack Bourne, the slab church in the Indian Village on the lakeshore; and until the ice cleared, even that was unreachable.

At one time, Sarah had been Mrs. Patrick O'Mahoney, and had lived in a Boston suburb, where within walking distance were a dozen stone churches. During Holy Week, immediately following Mr. O'Mahoney's death, she had attended mass at all twelve. Shortly after her first husband was buried, Sarah had gone into housework. She had been at it forty years when, with tumult and with shouting, Zachariah Bourne came into her life.

Zack Bourne was a widower of about Sarah's age. Sarah had met him while he was carpentering on an addition to the home where she cooked. Zack was many things besides a carpenter. He was tall, stooped, and mammoth-handed. He was boisterous, kindly, profane, bold, honest, and a giant. When his wrist was infected from the stab of a rusty nail, Sarah had prayed for him. Zack was no Catholic, but the prayer worked. He recovered, married Sarah, and took her off with him—back to the wilderness whence he had come.

Returning to the lakes and forests as caretaker of Mr. Reuben Usher's cabin was to Zack Bourne like an unexpected opening of the gates to heaven. He was on the verge of thanking God, when he remembered to congratulate *himself.* Along the Mopang watershed were many of Zack's boyhood friends—Ap Ireland, father of Steve, Jeff Coongate, the one-eyed poacher, old Joe Keegan, and others. But to Sarah, who had never been far from the city, the pilgrimage to the north was a strange and terrible experience.

When Mr. Usher voiced doubts of Sarah's strength to withstand the loneliness and the deadly waiting for spring, Zack had replied, "Mr. Usher, never you fear. Old Sarah's tougher'n a link of boom-chain."

"But I was thinking also of emergencies, Zack. What of sickness in the winter?"

"She'll pray her way out, like a snowplow bustin' through a drift." Gesturing with his slablike hands, Zack had offered irrefutable proof: "Why, God damn it, Mr. Usher—one time a cousin o' hern took sick in San Francisco, an' Sarah lit a few candles, kissed the daylights out of her crucifix, an' prayed her cousin back to life three thousand mile away."

"Are you a Catholic, Zack?"

"Me? Hell, no—but I believe in it."

In the beginning, Sarah felt that anyone living in this ruthless country must be an escaped convict or have some other sinister reason for renouncing a paved world. Four or five seasons passed before she accustomed herself to the visits of the savage, one-eyed Mr. Coongate, who cursed more fluently even than Zack, and threatened the lives of game wardens near and far. But Uncle Jeff called Sarah by her first name immediately after introduction, and in time quelled her fears with flaming compliments on her cooking, crocheting, and choice of husbands.

"Why, Sarah," said the outlaw, "—anyone that'd marry that old tomcat's pratickly noble."

After that, Zack and Jeff had thumped each other on the back, scuffled a little, and settled down to exaggerating Mopang log-drive adventures, and their own personal superiority from childhood to the present.

Gradually and foggily it came to old Sarah that her giant of a man was actually gentle. He blasphemed, and laid roaring plots against his enemies, but he loved the loons nesting in the cove. He grew sentimental over the bald eagles in the sky, and tolerated the old does who cautiously ate all the lettuce in the garden in the summer.

Whenever Uncle Jeff stopped by on his illegal moose hunts, he and Zack lay in the grass devising fiendish tortures for any game warden that came to mind.

"We could take an' tie Tom Corn in his canoe," Jeff said, once, "an' anchor it in a hundred foot of water off Headworks Island. We'd come by in our canoe ever' hour or so, an' heave rocks into the warden's canoe—jest a few to a time, till it sunk, an' him tied in it."

Uncle Jeff closed his one eye blissfully, but Zack had objected to the scheme. "It'd be a shame to waste a good canoe on a warden, even his own."

"Well, we could locate her by the bubbles."

"No, I got a better way," Zack said, earnestly. "We'd wait till the height of fly time, the almighty peak of it. Then we'd tie him bare-nekkid with haywire between two trees, with the wire looped around his neck, an' a turnbuckle rove in. We'd come by when we was a mind to, an' give that turnbuckle jest a little tightenin'—"

"Till his eyes podded out!" sighed Uncle Jeff, in ecstasy.

"By God, yes—an' look: once a day we'd feed him a crust of bread."

"Buttered with—"

Sarah had approached to announce that she was dishing up, and they had better come to the table. Rising, the two assassins exchanged glances of mutual understanding. *They* knew how they would butter the warden's crust.

Sarah no longer lived in terror that they would execute their conspiracies. She had had wardens to meals many times in the last six years. Hadn't Zack talked and joked with young Tom Corn, the very warden he claimed to hate to death? Zack had made Tom a new axe handle, urged a hot mince pie on him, and helped him launch his canoe. After Tom paddled away, Zack had showed signs of being lonely for him, saying, "He's a good fellow, the son-of-a-bitch. Mighty able an' square, that young Tom Corn. He knows damn well there's moose meat in that pie-fillin'. I hope he fly-blows, an' rots out—but I wisht he'd come back soon."

Merely to be on the safe side, Sarah continued to pray God to stay the murderous hands of Jeff Coongate and her husband. She beseeched Him to reduce the percentage of Zack's swearing, and to prevent his playing cribbage on Sundays. Once, during Lenten season, Zack had gone two whole days without smoking. Feeling that the spirit of righteousness had at last steamed its way into him, Sarah complimented Zack for his sacrifice. But, irritable from the itch to feel a hot pipe bowl in his fingers, Zack had turned on her, fuming: "Lissen, ole lady: I done it to please you, not to please God."

Before freeze-up, as the seventh winter faced them, Zack sent Sarah back home to visit her old friends. She was gone six unbearable weeks. In his loneliness, Zack worked in a kind of fury. He cut wood in the clearing, and while he chopped and sawed, he planned surprises to gladden Sarah's return. From the catalog he ordered a new cook stove, and a radio and battery. He laid congoleum on the kitchen floor, rechinked the cabin, and banked the sills with spruce boughs.

To Zack's two hound dogs, Buck and Slats, the new stove was anathema. They couldn't quite get under it, and had to sleep by the wood box, where it was drafty, and where, if they happened to be smelling extra strong, Zack could reach them with a sharpshooting toe.

When Sarah returned, just before Christmas, Zack hauled her from Privilege over the ice on a handsled. Along with a winter's supply of crochet needles, thread, yarn, and pattern books, Sarah had imported a small, outrageous dog. Buck and Slats had been too boisterous for the old lady. She wanted a comfortable pet—but no creature such as this had ever been imagined around Mopang, much less darkened the door of Zack Bourne's cabin.

"Zack—look," Sarah asked, holding up the trifling ball of fur from which glared two impudent and conceited eyes. "Ain't she cute?"

Zack's idea of a dog was something which would run a deer to water if it took two days. Glowering at Sarah's importation, he snorted: "Huh! What you call it, old lady?"

"Rosie," she answered, stroking the creature.

"No—I mean, what kind of an *animal* is it?"

"Why you, Zack! It's a dog!"

"The hell you say. Look out it don't kick you."

"Now, you be nice to Rosie."

"Rosie," Zack growled. "God a'mighty. Rosie. Her ancestors must of been mighty casual strangers."

"Now, Zack."

Fortunately for Rosie, Buck and Slats were off somewhere — doubtless on a deer trail — when Zack had arrived drawing Sarah and her pet on the sled. Sarah's simpering attention to Rosie's welfare diluted Zack's pleasure in displaying the radio, the new stove, and the congoleum. But he pointed to them, one by one, and said: "Look at that, an' that, an' that — what I done for you."

"Why, gracious goodness," cried the old lady, her eyes watering. "Just let me get my bearin's a minute. Here — you hold Rosie. Gentle now."

"You sound like a settin' hen," Zack grunted, holding Rosie at arm's length by the scruff of the neck.

"Careful! Careful!" Sarah implored.

Reluctantly Zack cuddled the degrading dog against him. Promptly and silently she bared her teeth and bit him on the thumb. Zack yowled, and snatched his hand back. The motion flipped Rosie half across the room. She lit running, and crawled under the stove, whence she peered vindictively at Zack.

"I go an' buy you all these nice things, so's you'll winter good," protested Zack, between sucks at his injured thumb, "an' what do you do for me? Bring me a dog that bites me!" Abruptly Zack's chin stuck out, and he lowered his head, to stare accusingly at Sarah. "Is Rosie housebroke?" he asked, in a foreboding voice.

Sarah backed away, uncertainly. "Well — practically — you might say — maybe."

Temporarily, in the gladness of reunion and in the goodness of a chicken supper, the old people forgot that Rosie had come between them. They talked happily together, and there was warmth, and a sense in their hearts of homecoming.

"Did you miss me, Zack?"

"Honest to God, Sarah — I like to died. Nights I'd wake up in bed an' make a glom for you, an' you wa'nt there, an' I'd lay awake prayin' for mornin', so's I could cut wood, an' make myself forget you was away."

"You prayed, Zack? *You?*"

"Sure I did."

"What'd you say in the prayer?"

"'God damn it to hell, I wisht the old woman was here beside of me.'"

"Well," sighed Sarah, blinking at the volcanic fervor of her man, "I — I guess you meant it, anyway."

It was the unexpected return of Buck and Slats that reopened the subject of Rosie, and established her as a lasting grudge. The two hounds announced themselves by snuffling in the crack under the cabin door with a sound like a cow drinking from a near-empty pail. Rosie emerged from under the stove, and cake-walked toward the door, every hackle perpendicular. A look of passionate, anticipatory glee illumined Zack's eyes. But Sarah seemed suddenly to have recollected that ghouls were abroad in the land.

"Don't let 'em in, Zack! Let 'em lay out a few nights!"

"Why, they jest want to befriend little Rosie," wheedled Zack, in a sugary voice. "They'll jest love her. They figure to welcome her to their home."

Zack sidled to the door, lifted the latch, and braced his foot above the sill as the hounds hurled themselves against the outside. He grinned coyly at Rosie, saying: "Nice little Rosie — wants to meet her big brothers, old Buck an' Slats, don't she? Ye-e-e-es."

Rosie responded with a soprano snarl, and Zack flung wide the door. The inrushing torrent of hounds parted around Zack's knees, and converged beyond on the spot where Rosie had lately been standing. But Rosie, her eyes popping from her skull, had risen straight into the air, like a flushed mallard. It appeared that her frantic clawing might suspend her indefinitely, but at last she came down on Buck's back. With Buck for a takeoff, Rosie next came to roost on the kitchen table in the platter of fricasseed chicken, lush with gravy. Buck was with her in an instant, but Slats hit the edge of the table coming up. Falling back, his front paws tangled in the red tablecloth, and the resulting avalanche of crockery set the lamp to jiggling on its chain.

The new congoleum saved Rosie. Lighter, and more accustomed to smooth surfaces than her pursuers, she was under the stove in a twinkling. Buck and Slats, their toenails vainly scrabbling for traction, got started late, and couldn't stop in time. Back-pedaling, haunches down, they both cracked their noses on the stove. From her retreat, Rosie hurled insults in a shrill, pipsqueak voice.

"Zack!" Sarah screamed, trying to make herself heard above the furor. "You see to them hounds! They'll kill Rosie!"

Zack was no longer able to control his delight or conceal his motive in bringing the trio together. "I was just fixin' it so's they'd meet sociable," he chortled. "May I drop dead in my tracks if—"

"Zachariah Bourne! You're lyin' to me! You wanted them to *kill* Rosie!"

"No sech thing," denied Zack, choking. "Say — did you see Buck make that grab for her? His neck stretched clear'n out till I thought his head would snap off."

Quailing at the memory, Sarah lifted her apron as though to blot the scene from mind: "You're just plain brutal," she moaned.

"Now, now, old lady. Quit carryin' on."

Zack's efforts to make peace were unsuccessful. He tried for an hour to regain the lost warmth of homecoming. He pointed again to the virtues of the new stove, traced with a hopeful toe the weeping willow patterns in the congoleum. Then he turned on the radio, and looked ingratiatingly toward his wife while the static, generated by the northern lights, crackled hideously in the cabin.

"I guess, now you got that thing up here," Sarah whimpered, "it ain't goin' to work good. Least you could do is try to get some hymns — it's Sunday — case you forget."

Zack's throat knotted with melancholy. He gulped, spun the dial, and, after ten minutes manipulating, isolated a dolorous voice, singing:

> "What a friend we have in Jesus,
> All our sins and griefs to bear—"

"Well, how's that suit you?" inquired Zack, in tones which indicated faith that all his sins and griefs would be borne by himself.

Sarah's answer was to settle on her knees and commence the work of clearing up crockery and spattered gravy. While she worked, she sniffled damply, and Zack Bourne's heart was a pain in his breast.

"My — my first husband —" Sarah mumbled, "— Mr. O'Mahoney — never treated me like this."

"You couldn't remember if he did," grunted Zack. "He's been buried forty-six years — so forget him. An' I might as well say that my *first* wife never would of brought home a miserable whelp like that Rosie."

Sarah responded with a sobbing dissertation on the beauties of city life. Zack interrupted her just once to ask, "Then why for Chris' sake don't you go back there an' stay?"

Thereafter, whenever Sarah fondled Rosie, or Zack took a passing kick at her, the gulf widened. Christmas Day in the cabin was characterized by a kind of arctic courtesy, but Zack made one wavering attempt to straighten things out. There was a half-pint of brandy he had been saving for the occasion. With guarded overtures, he got out the bottle, uncorked it, poured Sarah a small drink, and blurted: "Here. Take a shot of this, old lady."

Sarah almost melted, but memory of the panic-stricken Rosie congealed her heart. She caught herself in the act of reaching for the brandy glass, and murmured: "It only makes me dizzy."

"Then I'll save it for someone that'd 'preciate it," said Zack, pouring it back into the bottle. "Like that widow woman over to Mopang —"

The widow of Mopang was fictitious, but Sarah didn't know it. She began to read the widow into Zack's previous trips to Mopang. This was the last straw. Their estrangement was complete, and winter setting in.

Sometimes, in bed, forgetful of their feud in the sleepy need for companionship, the old couple would draw close, each gathering warmth and comfort from the other. In the loneliness of night, they could forget. But in the cruel cold of dawn, when Zack rose in his red merinos to build the fire, he often discovered evidence that Rosie was not even partially housebroken. Whittling his cedar fire-stick, and lighting the fire, he dreamed of tying Rosie in a sack and easing her through a hole in the ice. He yearned that his heart might harden to the deed.

It troubled Zack that Buck and Slats had made their peace with this insufferable creature, this focal point of hell on earth. True, the bold hounds gave Rosie an occasional workout, but it was not real sport for them. Rosie couldn't run in snow. She simply bogged down. They had to retrieve her out of drifts and carry her squealing to safety. To Zack's further revulsion, Rosie seemed to have taken a fancy to *him*. Lately, she had scuttled from the stove mornings and licked his cringing, upcurling toes.

"God A'mighty," whispered Zack one morning, as, unthinking, he reached down to stroke Rosie's ears. "A man can learn to stand most anything." Then, hopeful that Sarah would be awake and listening, he had roared: "G-r-r outa here, you whelp!"

Always, when ridding Rosie's messes with dustpan and ashes, Zack would mutter: "I'll never do this again, so help me. I'll get my keyhole saw, an' I'll saw right 'round it, an' jest let it drop down through. Only in a month or so, we'd have to lay a whole new floor."

That winter there was almost no travel on the lakes. The ice buckled and reefed badly. The snow piled in drifts, melted, slushed, froze, and melted again. Dreading sickness or accident, Sarah prayed each night, fingered her beads, and remembered the faces of priests she had known. To keep himself busy, Zack got out some maple butts in March, quartered them, and made paddles and axe handles. He recanvased all Mr. Usher's canoes, and steamed out new ribs for them wherever a blemish showed. Sarah crocheted, and nursed her plants in the row of tomato cans on the window sill. She was starving, desperate for friends, for the sound of a new voice, for the look of open water instead of the deathly waste of snow and ice. One day she finished a sampler, into which she had stitched the words THE ROAD TO A FRIEND'S HOUSE IS NEVER LONG.

The meaning she had made rose mocking her mind. There were no roads. There were no friends. There was no world but that of stillness and of cold. Desperate, she cried out: *"Zack—!"*

Her voice cut into him, and he looked up quickly, saying, "Yuh?"

She stood up, and started toward him, pleading: "Zack—can't we be friends again? I can't stand it any longer. We won't ever see anyone again. The ice—*the ice!*—it will never go out again."

"It'll go," Zack said.

"Zack—take me back to you, oh please, oh please."

"Damn right I will—if you jest say so." He wrapped his arms hungrily around her, and patted her head with his enormous hand. While she lay sobbing against him, he whispered to her: "Honey—jest you rest easy, now. Then you tell me what you want, and I'll get it for you, if I have to go to hell after it."

"I haven't been to mass in five months. I want to go to church. I want to go to confession. I want to see people, *people!*"

"I know, old lady," Zack said, his voice thick with tenderness. "But the way the lake is, we jest can't get out. Eighteen inches of slush." He stroked her head, touched her cheek with his lips, and added from the depths of his heart, "You're gettin' wrinkled, honey."

She clung to him, as if he were an anchor for her sanity. After a long time she said: "I can't get used to it, ever, Zack. Sixty years of my life was in the city, or near it. I—I could always go to church, an' 'specially Easter, an' Holy Week."

Over her shoulder, Zack peered at the calendar, and located Easter Sunday. "Say—here's what: we'll go to Easter service right here on the radio. We'll tie into some big church—maybe Boston, or New York—we'll hear the singin', choirs an' organs an' sech as that. An'—by God, say! We'll put on Sunday clothes, so's to make it more realer, too. Only ten days to wait."

That night Zack Bourne boiled an egg for Rosie and fed it to her with a spoon; and for the next ten days he and Sarah created for themselves a new world, inventing great things out of small. Sarah constructed three pots of paper lilies with green stems, and quit drinking tea. Zack took his broad axe and hewed a cross five feet high. Sarah thought it should be red, but there was no red paint, so Zack cut some underwear into strips and wound the cross in spirals. The effect on Sarah was worth it, tenfold. She told Zack it made God seem near, and she was no longer afraid.

The day before Easter, Zack spent nearly five hours tuning in the radio, checking times and stations for the holiest and most gratifying broadcasts, and lining things up so they'd run off without a hitch.

On Easter morning, they awoke early and lit candles. Outside it was snowing. On the lake were twenty inches of black ice. As yet there had been no geese, no ducks, no robins, no forerunner of spring.

In the gloom of the blizzard, the ghastly thought formed again on old

Sarah's lips: "Maybe spring will never come. Zack—would that be possible? Maybe we'll never see leaves, or open water. Maybe we'll never get outside, never see anyone or talk to anyone again, and—"

"Hush, now, honey—it's always like this, waitin' for the ice to go. You get to thinkin' you can't wait no more, but you wait just the same, and then—bang—out she goes, an' we're in a canoe, an' paddlin' down to the church in the Injun Village."

"Church—church—," murmured Sarah, making the sign of the cross over her breast. "Mary, Mother—Jesus, Savior—I'm waiting—waiting. I am an old woman, and can't wait much longer."

Zack hugged her, and rested his cheek on her hair. "Come on—let's get ourselves dolled up fit to rise from the dead. If *He* done it, we can do it."

"Zack—don't talk like that, today."

"All right. Nor I won't smoke the whole day, neither, nor swear. But hell, seems though we'd ought to have some wine to drink."

"Don't talk about things we haven't got. There's too many."

"That brandy!" said Zack, emptying the moth balls from his black suit. "It's made out of grapes, same as wine. It'll do us all right. We'll drink the whole jeesely bottle. We'll get lit up, an' dance—"

"Zack, hush."

Sarah put on her aging Easter bonnet. She dressed with great care, and at last hung the silver crucifix against her breast. Together, in the cabin on the shore of the frozen lake, the old couple kneeled before their homemade altar. Zack turned on the radio switch. They bowed their heads to the yellow eye of the dial, waiting for the tubes to warm, waiting for the sacred chants to flow into the room.

Sarah's lips moved in prayer. She closed her eyes, waiting, waiting for the music to come. It came. It came so faintly she could scarcely hear it. It swelled, then faded away altogether. Zack turned the volume full on. There was no sound but a waning hum. The battery had gone dead.

Zack was frightened. Sarah kneeled, swaying a little, beside him. He stood up and lifted her to her feet. Numbly she removed her Easter bonnet and handed it to him. He hung it on a wall peg, and said: "Don't you care now, honey. Don't let it get you, see?"

The old lady's eyes were half glazed with disappointment. Zack led her into the kitchen, sat her gently in a chair near the stove, and put Rosie in her lap. Then he went back into the front room, and closed in on the radio, holding his vengeful fist close to the dial. Baring his teeth, he hissed softly to the dead instrument: "God damn your stricken spleen an' belly, you lissen to the Easter prayer of Zack Bourne! May you rot an' fry in hell, an' explode an' burn, an' die in convulsions with a maggot in every pore. May you—*no!* Wait a minute! Take it all back!"

Starting swiftly toward the kitchen, Zack cried: "Hey! *Sarah!* Steve Ireland's got a batt'ry recharger! Steve Ireland, down to Privilege. I'll charge this jeesely thing so's you'll have the Pope right here in the cabin—"

"Zack—please," the old lady called, weakly. "It'll take you four days to get to Privilege an' back, through the woods."

"Huh, that's so," said Zack, wilting. "I never give it a thought. They wouldn't hold over for us neither."

"We can just pray for strength to wait, Zack." She looked up, smiling into his eyes, and murmured: "You—you know, you been awful sweet to your old lady."

"Well, I'd *ought* to be." He had come close to her chair, and was resuming his gruffness with great effort. "Why wouldn't a man be good to the best damn cook in the county?"

Sarah's eyes lowered. "It ain't so, an' you know it."

"Well, it *is* so. Even Rosie—she's gettin' paunchy on your grub. Look at her."

Zack leaned over, prodded Rosie, and suddenly peered closer, his eyes puzzling: "Fat—*no* sir! 'Tain't that so much. Sarah! That dog's goin' to have *pups!*"

"You don't say!" Sarah clutched Rosie to her bosom, and murmured soothingly: "My sakes, I do believe—"

Zack drew himself up and scowled at Buck and Slats who lay snoring by the wood box.

Sarah stared at the slumbering hounds with a look of mingled approval and indignation.

On the second Sunday of May, two days after the ice left the lake in a northwest gale, Sarah Bourne kneeled in the slab church in the Indian Village.

Outside on a fence rail sat Zack Bourne, gloomily holding in his fingers a series of cords, odd bits of haywire and rawhide, to each of which was attached one or more puppies about three weeks old. In all there were seven puppies, some resembling hounds, some resembling Rosie, some resembling nothing at all.

"What in hell you got there?" inquired Uncle Jeff Coongate, ranging close, and inspecting the puppies from under a perplexed brow.

"There ain't a one amongst 'em won't run a buck to water," defended Zack.

"What'll you take for the spotted one?"

"He ain't for sale."

"How about the black one with the ears?"

"Same goes for him."

"Goin' to keep 'em all to your own self?"

"It ain't that, Jeff." Zack motioned as best he could toward the church door. "It's up to my old woman. She figures them pups are hern. You can talk to her when she gets done prayin' in there."

Inside the church, as she breathed a paean of gratitude, old Sarah kneeled, and her cheeks were wet with tears.

There were so many things to worship, so many blessings for which to be thankful, that God must surely listen to her with an unusually attentive ear.

"Holy Father, I thank Thee for the springtime, for the open water and the sun, for the salmon fishermen who will come, for the people we will talk to. Oh, Father in Heaven, I beg Thee to forgive my sins, which are many. I do not deserve Thy kindness in sending out the ice at last. I do not deserve a husband as kind as Zack; and even though he has no faith, please forgive him for his sins, and let him outlive me. Father, may Mr. Usher always be pleased with Zack, and hire him every year to care for his cabins on the lake, which has been our lovely home for seven years. Let us spend our last few years together there, Father in Heaven. I am grateful to You for bringing me at last to this beautiful land which I love so dearly. Amen. Zack shot a moose last August and I ate some of it on a Friday, but I thought it was a Thursday. Forgive me, I implore You. Amen."

# The Warden, the Rum, and the Preacher

After they picked up the drowning game warden, Uncle Jeff Coongate and Zack Bourne had the whole lake to themselves. Considering the storm, they wanted the lake not at all. They wanted just once again to feel the stones under their feet and sniff the smoke of a little fire on shore.

As for the game warden, they wanted him even less than the lake itself. They felt that he belonged not only with, but in the lake. Aside from the fact that the warden overloaded the canoe they had kept upright in the gale for two hours, there was a matter of six hundred pounds of illegal moose meat hanging in the shed back of Zack's cabin. However, it seemed that the waves would shortly solve the whole problem by swallowing them all, including the warden, who sat shivering amidships, bailing when he wasn't balancing.

Uncle Jeff Coongate had argued in the beginning against picking up the warden, whose canoe had swamped. The one-eyed poacher reasoned that word had got around about the moose, and that the warden had started uplake to investigate. Uncle Jeff did not believe in aiding an enemy, especially under these particular circumstances. Besides, the warden was a strange one.

Jeff and Zack had paddled down to Privilege to get a quart of rum with which to celebrate the killing of their winter's supply of meat. The gale had caught them on the way back. Their precious bottle of Hernando's Fiery Dagger, untouched, lay tenderly swathed in a coat under the stern thwart. Its presence had cheered them on through the storm, giving them strength and purpose.

"I'm brave jest from thinkin' about it," old Jeff had yelled from the bow.

"Let alone from really drinkin' it!" Zack had roared.

Shortly after this they had sighted the drowning warden. He was nearly exhausted, but his plight drew from the one-eyed poacher only the briefest sympathy. It was tough luck, but it was the warden's tough luck, Uncle Jeff believed. And to look at it squarely, you couldn't have a warden in the cabin where you aimed directly to celebrate the killing of a moose. This much was clear to anyone. The old poacher was for giving the warden a merciful push downward and holding him under till his misery was over.

But Zack Bourne would have none of it. To help a man drown, even a strange game warden who had come to spy on you, would weigh upon the conscience and dull the delights of wassail. Surely, in case they reached shore alive, they could figure out a way to keep the warden from snooping around the woodshed.

By a miracle of canoemanship, the two poachers worked their craft to a position where the warden could clutch the gunwale. Uncle Jeff's eye lighted balefully, but he gallantly refrained from banging the warden's knuckles with his paddle blade, and even helped him crawl over the side into the canoe.

"Take that tea can an' bail," ordered the one-eyed poacher, "or back you go a-swimmin'."

The warden numbly bailed, keeping about even with the waves which raked over the gunwales.

Quartering into the seas, Zack and Jeff stared straight ahead, watching the creeping approach of their destined shore. If they reached that shore, Zack realized that he must caution his wife, Sarah, about the warden. Sarah was a good cook, and mighty religious, and the loneliest times of Zack's life were when Sarah was away. But unless you talked firm to her, and drilled a notion into her good and hard, she'd forget where she was and who was around. It would be just like her to say to the warden: "My stars an' body! Did you see the lovely moose Zack an' Jeff Coongate jacklighted night before last?" Or she might just absent-mindedly slice off some of the loin and serve it to the warden for supper.

In the bow of the canoe, increasingly vigilant as they approached the narrows where the swells piled furiously, Uncle Jeff Coongate fought his weariness with dreams of rum and a safe arrival. And he, too, laid plans for thwarting the warden. The moment the canoe touched the landing at the cabin, Uncle Jeff decided he would leap out and go to warn Sarah Bourne, leaving Zack to stall the warden. After cautioning Sarah, Uncle Jeff would duck around to the woodshed, cut the moose meat down, and pile stove wood over it.

Steadying with his paddle, as a tremendous wave lifted the bow, Uncle Jeff kept on in his mind, elaborating his plan. When the warden came up to the cabin, he would be very considerate of him. He would suggest that he drink some hot tea and retire at once under five blankets. On second thought, he would offer the warden a big, double jolt of rum, because the warden would have to refuse it. It was strictly against orders for him to drink on duty.

After the warden turned in, Jeff dreamed, he and Zack would take the bottle and go down to the root cellar. They'd have the lamp turned low. They'd sit on the vinegar keg and lard tub amidst the winter's provisions. They'd drink till the rum was 'most gone, and sing a little, and lick their chops thinking of feeding off the moose meat through the cold weather. It would be mighty fine and cozy down there, celebrating a moose, and a warden asleep upstairs. It would tone things up just nice.

The canoe pitched crazily as it came into the cross-chop in the throat of the narrows. A wave poured in. The warden's face, except for the patches of purple veins over his cheek bones, went livid. Zack swung the canoe at right angles, and as they ran for shore, a ragged swell chased them into the gut, broke, and swamped them full length from the stern forward.

Taking to the water head first, Jeff Coongate came up gasping: "Save the rum, Zack!"

Zack got hold of the coat and held it up triumphantly as his feet touched bottom. They floundered to the beach, and dumped the canoe. Through the narrows, and sheltered by an island a quarter of a mile to windward, they were safe. Half a mile up the shore the cabin was visible. They saw the wind-ripped smoke scattering from its chimney.

Jeff took the rum bottle from Zack, unwrapped it, and read the label in an enticing voice: "Hernando's Firey Dagger, hundred an' ten proof."

"A whole damn quart," breathed Zack, wringing water from his mackinaw.

Jeff, his eye gleaming villainously, offered the bottle to the warden. "Care for a swallow?"

"Well — I — no." The warden gulped. He shuddered in the cold, his wet clothes clinging to him. "I'm on duty."

"What a pity," sighed Jeff, hugging the bottle. "What duty brings you clear up here?"

Jeff had rewrapped the bottle and placed it back in the stern of the canoe, but still the warden said nothing. He seemed entranced by the bottle neck which peeped brightly from the folds of the coat. Uncle Jeff repeated his question in a sharper voice.

"What?" asked the warden, vaguely.

"I was just wonderin' why in hell they'd send a warden clear up here."

"The department wants to find out if moose are workin' back in," said the warden.

"Oh. Moose?" Jeff casually wiped the water from his eye socket. "Hain't seen hardly any signs. Was they thinkin' of declarin' an open season?"

"No."

"That's fine. Moose had ought to be protected permanent. Mighty fine animal. Pratickly exstink, you might say, too. Shame to kill the few that's left. Let's get a-goin'."

"Yes," the warden said.

Zack's wife, Sarah, came out of the cabin and hurried down to the landing before they reached it. She had been watching for them anxiously. She was in a great state of excitement, and she was wearing her black dress. She began speaking the moment the canoe sided in to the log wharf. She kept looking over her shoulder toward the cabin, apparently fearful that someone there might overhear.

"Zack Bourne, did you get that rum? Where is it? May the Lord forgive you, riskin' life an' limb on the lake just for the evil purpose of—"

"We got the rum," said Zack. "An' we got a game warden, too."

Zack intended his remark to warn Sarah, but she went on unheedingly. "You give me that rum, Zack. I don't want it to appear in sight."

"Why not?" inquired Uncle Jeff, bristling. "We all seen it. Why hide it?"

"Because they's a preacher here, that's why! Right after the wind come up, he got blowed ashore. A lovely little preacher, too. Interested in rocks, and trees, and—"

"A preacher!" wailed Jeff, outraged that Fate in a single hand had dealt him the cloth and the law.

"Yes. A preacher. And mind your language before him."

"Honey," said Zack morosely, "where in hell is this preacher, now?"

"In the cabin washin' for supper."

Zack had turned the canoe over and was holding the rum under one arm. "Couldn't Jeff and me have a little snifter before we meet him?"

"'Course not!" Sarah's eyes blazed indignantly. "Give me that rum. Not a drop till he's abed an' asleep. I'll just put it in the root cellar."

When Zack hesitated to relinquish the bottle, Sarah held out her hand.

"Come on, hurry up! I got some of the meat fryin', and' I got to get right back to the stove."

Jeff Coongate stiffened, and the warden sniffed curiously.

"Oh, good thing we had some of the beef left," said Zack pointedly.

"I told the preacher that's what it was," said Sarah.

The warden watched narrowly as she tucked the rum under her arm, and he seemed attentive as she explained: "I told him 'twas western corn-fed beef."

"What else would he think it was?" croaked the one-eyed poacher.

The warden shrugged. They all followed Sarah to the cabin. Zack opened the bulkhead outside, and Sarah went down into the root cellar and came back without the rum. The warden leaned over and peered into the dark interior of the cellar. He wore a patient look when Zack let the bulkhead doors down. Sarah faced them, a finger to her lips. "Mind, not a drop till he's abed."

"Never you fear. Jest trust us," said Jeff, sidling toward the woodshed out back. "I'll fetch in some wood for you, Sarah."

"I'll help," said Zack.

"I'll help, too," said the warden.

Before closing the kitchen door, Sarah called: "The wood box is full. The preacher filled it."

"May hell receive his stricken soul!" said Uncle Jeff.

"So it's in the woodshed," observed the warden. "Let's take a look at it."

Quite clearly no one was fooling anyone any more. They walked slowly to the woodshed, and in the dusk stood gazing at the contraband.

"We got him plumb through the neck," said Jeff. "Dropped where he stood."

The warden remained silent. Zack said to him: "Mind we done you a little favor out on the lake this afternoon?"

In the dim light the warden's face showed pale. He trembled a little. It was cold, and he was thinking of the lake. "Yes," he said.

"Well, so now you got us. You'd pinch us, even if we saved your life, wouldn't you?"

"I'd pinch my own mother."

"I know it. But jest 'cause she borned you, you would do her a favor before you took her to the gallows, wouldn't you?"

"Maybe."

"Then for cryssake don't let on in front of the preacher that you got us for poaching. It would jest about kill Sarah."

"All right," said the warden.

Filing through the back door into the kitchen, the three men stood blinking in the lamplight. At the table, a napkin tucked in his collar, the preacher sat before a platter of moose meat and a mound of hot biscuits. He was a small, happy man, as loquacious as the game warden was taciturn. No ill wind had ever blown so flattering a prize ashore at Sarah Bourne's lonely doorstep. Sarah hovered and fluttered, praying that her menfolk would make no glaring social blunders.

They didn't. The game warden was still as death. Zack and Jeff gloomily wondered where they could get five hundred dollars to pay their fine, and, if they couldn't, how it would be in jail. They sat down, silently wishing their clerical guest would finish his meal quickly and retire. Their rum, originally for celebration, was now essential to the cushioning of woe, but even for that purpose, it was denied them so long as the preacher remained awake.

When Uncle Jeff reached with his fork to spear a biscuit, Sarah rapped his knuckles with her knife. "Leave them be! There ain't only enough for our guest. Ain't bread good enough for you?"

"I always say," said the preacher, "that there's nothing like bread dipped in nice beef gravy. Do try some, Mr. Coongate."

"Thanks."

The preacher unselfishly passed the platter of moose meat to the game warden. The warden declined. The preacher then gave a brief discourse on the staying powers of red meat in the human system. Sarah listened worshipfully, as if his every word were gold. Zack and Jeff exchanged sad, thirsty glances, but the preacher showed no signs of drowsiness. In fact, he grew wider awake by the minute. He was enthusiastic over food, nature, people, and his own voice. Uncle Jeff tried mental telepathy and open yawning, but they didn't work.

Sarah kept prompting the parson. Zack feared that Sarah might take it into her head to tell him the story of the death of her brother Jonas. It was a long, harrowing story, but the preacher had a lot of stories of his own. While he was telling one, Zack dreamed of the first, cool feeling of rum in his mouth, then the shock and fire in his throat, then the strangling sensation, and at last the huge glow in his belly and the roaring in his brain.

The parson was off on a new tack. Uncle Jeff stood brooding by the wood box. The game warden seemed lost in cold, black thought. But it was the game warden who first succumbed to weariness. "Guess I'll turn in," he said.

"Very wise decision," approved the preacher. "You have been through a terrible experience. Nothing like long and dreamless sleep to reknit the fibers sundered by terror, chill, and immersion."

The warden looked as though his fibers needed reknitting. Zack showed him to the front room of the cabin. There wasn't any bed. The spare bed was for the preacher. Zack spread some bearskins and got some blankets. The warden took off his boots and his pants and lay down, and Zack returned to the kitchen, closing the door gently behind him.

The preacher had opened up a new vein of conversational resource. He had arranged a peck or so of rocks on the table and was going nicely on geology and Indian relics. Sarah, her face ruddy in the lamplight, looked as if her soul were filling rapidly with wisdom. Uncle Jeff, now hunkered inside the wood box, thought only of the sound of a cork squeaking out of a bottle neck.

"Should think," said Sarah, "that warden would of wanted to stay up and listen to these educational things."

"Guess he's beat out," said Zack, taking a chair. "He d— dang near drowned."

"I can readily understand his exhaustion," the preacher said.

"Ain't you a little mite tired yoruself, Reverend?" graciously inquired Uncle Jeff. "We don't aim to keep you up. Any time you want to hit the hay, why—"

"I get along on very little sleep," replied the guest. "I attribute it to exercise in the great outdoors, and to the stimulus of exchanging ideas with people."

"Oh."

Zack ran his tongue along his lips. There was only one thing to be thankful for: Sarah had not started about her brother Jonas. She didn't seem to have much chance. The preacher had selected a fresh rock from his collection and was holding it up to the light.

"This," he said, "is a specimen of jasper, rather rare in these parts. Frankly, I was surprised to find it."

"My!" Sarah exclaimed. She looked around at Zack. "Ain't it interestin' to hear a man talk like this? It's very educational."

"Yuh."

Thus encouraged, the preacher dropped the jasper and picked up some other rocks. "Now here we have a very interesting quartz relationship. I—"

"Quartz?" said old Jeff, to whom the word had but one meaning. "Where?"

"Here. Now a crystalline schist, as you no doubt fully appreciate, is—"

"A rock is a rock," said Zack sullenly.

"Don't show your ignorance!" Sarah blurted. "Hold your tongue."

The preacher smiled tolerantly. "A rock, as your husband has pointed out, is, of course, a rock. But how was it formed? When was it formed? And under what conditions? These are the great questions."

The parson answered these questions at some length. He propounded others, and answered them. He spoke weightily of pyrites, lignites, chalcedony, fault scarps, moraines, stalactites, stalagmites, sedimentation, silica, and the great ice sheet. The two poachers suffered in silence. Not that they wanted to speak. Their throats were too parched. They were far less interested in rocks than in the cruel Fate which had first brought them a game warden who would jail them, and second a preacher who had kept them from their rum. Their mercy and hospitality had brought them misery tenfold.

Just as the preacher packed away his rocks and looked as if he might consider going to bed, Sarah's eyes lighted, and she began about her brother Jonas. Old Jeff settled deeper in the wood box, too weak to sigh. Zack swallowed, and his throat made a dry creaking sound.

Sarah's brother Jonas had fought in the first war, and had died on the nineteenth anniversary of his shrapnel wound, just at sunset, when a neighbor's boy, a Scout bugler, happened to be playing taps. To Sarah the coincidence had a deep religious significance. Here was her great chance to get a clergyman's opinion.

Zack and Jeff had heard the story so many times that they could clock off the points accurately. Five minutes for Jonas's patriotism and character; seven for his *croix de guerre;* nine for his hospitalization; twenty-two for his operations; three for the neighbor's boy who had joined the Scouts at Jonas's suggestion; two for Jonas's kindness in buying the boy the bugle; and from eight to twelve for the death scene. Sixty minutes might cover it for an ordinary guest, but Zack figured Sarah would take close to eighty for the preacher. He estimated that, with luck, he could live an hour and a half more without rum. But over in the wood box, Uncle Jeff Coongate looked as if he couldn't hold out, that death by thirst would claim him before Sarah got Jonas out of the veterans' hospital.

Sarah had progressed as far as Jonas's second operation, and the preacher was listening in an attitude of deep thought, when they first heard the bumping noise. Sarah paused, annoyed. "That's your canoe blowin', Zack. Didn't you tie it?"

"The wind's died out," Zack said.

The preacher said: "Listen."

They listened for some moments, but the night was still. Sarah resumed her story: "Well, then Jonas says to the doctors: 'I'm willin' to undergo anything.' Jonas was brave, always brave. He says to them: 'You cut me open before, an' you can do it again.' So then they cut Jonas open, and—"

They heard the bumping sound again, this time much nearer against the outside wall of the cabin. Jeff Coongate looked up at the deer horns where his rifle hung. Zack had stood up and started toward the door, when a doleful, singing voice reached them:

> I'll go where you wan' me to go dear Lor',
> I'll travel o'er lan' an' sea.

I'll do what you wan' me to do dear Lor',
I'll be what you wan' me to be-e-e-e-e —

When Zack opened the door, the game warden almost fell into the kitchen. He caught himself with one hand. In the other he held the rum bottle, which was nearly empty. It was obvious to everyone that the warden had gone out through the front door of the cabin, and down into the root cellar to the bottle. Judging by the pittance of rum left, the warden had been in the cellar a long time. He was minus his pants and boots, and his long underwear lacked crucial buttons.

"Re-knitting fibersh," he said. "Fibersh fine now."

"Mrs. Bourne," said the preacher gallantly, "shall I show you to your room?"

"He got into our medicine that we keep in the root cellar," wailed Sarah, determined to explain the rum bottle on high moral grounds.

"It was for Mr. Coongate's cough," Zack softly added.

Jeff gulped out loud. "Zack sometimes coughed a mite, too."

The game warden reeled, aimed for a chair, and just made it, as his underwear opened all the way down the front. The preacher stepped between him and Sarah. Sarah fled to the bedroom, and the preacher turned to deal with the drunken warden. He placed a hand firmly on the warden's shoulder. "Listen to me," he said severely. "Are you able to understand me?"

"Shernly," said the warden, looking up gravely. "Shernly I understand."

"These men saved your life on the lake today. They brought you to their home."

"They had to," the warden mumbled. "Only place on the lake."

"They fed you. They gave you of their hospitality — their food and meat, their shelter."

"Didn't eat any meat," the warden said thickly.

"And in return, you steal their medicine, and get helplessly intoxicated."

"Unh," said the warden.

"I am therefore in duty bound," continued the preacher, "to report you to the authorities. An officer of the law, drunk. A serious offense."

At this moment, Uncle Jeff Coongate, climbed from the wood box and sidled forward. "Reverend," he said, "this man went through a mighty turrible time in the lake till we come along. He swum an hour in the cold water, with the fear of death on him."

"His poor wife an' children are dependent on him," said Zack Bourne.

"Lookin' at it one way, he wa'n't hardly responsible for what he done, Reverend," Uncle Jeff went on. "'Course it's a turrible thing, jest the same. Shocked me awful. But I say he should be forgiven. On account of his wife, an' children, an'—"

"An' the work he does protectin' this counry from the ravidges of lawless poachers," said Zack.

"Jest the very words I was goin' to use," said the one-eyed poacher. "So I say we forgive this poor man. But if we ever had cause to change our minds, we could always get you to witness what he done here tonight. Couldn't we, Reverend?"

"Indeed you could," said the preacher enthusiastically. "And I may say that you men have demonstrated remarkable forgiveness. I shall remember it as long as I live."

"Shame here," said the warden.

"You are a very fortunate man," the preacher told the warden.

"Shernly am," repied the warden.

He went carefully to the front room, closed the door, and sank down on the bearskins, knowing that he could sleep, for the cruelty of cold and the fear of death were no longer in him. "Everyone's very forshunit," he muttered, pulling the blankets around him.

# The Long Night

*I*n the morning, some hours after the last jug had fallen, Uncle Jeff Coongate opened his one eye, sniffed, and, through the stronger fumes of rum, detected the odor of sweet grass. This reminded the old poacher of Indians weaving baskets in the sun. Next, he thought fondly of Tom Compus Mentis, who was still asleep beside him in the spare room in Zack Bourne's cabin on Mopang Lake. Finally, with a wave of grief, Uncle Jeff recalled his tragedy: Zibe, his beloved hound dog, was dead.

It was Tom Compus Mentis, the gentle and ancient Indian, who, on the day before, had brought Zibe home to Jeff. With the crippled hound lying in the bow of his canoe, old Tom had travelled the twenty-nine miles from Hedron Lake to Mopang in seven hours. It was a feat of loyalty and endurance which signalized a long and dignified friendship.

Zibe had been shot in the spine. His hindquarters were paralyzed, and as the old woodsman gathered him in his arms, he had whimpered, and pressed his fevered muzzle to Uncle Jeff's neck.

"Zibe," Jeff whispered, "Zibe — what hellbird done this to you?"

"Red Hackett," said Tom Compus Mentis. "I find tracks. And empty shell—.35 auto."

The one-eyed poacher carried Zibe into Zack Bourne's cabin, and the Indian stayed in the doorway. Zack, Jeff Coongate's lifelong comrade in enterprise against the game laws, looked once at Zibe's wound, and shook his head in sorrow.

"It's mortal," he said. "Poor ole Zibe—best hound ever run a moose to water."

Zack's wife, Sarah, began to cry. She had never truly loved Jeff's hound, fearing him as a primordial and fiercely roaming adventurer, like his master. But Sarah was so tender-hearted that she was touched by any misfortune.

Zibe moaned softly, and a shudder of pain racked the sleek and rangy body. It was plain that the hound was beyond hope, and suffering needlessly.

"Hand me my rifle, Zack," said Uncle Jeff.

Zack silently obeyed. Carrying Zibe and the rifle, the old woodsman stalked across the back clearing into the cedars. Presently, those in the cabin heard a shot—a sound both grim and merciful.

"Sarah," said Zack, tonelessly, "get out the rum."

"I was a-goin' to, by my own self," said Sarah, "jest this one, dreadful time."

When Uncle Jeff Coongate returned, the first jug was opened before him—and Tom Compus Mentis no longer stood in the doorway, but had drawn in a little toward the jug, his dark eyes having a look of sorrow and horizons.

Tactfully avoiding the Indian's gaze, Jeff and Zack both drank. Sarah, herself, turned a half-ounce into a wine glass, and sipped. Touched by this breaking of precedent in homage to Zibe's passing, Uncle Jeff had bowed to Sarah. Then he nodded to Zack, and together they went out into the cedars with a shovel.

While they were gone, Sarah graciously bethought herself of the old Indian, who stood so patiently by the jug.

"Why, Mr. Mentis! You ain't had any of the rum—after that terrible trip, an' all. Here. I'll get you a glass.

"No thanks glass," said Tom. He enfolded the jug in both palms, and tipped it upwards. When the two woodsmen returned, the damage was begun—and they knew how dismally 'twould end.

"Honey," Zack hissed, in an aside to Sarah, "You lost your mind? Don't you know how ole Tom'll suffer? In the mornin' he'll see bugs a yard long, an' ravens perchin' on his wrists."

But morning was not yet. Nor had Tom Compus Mentis told the story

*The Long Night*

of the Hacketts, the great moose of Hedron Lake, and the wanton shooting of the far-wandering Zibe.

The Hacketts were three brothers, successful evaders of the draft, the income tax, and the obligations of gentlemen. They lived in Hedron, which, cross-forest, was twenty-four miles from Zack's cabin on Mopang — twenty-nine by canoe. One of the Hacketts ran a restaurant and bar. The other two had a farm planted to kale, which attracted deer. During the war, and currently, they killed moose and deer, put down the meat in mason jars, and sold it for a dollar a pint. They took the loin and hindquarters of a critter, and left the rest to rot. It was this practice which filled Uncle Jeff Coongate with fury and contempt. Although he personally excoriated game laws, and the minions thereof, he despised the wasting of the fruit of the wildlands.

The one-eyed poacher and the butchering Hacketts differed in all their practices. Between Uncle Jeff and the successive game wardens who pursued him, there was a spirit of respect, as among duelists. Whenever they caught him, the old poacher went majestically down to jail in Mopang, where the first cell on the left was usually reserved for him. When he didn't get caught, he feasted royally with Zack Bourne, and if there were so much as a shank left over, it was dropped on the doorstep of some needy family.

But there was nothing of Robin Hood in the Hacketts of Hedron. To the Fish & Game Commissioner, they were known as the wantons of the wilderness, and he would rather have caught them even than Thomas Jefferson Coongate. Privily, the Commissioner himself would have agreed that the Hacketts' shooting of Zibe was most wanton of all. When the shooting occurred, Zibe had been deep in the sweet obsession of a fox track. As Tom Compus Mentis explained, nothing else could have lured him so far from home.

"But those Hacketts," muttered Tom, reaching for the jug, "they think maybe Zibe come to drive big moose away."

"Moose?" said the one-eyed poacher, keening. "Do you know where they's a big one, Tom?"

The old Indian's face wrinkled like a scorched moccasin. "Big! I say big. Hacketts try to bribe me tell where he is. No tell. They got big order for moose meat — dollar pound."

Tom told how the Hacketts had tried to follow him to the moose's haunts, and how he had eluded them. As the rum became fire in his veins, he laughed reminiscently at their attempts to trail him. Early that very morning, before the wind had wrinkled the lake, Tom had been playing cat-and-mouse with the Hacketts. He had heard a rifle shot. Half an hour later, he had cut back through the dense growth, picked up the Hacketts' trail, and found the empty cartridge from Red Hacketts' .35 autoloading rifle. Nearby, from the spruce blowdown where he had crawled to die, Zibe had dragged himself on his forefeet to Tom's side.

It was night, now, and Uncle Jeff Coongate, listening to the Indian's tale, stood tall in the lamplight, as he planned revenge. The oaths slid wondrously from his lips, and his mustaches gleamed white. Zack fervently echoed the oaths, while Sarah covered her ears.

"Hacketts!" said the one-eyed poacher. "May they rot and fry, stricken in spleen and paunch, an' blowflies in every pore."

After Sarah went to bed, they began on the second jug. Presently Zack suggested that they simply go over to Hedron in the morning and shoot the Hacketts in a bevy.

"No!" cried Sarah from the bedroom. "Oh, no, no!"

For years she had listened to her husband and his crony conspiring against the lives of game wardens, but had realized it was merely a form of play, or entertainment for them. But this business of the Hacketts had a serious ring that made her blood run cold. Surprisingly, it was Jeff Coongate, who, this time, eased her mind.

"Sarah's right, Zack," said Jeff. " 'Course, I can see where it'd be pleasant to kill them Hacketts — angle shots, we could take on 'em. Clip off a little flesh to a time, till they was whittled to the bone. But I don't like to spend my whole life in jail — jest winters. Spring, I like to get out in time to spear a few salmon before fishin' season opens. *But—*"

It was not so much Jeff's voice, as his posture that underscored the word. Zack saw the light flaring in his comrade's eye. He sat back, waiting for Jeff to unfold, while Tom Compus Mentis, unnoticed, took a long, silent pull from the jug.

"What d'you aim to do to them Hacketts?" Zack asked, finally.

"I aim to kill their moose — that big one Tom tells about. I aim to kill it right in their face an' eyes."

So far, the idea was mere nebula; but, inspired by the rising fires of rum and glory, the avengers leaped lightly over hazards, and had the moose down.

"He'll dress out around six hundred," estimated Zack.

"Eight hundred, easy," corrected Jeff.

In the light of the many lamps which had seemed to multiply in the cabin kitchen, the moose finally tipped the scales at a thousand pounds, clear meat.

"It's too much," said Zack, sadly hefting the jug. "Some of it'll spoil, sure."

The one-eyed poacher gazed loftily at his less imaginative comrade.

"Too much? Spoil? Are you thinkin', like always, jest of your own self,

Zack? Ain't there other folks goin' hungry, same as me an' you. Give, seth the Lord. Blessid is the poor."

Heads together, hands clasped in the emotion of selfless giving, they outlined a vast program of philanthropy, while Sarah listened in terror in her dark bedroom, and the old Indian's hand strayed more and more helplessly toward the jug.

"We shall feed the entire offsprings of Jumbo Tethergood."

"An' the pore li'l orphans of Tim Preston."

"With the Hacketts' moose, we shall pervide for the fam'lies of Mopang."

"An' Boomchain Junction, an' New York, an'—"

Further expansion was checked by the thick, uncertain voice of Tom Compus Mentis.

"Game warden," said Tom. "New game warden. Comin' Hedron—tomorrow."

At the time, a new game warden, zealous though he might be, seemed less like an obstacle than an added attraction.

"Good," said the outlaw of Mopang Forest. "Perfick. Spice things up a mite."

But in the morning, the new game warden loomed large, especially in the eyes of Sarah. She had read in the game laws that the penalty for killing a moose was five hundred dollars fine and three months in jail.

"Almost like for murder," she wept. "Don't you go, Zack. I beg you. Oh, Zack—please."

Ever since his marriage to Sarah, Zack had been emotionally torn. Subtly influenced by Jeff to maintain the old status of the devil and the demijohn, he was as subtly swayed by Sarah's prayers for his reform. Now, acutely miserable, he looked from one to the other. But this time, it was the one-eyed poacher who was moved by Sarah's pleading. Moreover, as Uncle Jeff savored the drama of the situation, he saw opportunities dear to his heart. Head bowed, he stood in the open doorway, and spoke.

"Zack—Sarah's right. You can't go. This mission is for a single man, with no dependints, no one to mourn for him."

"Dang it, Jeff! You always took me. We always done things—"

Jeff raised his hand in a gesture of sacrifice. "No. Zibe was mine."

So genuine was Jeff's grief for Zibe, that he no longer felt himself playing a role. Reality threw him off for a moment, and he gulped, and said: "Zack—you got any .45-70 ca'tridges? I—I used my last one—out in the cedars—yest'dy."

"No, but take my rifle, Jeff. You got to let me help that much."

"No," said Uncle Jeff, "'cause if that new game warden gets me, he'll confiscate the rifle. I couldn't bear to have that happen. Don't want to have my personal affairs hurt you, in no way whatever. No, Zack, this time it's a big thing. I can't take you with me. It's so big I got to play a lone hand."

The crestfallen Zack slumped into a chair, his elbows among the breakfast dishes. He resembled a boy plucked from the very entrance to a circus, and he was unappeased by Sarah's grateful murmurings.

By the lakeshore, in the sand, Tom Compus Mentis drew a map of Hedron Lake, showing a hidden inlet, an unknown dead water, and the great moose's range. As he noticed the wavering lines of the sand map, the one-eyed poacher's heart ached for the suffering Indian.

"Tom, your hand's a-twitchin' like a chicken's foot in the mud."

"You got a little bit rum left?" begged Tom, abjectly. "Me bad sick."

"No, Tom. We killed her all. You go straight home in your canoe. I got to go down to Mopang to buy ca'tridges. I'll be to your shack tonight. I'll bring you a dite of rum, but that's all. An' listen: don't you tech a drop in Hedron — not till I get to you. Mind that, Tom?"

The Indian slid away in his canoe, and Uncle Jeff Coongate saw despair in his wake. "Poor ole Tom," he muttered, and strode forth on the Mopang trail, already longing for Zack's companionship, his pleasure at Zack's frustration diminishing as he realized to the full that he had trapped himself into a considerable adventure, what with a moose, three murderous Hacketts, and — and — what was that other thing? Oh, yes! A new game warden!

In the afternoon, as he left Mopang and struck through the forest for Hedron Lake, it began to rain. His tireless stride brought him to Tom Compus Mentis's shack before midnight. But the Indian was not there — and his stove was cold.

"Tom," he muttered, "the demons was too much for you. I got to find you."

Drenched to the skin, the one-eyed poacher turned back toward the hamlet of Hedron, scorning the road, cross-cutting through the woods. He came out on the road two miles from the town, and as he stood for a moment, the headlights of a car approached. The car drew up to him, and stopped. The door swung open invitingly, and a pleasant voice hailed him.

"Howdy, stranger. Want a lift?"

Although bone-weary from the miles he had covered, the old woodsman replied with prideful reluctance: "I don't want to put no man out."

"Get in. It's raining."

Not till he had seated himself did the one-eyed poacher take full cognizance of his benefactor. But in the dim light from the instrument panel, the identity of the fellow was plain — the badge, the service cap, the uniform.

"Jest a moment, son," said Uncle Jeff. "Let me out. I never ride with game wardens."

The young warden smiled. His name was Steve Engle. He was a graduate of Anzio beachhead, the State Wildlife Training School, and a boyhood spent in Hedron, where a certain old Indian had taught him to love the woods, pound ash withes for baskets, and showed him where an otter family played. Tonight, on his first solo assignment as game warden in the Hedron district, Steve Engle had met and befriended that same old Indian. To meet the celebrated one-eyed poacher on the same night, within a few minutes, was to Steve like hitting the jackpot. He proposed to make the most of it.

Steve had never seen Uncle Jeff. But the old poacher's features, physique, and personality were unmistakable. The sweeping mustaches shone wet, the huge right hand held a Winchester between the peaked knees, and from the high-boned, imperious face, the one eye glowed like a blowtorch.

"Mr. Coongate," said Steve, almost reverently, "I haven't been a game warden very long. So maybe I won't contaminate you."

"In that case, maybe you ain't tainted yet. But hurry, son. Get me into Hedron fast. I don't want to set with you too long."

As they drove along, Jeff drew himself delicately away from the young warden as far as the seat would permit.

"Aren't you a long way from home?" asked the game warden. "What brings you here from Mopang?"

"I ain't accustomed to answer questions. But since you're new, I'll tell you: I come over here to see a sick friend."

Steve chuckled in his disbelief. "Did you find the friend well?"

"No. Didn't find him at all. So I come on back. He's prob'ly in Hedron."

Steve rapidly guessed at the miles the old man had covered afoot that day. It was incredible! He glanced with increasing respect at his passenger — and at the highlights on the rifle between his knees.

"Mr. Coongate," said Steve, "who is your friend — the sick friend that wasn't home?"

Although disdaining the impertinence of the warden's questioning, Uncle Jeff decided to be tolerant. The boy was young, and would grow up to have trouble enough.

"Tom Compus Mentis," said Jeff.

"Who? Did you say — ? Why, Tom Compus is a friend of *mine!*"

"No. It ain't possible. No friend of mine could be the friend of a game warden. It jest wouldn't work out."

"It was when I was little," Steve hastened to explain. "Old Tom showed me the forests, and made moccasins for me. And—but—! Say, wait a minute!"

Drawing the car to the side of the road, the warden stopped, and glanced at his saturnine passenger. "Tom Compus Mentis *is* at home. I just left him in his shack, ten minutes ago! How come I didn't meet you on the road?"

These tidings had a sharp effect on the one-eyed poacher. He feared the worst. "When I left Tom's shack, I cut through the woods to the road—where you picked me up. That's why we didn't meet. How'd you happen to drive Tom home?"

"He couldn't walk too well."

"Was he drinkin'?"

Steve nodded. "Yes—Hackett's restaurant. The Hacketts had him in a booth, and they were loading his drinks."

"Let me out of here!" said the old-timer.

Steve reached across and opened the car door, and the outlaw of Mopang Forest disappeared in the darkness toward Tom Compus Mentis's shack.

Driving on toward the warden's cabin on Hedron's outskirts, Steve Engle smiled elatedly. It seemed dead certain that his first solo assignment was going to be a success—with cream and sugar on top! He was holding a fistful of aces. Through the rain-wet window of Hackett's restaurant, he had seen the Hacketts lay a map of Hedron Lake under Tom Compus Mentis's eyes, and he had seen the sad, old Indian, dazed with drink, point to a hidden inlet in Anchor Island Cove. Now, *why?* What with moose meat selling for a dollar a pound, Steve thought he knew. He also thought he knew why the one-eyed poacher had appeared in the Hedron district. What a chance, thought Steve. Mine, all mine: to gather in the butchering Hacketts and the legendary Jeff Coongate—all in one swoop! What a tale to tell the Chief! The arrests would be simple, if he just remembered the advice old Tom Compus Mentis had given him, when he was a boy: look, listen, be still, and wait long in the night time.

In Tom Compus's shack, Uncle Jeff Coongate was indulging in similar, if craftier dreams. He had built a fire in Tom's stove, and made tea, and as he fed the Indian steaming spoonfuls, his heart was big with forgiveness.

"Hacketts make me tell about moose," Tom moaned. "Awful bad, Jeff. Awful sorry."

"Now, jest you rest easy, Tom. It's all right. I aim to get that moose, jest the same."

Uncle Jeff's one eye rolled beatifically, as he put together the pieces of his greatest and simplest conspiracy. In a single trick, he would wreck the Hacketts, avenge Zibe, outwit a game warden—a nice, pleasant new one—and possess a moose. Poor old Zack Bourne would shrivel and grow the green mold of envy.

"Tom," said Jeff, tenderly, "'member what you used to tell me, when we was huntin' an' trappin' together, in the old days? 'Look, listen, be still, an' wait long in the night time.' Well, sir, Tom—that's what I aim to do."

"Look out new warden, Steve Engle. He smart."

"He did seem above average, for a warden," mused the one-eyed poacher. "Now, tell me how he come on you tonight in Red Hackett's place."

The Indian told his story. It was as Uncle Jeff had surmised. Putting two and two together, the young warden would be on the Hacketts' trail.

"An' wouldn't that boy jest love to catch me, too, Tom? Why, think what it'd mean to him! The Hacketts, an' ole Jeff Coongate, with a moose down—singlehanded."

Blissfully, the old woodsman slipped a spoonful of hot tea between the Indian's lips. Tom swallowed it unhappily.

"You bring old Tom little rum, Jeff?" he implored.

"Yes, a little, Tom. But not now." Before retiring, Jeff patted his friend's shoulder, and added philosophically: "Man cannot live by breath alone."

Beside the deadwater, beyond the hidden inlet in Anchor Island Cove, young Steve Engle waited long in the night time, and loneliness invaded his heart. Perhaps, in his zeal, he had assumed too much. Perhaps the Hacketts were suspicious, and Jeff Coongate gone his kingly way homeward to Mopang. Perhaps the moose was a myth—but there was no mistaking the great creature's track. It was, thought Steve, as long as a snowshoe and as broad as a stove lid. But when would the Hacketts make their kill? And where, oh where, was the one-eyed poacher?

Steve visited Tom Compus Mentis one day, and casually inquired. Tom shrugged.

"Jeff Coongate go," said the Indian, and blew to indicate a puff of smoke. He spoke the truth. He hadn't seen Jeff since the rainy night of his arrival.

"Guess I must have scared him off," thought Steve, with no special conviction, as he resumed his vigil.

The fifth night, or the sixth, Steve couldn't remember, began like all the others. In the dense cedar growth, in the darkness, the Big Silence weighted his spirit. He heard a mouse in the leaves, and tried to guess whether it was near or far. He heard a loon calling, then silence again, and the night wrapping itself around him. And then, unmistakably, the soft, hollow thump of a paddle against the gunwale of a canoe.

He tried to locate the sound. He couldn't be sure of the distance—but the direction was to his left. He lay waiting, his heart pounding. He remembered what the Chief had told him. "You'll be alone, Stevie. Watch it."

The first rifle shot came from down the deadwater, around a small point, about three hundred yards away. The echoes rolled back from the ridges, and died, and then Steve heard the second shot. He inched up on his hands and knees and crawled through the cedars. He got across the base of the little point to the edge of the deadwater, and lay still. He knew the Hacketts were waiting – and he steeled himself to wait longer.

Not over thirty yards away, he saw a match flare. He shivered to think how close he had figured it. Next he saw the steady glow of a lantern, and heard the sound of men moving. He squirmed toward the lantern, his service revolver in his right hand, his flashlight ready in his left, in case they heard him and kicked out the lantern. Then he stood up and walked in, his gun ahead of him.

They had the big moose down. Its head was pointed toward Steve, antlers palmed out wide. But – not a man was in sight! The young warden realized too late that they had trapped him into the light. He started to jump back. A crack on the side of his head made him see star shells, and he lunged forward, hitting with his elbows.

Someone got an armlock on his throat. He saw a man's head within reach, and he whipped it with his gun barrel, and felt the barrel hit solid. The man went down. But there were two others. One had the armlock, and was bending his head back. The other stood in front, with a rifle at his hip, the muzzle on Steve's belt buckle. He wondered if they would finish the job, or knock him cold. He would never be able to identify any of them in court. Was that what they figured on?

The armlock tightened, and Steve felt himself blacking out. Then, to the right, he saw a jet of orange flame, and heard an explosion like a howitzer. He was sure he smelled black powder. His vision cleared. The man in front of him wasn't holding a rifle any more. It had disappeared, and the man was hugging his wrists to his sides, and howling with pain.

A flashlight blazed where Steve had seen the flash of the rifle, and a man of majestic height stepped calmly forth from the cedars. The flashlight he carried was the long, heavy, five-cell variety, and he flashed it in the eyes of the Hackett whose armlock had but lately loosened from the young warden's neck.

"I jest wanted to make sure," said the splendid voice, "that you was Red Hackett." With that, the one-eyed poacher brought the flashlight down solidly on Red Hackett's head, and Red settled deeply into the moss.

"Jeff Coongate!" said Steve.

"What's so strange about that?"

Steve laughed in nervous relief. The one-eyed poacher examined his flashlight, grinning at its dented barrel.

"That's one for old Zibe," he muttered, and straightway began the pleasant work of trussing up the Hacketts with the assistance of Steve, one pair of handcuffs, and the rawhide laces from his own moccasins.

Two hours later, the three Hackets were in the Hedron jail, and Steve had telephoned his Chief long distance. A few minutes after that, in the game warden's cabin, Steve was playing host to Uncle Jeff Coongate. He was strangely impressed by the old-timer's dignity, reticence, and superb manners.

"Mr. Coongate," said Steve, gratefully bringing out a bottle, "here's some rum. Don't know if you like the particular brand. It's Hernando's Fiery Dagger."

Coyly concealing the gleam in his eye, the old woodsman waved the bottle away. "I don't often tech intoxicatin' bev'ridges, son. But—" the great hand stole daintily forward—"to celebrate your triumph tonight, I'll take jest a small portion."

Steve watched, while Jeff drank to the extent of four bobs of his Adam's apple.

"Well—Uncle Jeff—" said Steve, haltingly. "I want to thank you for helping me out of a tough spot."

The one-eyed poacher scowled indignantly, and took a small chaser of Hernando's. "Me? Help a *game warden?* Let me set you straight, son. I have never shot a legal piece of game in my life—except by mistake. An' I have never helped a game warden."

"But you did tonight, Mr. Coongate."

Uncle Jeff shook his head. "No. An' I don't want you to tell it 'round that I helped you, neither. That's the way rumors get started. Why, son, what would Zack Bourne think of me, if he heard I'd helped a warden? I wasn't there to help you. I was there to get the man that shot my ole hound, Zibe. I'd intended to do battle with him, but you come along an' spoilt it for me. An' I may's well tell you I was also there to get that moose. That moose, you could almost say, was really *my* moose."

"So I almost thought," mused Steve. "And—doggonnit, Jeff, I'm glad the Hacketts killed it, instead of you. It leaves you in the clear."

"Yes," said Jeff, with mixed emotions, "I persume it does. Well, I got to be getting along."

"Wait. I'll drive you back to Mopang. It's nearly three o'clock in the morning."

"No. That's all right, son. It'll be daylight, time I get to Leadmine Cove, on Mopang. I'll have breakfast with Zack Bourne. Keep out of my way, Steve—an' you'll never have any bad trouble."

With that, the one-eyed poacher was gone. Steve sighed, and turned in for a few hours, till the Chief Warden arrived. Not long after daylight, they went down to haul the carcass of the moose away to the nearest hospital, for the delectation of the patients' diet. The moose, of course, was still there. As they stood looking down at it, Steve said to the Chief:

"They don't make 'em any more like Jeff Coongate. Just imagine — footing it in the dark clear to Mopang Lake, at three in the morning."

"He's quite a man," said the Chief, somewhat guardedly, as he bent over the moose. "He's — why blast his old soul! This moose has been bled, and dressed out, and the hide folded back on!"

Dumbfounded, the two wardens lifted off the hide. The creature had been dressed by an expert hand. Choice portions of the loin had been sliced off with surgical precision.

"Looks to me," said the Chief, sardonically, "as if Jeff Coongate made a small detour on his nocturnal trip to Mopang Lake. Wonder what he and Zack Bourne are eating for breakfast? I'll bet the gravy's good!"

Steve Engle's look of consternation changed slowly into a smile. "The old master's touch!" he said.

"You called it, Stevie. Save a game warden's life, and steal a moose under his nose. That's Jeff Coongate. And say, I'll need a drink, when we get this job done. Got anything up in the cabin?"

"Why — uh, why, yes, Chief," said Steve. "There's a little bit left — Hernando's Fiery Dagger, it is."

# The Diary of Death

On a winter's evening, in his apartment in Boston, Mr. Usher sat down to read the record of events which had transpired during the previous year at his camp in the wilderness on Mopang Lake. The record was kept in diary form, with daily entries by the resident caretaker. Mr. Usher opened the volume at hand with marked anxiety. He had been able to spend but two weeks at his camp during the previous year, and this diary, which he had just received, represented the first twelve months' residence of a new and untried caretaker, Zachariah Bourne.

Mr. Usher had hired Zack Bourne with strong misgivings. There had been no doubt as to Zack's woodsmanship, or his qualifications to live happily in the wilderness. He was a magnificent physical specimen, and he had lived in the wild lands most of his life, but he had a reputation for lawlessness, and a primordial sense of justice which both attracted Mr. Usher and frightened him. Moreover, in his desire to protect Mr. Usher's interests, Zack had seemed overzealous from the start.

"Jest you rest easy, Mr. Usher," Zack had said. "I'll shoot the feet from under anyone I see fishin' in our waters, or huntin' in our territory."

"But you can't do that, Zack."

"I'm the best rifle shot in Mopang."

"So I'm told. I simply mean that the lakes and the forests are free to anyone. Part of your duty would be to keep the peace, as I have always tried to keep it here."

"Sure, Mr. Usher. I'll jest fix it so things'll seem peacefuler to trespassers if they stay away from here."

Mr. Usher probably would not have engaged Zack if it hadn't been for Zack's wife, Sarah. Sarah was city bred, and Mr. Usher saw at once that she would have a gentling effect on her tall, tough-minded husband.

"Zack Bourne!" Sarah had reproached. "Hush that wild talk."

Turning to Mr. Usher, Sarah had then explained that Zack had lately returned from visiting a crony who was in jail down in Mopang. The crony's name was Thomas Jefferson Coongate, and he was an evil influence on Zack, and a menace in the community.

"Coongate?" Mr. Usher had inquired. "I seem to recall the name. Isn't he the one-eyed poacher of Privilege?"

He was indeed, said Sarah Bourne, and briskly sketched the Coongate character. Old Jeff Coongate, according to Sarah, was composed solely of vices. He was a chewer of tobacco, a drinker of bottled goods in any alcoholic form, and a kind of marathon blasphemer. He was a sworn breaker of game laws, and an enemy of the State. He was a jacklighter of deer, a gill-netter of salmon, a dynamiter of trout, and above all else a plotter against the lives of game wardens. In fact, he was currently in the clink for shooting the stern off a game warden's canoe with an automatic shotgun. Happily the warden was a good swimmer.

When Sarah paused to draw breath, Zack said, "But he's a good feller, jest the same."

"That's what you think," snapped Sarah, "because you an' him riverdrove, an' poached together, when you was boys. Every time you been in trouble, 'twas him got you into it."

This conversation more than half convinced Mr. Usher that Sarah had Zack under control, and he had hired Zack on the spot.

"I want you both to regard this place as your home," Mr. Usher had said to Zack and Sarah Bourne. "The canoes and all the equipment are for your use, as well as mine. I hope you will love this camp, as I do. I request that you do not leave the place alone for more than two or three days at a time, except of course in emergency. And there is only one thing on which I insist. That is the regular, and accurate keeping of the camp diary, day by day."

"You mean," said Zack, troubled, "that I'm to write somethin' down every day? Every single day?"

*The Diary of Death*

"Exactly."

"I'll tend to that myself, Mr. Usher," said Sarah.

Now, in his apartment, as he read Sarah's careful entries in the diary, Mr. Usher's mind gradually relaxed. Sarah had done an excellent job. From the simple facts she had recorded, Mr. Usher got a clear picture of the seasons, the work, the weather, and events. Mr. Usher read with absorption and fascination. The diary was vivid evidence of the reality of the place he loved beyond all others.

January and February told of blizzards, bitter cold, the crackle of northern lights, and the thunder of the ice at night. And always the loneliness:

"No one come by for seventeen days, too cold, 27 below today, mouse in back pantry, Zack has toothache, but hauled wood from choppin across dam."

March and April told of thaws and freezes which made travel on the lakes next to impossible. Then came May, and the last deadly weeks of waiting for the ice to leave. And on the 23rd, the joyous entry:

"Ice went out overnight in northwest gale, flock geese landed in cove at sunset, Zack took me out in canoe, wonderful. Salmon fishermen be coming soon, and will have company here in this lonely place at last. Zack leaving daylight tomorrow for supplies."

So read Mr. Usher — on through June, and the fly season. He read of three deer feeding in the back clearing, a family of otter living briefly along the stream, and a moose sighted across the dam. Mr. Usher's satisfaction with his new caretaker was first clouded by an entry in late August.

"Game Warden Tom Corn stopped by today out of tobacco. Zack would not give him any, mean I call it. It was Tom Corn's canoe that Jeff Coongate shot stern of off. The warden reported Jeff Coongate gets out of jail October one. Oh dear. Hope he don't come to see Zack, we been so happy here, even through this long and terrible winter."

Mr. Usher began to read more rapidly. He had a feeling that the inevitable was about to happen, that the nefarious one-eyed poacher would soon arrive and lead Zack Bourne astray. On September 11th a swallow flew through the open kitchen window. Sarah wrote that this was a bad omen, that it meant that someone would be very sick, or get hurt. But the dramatic import of this was lost to Mr. Usher. It was completely overshadowed by Sarah's description of the turning of the leaves in early October — and by the following entry under date of November second:

"A most awful day. Thos. J. Coongate come up lake in night, arrived here crack of day. He had whiskey, and offered to Zack. I would not let Zack touch it. He tried to get Zack to go to Little Mopang Stream to trap beaver, this against law. I would not let Zack go, as I know Mr. Usher would not like it. Finely I told that one-eyed poacher to go away from this place, and he went after darkness fell as he don't want no one to see him. Zack mad at me, says am not cordial to his friends. Cannot be cordial to that outlaw man, for fear Zack will get himself in trouble."

On November third, fourth, fifth, and sixth, Sarah reported that Zack had not spoken to her. But then on the seventh:

"Zack made up today, kissed me, so sweet, said he knowed I was right, and if it hadn't been for me he would of done something foolish. Was so sweet, hugged and kissed me, till I am bruised and squoze, he don't know his strength. My!"

The entry of November 10th told of Zack's last trip out to Privilege for supplies before freeze-up. Zack returned two days later with a canoe-load of provisions, and the mail. November 13th:

"Unlucky day, Zack brought letter from my brother saying my sister very sick in Bangor. Must go to her, as if anything happened would feel awful, and shell ice on lake now in many places. Must go, hate to leave Zack alone, as don't know what will happen. Do hope and pray that one-eyed devil Jeff Coongate don't come back this way."

As he finished reading the above entry, Mr. Usher stiffened in his chair. He, too, hoped and prayed that the one-eyed poacher would not, or had not visited his camp when Zack was there without Sarah. November 14th, 15th and 16th were blank, indicating the time required for Zack to get Sarah out to Privilege en route to Bangor. On the 17th, Zack had returned to the job. The handwriting was no longer in Sarah's clear, even penmanship, but showed signs of tremendous effort. Mr. Usher remembered that Zack had seemed troubled when he learned that he was to write something every day. The first entry in the labored, masculine handwriting, was on the 17th.

"Hellish trip back uplake after leaving Sarah in Privilege, broke ice clear from Caribou Ledge and chewed canoe canvas plumb to hell. Geese went South in night, big flock, wish was with them, lonesome for Sarah all ready, but brought plenty big supply medicine back with me, Hernando's Fiery Dagger rum an Old Blow-Torch gin, ha-ha!"

Mr. Usher's heart sank. This was the thing he had dreaded. But he had not realized that Zack would be so brazen as to write it down in his own handwriting. On second thought, he realized, Zack Bourne was exactly the kind of man who would do just that, and do it unblushingly.

From November 17th on to the end of the year, the diary of Mr. Usher's beloved camp was the plain, agonizing record of a bush-queer man going steadily and irretrievably to hell. It was both fascinating and appalling. November 19th:

"Cold for two days, ice four inches caught pickerl through ice, will say anyone that can stand up on this black ice after drinkin pint of Fiery Dagger rum is sure good balancer. Fell flat a dozen times gettin ashore, found camp door open wide when got back, someone maybe comin. Wish Jeff Coongate would come, would have hell of time. Plenty rum and gin left."

This entry was enough to sicken Mr. Usher, but he didn't realize to what depths a lonely man would sink until, on December 4th, Zack Bourne became a squaw man.

"Down to Privilege over the ice with hand sled. Stopped at Injun Villige on way back, got a squaw here now to keep me warm nights, her name Elsie Brown Blanket. Found old cat, Daisy, had kittens in cloze basket, five. Elsie thinks kittens might be good to eat. Some squaw, all right. Big bull moose workin over in woods near cove."

December 5th to 10th, inclusive, were quite clearly given over solely to debauch. Mr. Usher, reading between the lines, saw the desecration of his camp, and his wilderness. The handwriting for this period had become an illegible, drunken scrawl. December 11th marked Zack's return to partial sobriety. Mr. Usher read this day's entry, his stomach revolting.

"Elsie been keepin diary for me past few days, but I can't read what she wrote, but I know what she wrote about, ha-ha, thats all we been doin anyway. Snowed last night an covered most all empty bottles an tincans in front dooryard of cabin."

Mr. Usher was but slightly relieved to note that, on December 14th, Zack Bourne had tired of Elsie Brown Blanket's aboriginal charms.

"Elsie wants to get marrid to me and raise famly, can you beat it? That's a squaw for you. I said did not plan to commit bigmy with her, but only a little adultery, ha-ha. She got mad an threw hand axe at me, so am leavin today to take her back to Injun Villige. Good snow-shoein on lake, tempriture zero, wind north, clear."

There were only a few more entries. Zack's year, reflected Mr. Usher, his heart heavy within him, was almost over. So was Zack's job as caretaker of the camp on Mopang Lake. If the record of decay had so far sickened Mr. Usher, the last few entries did even more. They froze his blood.

"December 20th:

"My two dogs, Buck and Slats, been chasin moose in woods across dam. Will go after moose some day soon."

"December 25th:

"Merry Christmas, like hell. Buck an Slats dogged the moose out on ice. He dropped with first shot, I got the bastid right back of ear, some shot, as I had drunk 2 qts. rum yestdy an was shakin so couldn't hold rifle ver stiddy. Was dressin out moose when game warden Tom Corn stepped out of hidin in thick brush on shore, and got me for doggin moose. He drawed his service revolver and right before my very eyes shot both my dogs, Buck and Slats, best friends I ever had. Then he said for me to get ready to go to Mopang with him to jail, an I said would come peaceful, an told him I would get some things from cabin if he would wait. He waited all right, and will say that game warden will never shoot another dog in this world. How I know is my bisness, but wish Jeff Coongate seen it happen, as it would sure pleased Jeff, as this warden will never trail him nor anyone no more."

Mr. Usher shuddered, and closed the diary of death. He did not know whether to try and get in touch with Sarah Bourne, in Bangor, or to turn the diary over to the police. He finally decided to hire a plane equipped with skis for landing on the lake in front of his cabin door. His decision as to what to do about Zack would depend to some extent on what he discovered.

Taking with him the diary of death, Mr. Usher flew to Bangor the next morning on the regular transport plane. From Bangor he proceeded north by charter plane for Mopang Lake. He had been fortunate in securing the services of a pilot who tended the wants of trappers throughout the north. The flier knew the country well. He set his ship down smoothly on the packed snow on the lake before the cabin. Mr. Usher noted that no smoke came from the chimney. Had Zack left the country? Had the game warden already been missed? Apparently not, for inside the cabin Mr. Usher found the stove warm.

The pilot, looking from the kitchen window over the lake, said: "I guess there comes your man now. Prob'ly been cutting wood over on the island."

Even at a great distance, Mr. Usher recognized Zack Bourne. He had harnessed himself to a handsled, and he was leaning forward, his great shoulders straining. The handsled was loaded with wood.

"I'll pick you up at three sharp this afternoon," said the pilot. "That is, if the weather holds."

"But won't you stay and eat something?" asked Mr. Usher. He felt strangely lonesome, now, and uneasy. He wished the pilot would stay, and told him so.

The pilot shook his head. "I've got to pick up beaver skins for six trappers over in the Golroy River district. There's a bulge in the market, and if I don't catch it, I lose their business. I won't be gone long, unless a storm comes up."

The plane took off, circled for altitude, cleared the big ridge, and was gone before Zack Bourne arrived with his load of wood. When he recognized Mr. Usher, Zack slipped out of the sled harness and strode forward, smiling as if his conscience were as clear as a child's.

"Say, if it ain't Mr. Usher! I'm sure glad you could come."

As they shook hands, Mr. Usher felt bewildered, and a little frightened. Now that he had arrived, he did not know exactly how to proceed. Moreover, every time he turned his head, Mr. Usher noted a new bit of evidence which added confirmation to his worst fears. Zack's deer dogs, Buck and Slats, were conspicuously absent.

"What happened to your hounds?" asked Mr. Usher, gently.

"Buck and Slats?" While he answered, Zack calmly went about building up the fire and preparing a meal. "Well, I was afeared they might get to chasin' deer on the snow, where the tracks would show too plain. So I left 'em down to Privilege when I took Sarah out."

The smell of frying pickerel brought forth corroboration of another item in the diary of death. The cat, Daisy, and her five kittens emerged single file from under the stove, and, with tails high and backs arched, rubbed against Zack's legs. Mr. Usher's stomach turned over, as he recalled the entry in which Elsie Brown Blanket had pondered the kittens' edibility.

"I — I — uh — suppose it must have been lonesome here without Sarah," essayed Mr. Usher, miserably.

"Turrible! I damn near perished nights," Zack answered.

Now, for the first time, Mr. Usher observed that Zack's left hand was bandaged. Doubtless this wound had resulted from Elsie Brown Blanket's throwing of the hand axe. Zack had apparently shielded himself with his left hand, and had been cut.

"How did you hurt your hand, Zack?" asked Mr. Usher, fearfully.

"Cut myself with the hand axe," came the brazen reply.

"How?"

"Splittin' kindlin' in the dark."

Zack set a plate of fried pickerel and potatoes in front of his employer. But Mr. Usher's appetite was completely missing. He somehow could not bring himself to break bread with a drunkard, adulterer, and murderer. Zack himself ate with relish, and when he had finished, said: "I'd like to take you out 'round the place an' show you some things I done. Maybe you'd be pleased to see 'em."

Deciding to delay mentioning the diary until time for the return of the plane, Mr. Usher accompanied Zack on a tour of inspection. In between debauches, Zack had found opportunity for a prodigious amount of work. Mr. Usher smiled bitterly. Aside from the fact that his new caretaker broke all ten commandments, he was the perfect man for the job. He had built a cap-and-bunk fence around the garden, using dry cedar poles. He had cut the unsightly dead limbs from the great white pine which landmarked the place in Mr. Usher's mind and memory. He had shingled the shed roof with shingles he had split himself, with mallet and frow. He had recanvassed three canoes as smoothly as a factory might have done it. But most pleasing to Mr. Usher was the magnificent axe work which had gone into the hewing of new sills for every building on the place.

"That's beautiful, Zack," Mr. Usher had remarked, momentarily forgetting that this man was virtually a self-confessed murderer.

"'Tain't nothin' at all, hardly. You come in the workshop, an' see the paddles I made. Got six out of one big maple butt. An' I got the best one marked for you. It's got a spring, an' whip to it, an' the bird's eye in the wood makes it han'some."

Mr. Usher tested the spring of the blade, found it perfect, and set the paddle down with a sigh. "I am very sorry that your wife, Sarah, had to leave you alone so long, Zack."

"Me, too. But I think Sarah's sister'll die, an' that won't bother me a dang bit, neither, 'cause then Sarah can bury her an' come back."

As they left the workshop, walking toward the cabin on the path Zack had shoveled in the deep snow, Mr. Usher decided to have his showdown and get it over with.

"Zack," he said, "I have read the diary. I have read it all. That is why I am here, as you may have guessed."

At mention of the diary, Zack Bourne showed his first signs of uneasiness. His eyes no longer met Mr. Usher's squarely, and he replied irrelevantly, plainly avoiding the subject. Pausing at the cabin door, he pointed to the windows, and said: "I puttied every dang pane of glass this side of the cabin."

"Zack, I want to talk to you about the diary."

But Zack's reluctance to discuss the subject continued. His guilt was palpable. He looked off across the lake, and, after a heavy silence, said: "There's someone comin'. There's two men comin'."

Mr. Usher glanced at his watch. Plane-time was but half an hour hence, and the two men, who were approaching rapidly across the lake, gave him extra confidence.

"Zack, I'd like to go over the diary with you and ask some questions. I brought it with me."

They entered the cabin. Mr. Usher sat down at the kitchen table, spreading the diary open before him. Zack put some beech chunks in the stove, and sat down opposite his employer.

"Ain't the diary all right?" he asked, avoiding Mr. Usher's eyes by staring from the window at the approaching men.

"No. I am sorry to say it is not all right."

"Well, dang it, that's Sarah's fault then. She kep' it."

"She kept it perfectly. I refer to the entries made by yourself, in Sarah's absence."

Zack swallowed. His forehead glistened, as the sweat began to come. He stared steadily at the two men, who were by now less than two hundred yards away.

Mr. Usher turned the diary toward Zack, and pointed to the entry for November 17th, the first following Sarah's departure: "... brought plenty big supply medicine back with me, Hernando's Fiery Dagger rum an Old Blow-Torch gin, ha-ha!"

"What do you suppose I thought when I read that, Zack? What opinion could you have thought I would have, about the new caretaker to whom I had entrusted my place here?"

Zack's huge hands clenched. The red of shame suffused his face. He averted his eyes, but made no reply.

"And this entry," continued Mr. Usher, turning to December 4th. "With your wife gone, you turned squaw man. You brought an Indian woman here—the one who threw the axe and cut your hand."

Zack guiltily thrust his bandaged hand out of sight under the table. Then, with a groan, he stood up and walked to the cabin window, his giant shoulders slumped abjectly.

"Zack," said Mr. Usher, "I am afraid I shall have to terminate my agreement with you. As for the entry about the shooting of—"

Zack had suddenly straightened and glued his face to the windowpane. The two men were just entering the cabin dooryard. "Game warden!" said Zack. "A game warden with that—"

"The game warden," Mr. Usher asked gently, "couldn't be Tom Corn, could it, Zack?"

"Not unless it's his ghost," said Zack, turning fiercely. "He's been—transferred."

To Mr. Usher, the word "transferred," as it issued from Zack Bourne's livid lips, meant liquidated, purged, in short, murdered. But Zack's recent shame and guilt had suddenly dropped from him. He stood for a moment, tall, tense, savage. Then, with the quickness of a huge cat, he reached for his rifle, snatched it from the wall pegs, jacked in a shell, and flung open the cabin door.

"Zack! Zack!" cried Mr. Usher. "You can't kill another warden, Zack!"

"I don't aim to kill no warden," Zack snarled, as Mr. Usher followed him from the cabin door. "I aim to kill the bastid that wrote that diary for me. Step to one side, warden—jest a foot to one side, till I get a shot at that one-eyed Jeff Coongate!"

Standing behind, and a little to one side of Zack, Mr. Usher observed that the warden's body shielded the second man. As he watched, spellbound, a face of splendid and grinning malevolence appeared briefly over the warden's shoulder. One eye was missing from the face. The color of the other eye was a kind of baleful blue. There was also a stringy, white mustache, from which icicles hung, giving the one-eyed poacher of Privilege the appearance of a sardonic Santa Claus.

"Warden," said Thomas Jefferson Coongate, "it's your duty to pertec' me. I'm your prisoner."

The warden moved a little, not especially liking his view of the hole in the end of Zack Bourne's rifle. The one-eyed poacher moved with him, and for a second or two the warden and his prisoner resembled a dance team, shifting feet in perfect synchrony, no mean performance on snowshoes.

"Zack," said Mr. Usher, almost happily, "I think you better let me take that rifle now."

"Go ahead an' give it to him, Zack," said the game warden.

When the rifle was safely in Mr. Usher's hands, the one-eyed poacher cautiously showed his head and part of his body. "Git me down to that jail quick, warden," he said. "I ain't safe, loose, while ole Zack's mad at me."

"You'll have time to cool off, Zack," the warden grinned. "I think I can promise Jeff Coongate at least three months. He's been chloroformin' beaver over on Little Mopang Stream."

"An' to think," muttered Zack, leaning weakly back against the cabin wall, "that I dang near went with him, on'y for my wife, Sarah."

A few minutes after the game warden and his prisoner left for Privilege en route to the Mopang jail, Mr. Usher's plane landed. But Mr. Usher had decided to remain with his new caretaker for several days, so he paid the pilot off.

There were a few things that needed clearing up concerning the diary of death, but there was no longer any doubt about Zack Bourne. Zack's temper had cooled. Dark had fallen over the Mopang country, and in the light of the lamp in the kitchen, Zack read the one-eyed poacher's inimical work of art, and chuckled aloud.

"Why, that ole hellcat. There ain't a whisker of truth in him. What he wrote down, is jest what he wished was true, but knowed it never could be. It's a kind of a dream, like."

"Just how did it all get into the diary, Zack?"

Zack ruefully explained that Jeff Coongate had stopped at the camp for two nights, shortly after Christmas. To Zack, the writing of the diary had been an ordeal which he couldn't face. He had tried again and again, but in his fingers the pen had felt unnatural. As the days passed, and he had written nothing, the very sight of the pen had nauseated him, and he had continued his procrastination, brooding and ashamed. He had hoped that Sarah would return to fill in the empty days for him. But no. Instead came the one-eyed poacher of Privilege, who offered to take the whole thing out of Zack's hands and make a nice, interesting record. Zack hadn't even bothered to read what he wrote. Jeff Coongate had graciously wrapped the diary, sealed it, and addressed it.

"Then you really did cut your hand splitting kindling," laughed Mr. Usher.

"Sure did. And Daisy sure had them five kittens, all right. 'Twas 'bout three weeks before Jeff showed up. He'd been clear out to Carterville to get chloroform for them beaver he'd located on Little Mopang Stream. An' I really took Buck an' Slats to Priv'lige, too, so's they wouldn't cause no trouble here. An' it's a fact about that warden, Tom Corn — he's transferred. An' that Jeff Coongate! Well, he's a good feller, just the same. But I figure he put that in about the squaw a-purpose to torment Sarah. He hoped Sarah might read about Elsie Brown Blanket."

"Zack," said Mr. Usher, "by way of apology, I'd like to renew my agreement with you for an indefinite number of years. Would you be willing?"

"Yes, sir, indeed I sure would. Me an' Sarah loves this place like it was our'n. But there's jest on'y one thing: don't you never tell her 'bout that diary, nor who wrote it. I wouldn't want Sarah to know that Jeff Coongate spent a couple nights here. He ain't a man that women understand."

# *Envoy*

# Ghosts of Old Campfires

One wintry afternoon in my invisibly heated city apartment, restless for the bright moment of spring, I dreamfully unrolled an old tent; and on the wall-to-wall rug the tent was a forlorn and displaced personality, and so was I. Clinging to the tent were some pine needles from the forests of Maine, a cedar twig from the same beloved source, and, most poignant of all, the faint, elusive odor of wood smoke.

The ghost of that last campfire on South Branch Pond arose from the tent to haunt me. The remembered firelight walked the tent walls, and a stick of burning maple hissed a sonnet to the wilderness. It was a thousand miles and hundred days to the next campfire on South Branch Pond, an injustice which caused me to make cantankerous and ungrateful comparisons between honest fire and the ingenious system of combustion which warmed my city apartment.

Here is no pungent drift of wood smoke, nor flicker of flame, I brooded. Fire is no longer a work of art, but an unfeeling science, its warmth measured not in terms of the soul of man, but in something called British Thermal Units, which abhor tinder and matches and hide their light and beauty under a bushel—to wit, a concealed boiler. The woodpile is a gloomy oil tank in a cellar. There is no axe to be whetted, nor anywhere a litter of white, sweet-smelling chips; and the tree in the alley is not for wood, but a perch for improvident sparrows and a symbol of lament for a forest.

Along about here, I yearned to expound my anguish to a kindred spirit, and called to my wife who has developed a tolerance for these outbursts. I explained to her that it was an outrage, a human indignity, to have the home fires fed by an anonymous agent summoned by telephone, a crass stranger in uniform driving a fuel-oil truck equipped with an insidious black hose.

"We ought to be thankful for him," she said, looking from the window at the blown snow in the city's gutters. "He's due to arrive any time."

"I am *not* thankful for him," I said. "I consider him an emissary from Hell. Totally devoid of kindling and dry matches."

Unmoved, my wife returned to her ironing board. For the moment, I did not pursue my grudge, for I had glanced down at the unrolled tent, as though to apologize for its unseemly resting place.

And I had noticed a gleam of familiar metal. Leaning over, I discovered my waterproof matchsafe, opened it to disclose several noble, blue-headed kitchen matches—and lighted one on my thumbnail. As the match flared and went out, so did my one-man rebellion, for I was dreaming of true fires winking on wilderness lakeshores, and of their light on the rafters of cabins, or on the undersides of pine branches in the summer night.

No fire is like any other fire. Each has its own identity, its peculiar and original pattern of flame and smoke which is obviously patented in Heaven. Moreover, each fire makes you think of other fires—some you built yourself, some you sat beside, and some the classic fires of literature.

Do you remember the fireplace fire in Whittier's "Snowbound"? And the tragic one in Jack London's story "To Build a Fire"? A tenderfoot built it in Alaska in seventy-below weather under a snow-arched fir branch. The fire partly melted the snow, and the snow slid from the branch and put out the fire. The tenderfoot had used his last match, and he had made his last mistake.

Much happier was the fire Tom Sawyer, Joe Harper, and Huckleberry Finn built on Jackson's Island in the Big River. It warmed them, cooked their catfish, cheered their restless young souls; and when darkness fell they drew near to its flame and were brave because of its light.

The first fire I can remember was the one my father built in a wheel rut in an old cart road. Swinging the brown knapsack from his chubby shoulders, he said:

"I will now build a fire which does not smoke. Thus we will attract no hostile Indians."

There hadn't been any hostile Indians for a hundred and fifty years. The forest of that first fire was a Massachusetts woodlot within sound of church bells. It was nearly fifty years ago. My father and his sprightly imagination are both gone; but I can still wrinkle my nostrils to the smell of the acrid sulphur match, or lucifer, with which he lighted the fire. The fire didn't smoke. He had built it of dry, bone-white poplar, and I see its light reflecting from his merry face.

I scratched another of the fine, tall, blue-headed matches that I had found in my matchsafe in the unrolled tent. Before the match burned out, I had warmed myself by a hundred remembered campfires.

There was a sweet one on the Peabody River in New Hampshire's White Mountains. There are wonderfully shaped stones on the Peabody, and with these stones on a gravel bar Digsy Jones and I built a neat, new fireplace. We gathered dry pine and the resinous roots of a spruce, and the axe blows echoed clean and clear. For tinder we used a curl of birch bark, and at the touch of the match the bark gave forth its incomparable odor, and the flame rose bright in the spring gloaming.

On green alder skewers we broiled the trout we had caught, and at dark turned in. Our tent that long-ago spring was a tarpaulin strung over a peeled spruce ridgepole, and the night's sudden rain drummed on the fabric, reminding us that we were dry, warm, and consoled.

There were some memorable fires on a long canoe trip on the Machias River in Maine: the one on the old riverdrivers' campground, where the night hawks came swooping to the light, and the river sang mysteriously in the lap of outer darkness.

There was a camp under the giant pine at Rollerford Dam; and a beauty on the yellow scimitar of beach on Sabio Lake, where the firewood was abundant cedar which burned to a feathery ash. In the morning we awoke to see a moose wading in the misty lake in front of our tent.

The last campfire on that trip was on an island in the river. Island campfires have special enchantment, and this island was a gray, moss-covered ledge with a single Norway pine growing on it. We hauled firewood from the mainland in our canoe — and that night the light from this wood gave us a true sense of isolation, and the ledge under the moss was warm from the sun of yesterday.

I remember the sagebrush and cottonwood campfires in Montana. The sage flavor touched all the grub you cooked, and even the coffee, and you learned to like it.

One of the best campfires of my experience was on the shore of Mattagamon Lake in Maine. I was crossing the lake in my boat from the opposite shore in the early morning, and the lake was like black glass. A mile away, I saw the orange firelight in front of a white tent and the pale smoke in the still air. A man and his wife were standing close to the fire's warmth. I beached my boat nearby and said good morning.

"We're from California," the man said. "We always wanted to pitch a tent and build a campfire on a Maine lake."

This sense of our broad land, with its wagon tracks, tire tracks, footprints, and distance, reminds me of a night fire of sycamore limbs under a trestle over a river near Yellow Springs, Ohio. This was circa 1920, and I used to sneak away from my college dormitory every night and sit beside this fire. It burned for many nights, and it shed a wondrous light on the faces of the hoboes who kept it fed. The tales of these far-wandering men are romance in my ears to this day. The glow still lives in the sunken eyes of the old one who had never in his life paid a dime for railroad fare. Every time I hear a freight train in the night I think of Locky Colburn. Where is Locky, now? He might be squatting in a boxcar on this very freight, or shivering in a gondola – dreaming of his next campfire, and stew bubbling in a tin can under a bridge in Butte.

So I lit another wooden match, and thought how Old Pop Thornton, the magic woodsman, called these matches Roman candles. Pop must surely be the epic campfire builder of them all. On the St. Croix and Penobscot watersheds of Maine, they claim that Pop can build a fire in a downpour in a cedar swamp with two wet sponges and a twig of green beech. I half believe it.

Pop is now seventy-four. For campers he has guided, for their sons, or for his spirit's sake, he has been building wood fires for six decades. Even with discounts, it figures up to around twenty thousand nine hundred campfires – in sun, wind, rain, snow, or in historic stoves in cabins.

I reached once more for my matchsafe. It was empty. My ashtray was laden with tiny fragments of genuine charcoal. But the spell was broken. The scent of wood smoke and the loveliness of firelight on a tent wall never seemed so far away. The hiss of steam in the apartment radiators was a travesty, and I was filled with dull wrath at the thermostat, and at all things electrically equipped, including the apartment doorbell which gave off an abrupt and strident jangle.

I opened the door to admit a tall young man in a uniform bearing the insignia of an oil company. Here he was! The emissary from Hell, handing me a bill for *oil!*

"Twenty-three dollars and eleven cents!" I said. "Why, I could cut that much clean-smelling firewood in –"

"So could I," said the young man.

He was looking down at the tent on the apartment floor. He was kneeling down to touch its fabric, and then he was looking up at me, his gray eyes starry and wistful.

"I can hear the sound of the axe right now, Mister," he said. "I can see the chips, and the firelight — and the wood smoke."

I fumbled mistily for a cigarette, while the young man went on, filling the room with the music of his heart.

"My wife and I," he said, "we got a tent like this. Every spring we toss it in our car, and go. We take some grub, and the axe, and go till we find a little place with trees by a river, and — it's what we dream about all winter. Sometimes it seems we can hardly wait. But, listen — you know what we say to each other? We say, 'Spring will always come!'"

The young man suddenly noticed my unlighted cigarette. Reaching earnestly into a pocket of his uniform, he drew forth a noble, blue-headed wooden match, and across its flame we looked into each other's eyes with renewed faith in the coming of spring, and a knowledge of the beauty of campfires, which passeth all understanding.

# *Bibliography*

This list includes the final name of the story along with the periodical it first appeared in, as well as any previous anthologies it was part of. The stories in this book have been taken from the anthologies and may have some changes in the titles as well as in the work itself from the periodical version. However, these changes were all made by Smith and the works thus represent his changes, not those of an editor. Titles in parenthesis are those used in periodicals.

"An Ode to Spring Fever." ("Ode to Spring Fever") *Sports Illustrated,* April 11, 1955. *A Treasury of the Maine Woods*

"Jake's Rangers Hunt the Whitetail." ("Jake's Rangers and the White Deer") *Field and Stream,* October 1959. *Upriver and Down*

"The Saga of Third Chain Cabin." ("Pop's Last Hunt") *True,* December 1956. *A Treasury of the Maine Woods*

"A Rifle Named 'Sleigh Bells'." ("Sleigh Bells") *Outdoor Life,* February 1959. *For Maine Only*

"The Jinx and Uncle George." *Field and Stream,* October 1960. *Upriver and Down*

"Old Come-and-Get-It." ("Out of the Frying Pan") *Field and Stream* (March 1961?), *Upriver and Down*

"The Magic Woodsman." *A Treasury of the Maine Woods*

"Death of a Haunted Tent." ("My Horrible Haunted Tent") *True Fishing-Hunting Yearbook*, 1964 (1960?). *Upriver and Down*

"Jake's Rangers vs. Spring Fever." ("Ordeal in Capital Quest of Wilderness in Trout") *Field and Stream*, 1959. *For Maine Only*

"Appointment With Death." *This Week*, February 15, 1953

"Weather Prophet." *Tall Tales and Short, From Fact to Fiction, For Maine Only*

"The Tenderfoot Who Wasn't." *Liberty*, July 1937. *A Tomato Can Chronicle, For Maine Only*

"Last Trip Together." *Tall Tales and Short, From Fact to Fiction, For Maine Only*

"Some Have to Get Hurt." *McCall's*, February 1942. *From Fact to Fiction*

"The Last Hermit of the Maine Woods." ("The Last Hermit") *Field and Stream*, April 1963. *Upriver and Down*

"Old Lady in Waiting." *Tall Tales and Short, For Maine Only*

"The Warden, the Rum and the Preacher." ("Poachers, the Rum and the Preacher") *Esquire*, August 1940. *The One-Eyed Poacher of Privilege, For Maine Only*

"The Long Night." ("The One-Eyed Poacher and the Long Night") *Collier's*, September 1948. *The One-Eyed Poacher and the Maine Woods*

"The Diary of Death." *Esquire*, June 1941. *The One-Eyed Poacher of Privilege, For Maine Only*

"Ghosts of Old Campfires." *Lincoln-Mercury Times*, March-April 1956. *A Treasury of the Maine Woods*